Letters from Cuba

Adolf Hungry Wolf

CANADIAN CABOOSE PRESS

Canadian Cataloguing in Publications Data
Hungry Wolf, Adolf, 1944 -
Letters From Cuba
ISBN 0-920698-52-2
1. Hungry Wolf, Adolf, 1944-   --Journeys--Cuba. 2--
Description and travel. I. Title.
F1765.3.H86 1996   917.29104'64   C96-910642-4

Also by Adolf Hungry Wolf:

- TRAINS OF CUBA - Steam, Diesel & Electric: A Guidebook, with photos, rosters, maps and information

- MOUNTAIN HOME - Tales of seeking a family life in harmony with nature

- THE BLOOD PEOPLE - An Illustrated interpretation of the old ways

- RAILS IN THE CANADIAN ROCKIES

- CANADIAN SUNSET

- OFF ON A WILD CABOOSE CHASE

- SHADOWS OF THE BUFFALO

- THE GOOD MEDICINE BOOK
              ....and many more.

For a complete listing write to:

Canadian Caboose Press
Box 844
Skookumchuck, B.C.
V0B 2E0, Canada

*Zorro rides again! Along with old American cars and other ma-
chines, Cuba is also left with a lot of pre-revolutionary Hollywood movies and shows, including those of the masked crusad-
er who defended the poor from oppressive Spaniards - a highly
popular theme in this former Spanish colony. The hand painted
scene decorates the back of a red homemade carriage, whose
horse rested in the shade of a huge tree out in front of the old
railway station in Matanzas, waiting for the next passenger to
need a taxi ride.*

INTRODUCTION

It's an easy afternoon's flight from Canada to Cuba, yet in some ways the two are a whole world apart. The money it costs to make such a flight is a week's wages for the average Canadian, while for most Cubans it represents a fortune totally beyond reach. They struggle with the barest of food, clothing and other necessities, often watching with yearning as ever-more multitudes of tourists flock to their land for comfortable vacations, carrying suitcases full of unobtainable luxuries.

After thirty-some years of hearing little more than critical things about this little island nation and its unique leader Fidel Castro, I finally went to see for myself the only communist country in the western hemisphere, expecting to encounter its revolutionary masses either praising the results of their own ways or else scared to death to talk about them. In fact, the idea of making such a visit was long postponed because I value individual freedom and privacy very highly and could not bring myself to go through all the restrictions and red tape (so to speak) that visits to communist countries have generally required.

But Fidel's Cuba was making some remarkable changes by the time my 18 year old son Iniskim and I went there for our first visit in March of 1993. Earlier, we might have been limited to a few special tourist hotels and areas, getting beyond them only with escorted groups aboard tour buses, whereas *we* rented a little Korean four-wheeled drive car and went pretty well wherever we felt like. We ended up with many new friends - and an unexpected sympathy for their social plight - so I went back for a second and longer visit in 1994 with my older son Okan, who came again with me in 1995, after which I brought my wife Beverly in 1996, as a 25th anniversary trip, so she could also meet our friends. Four months of visits there have resulted in many new insights and experiences.

Those among our friends who practice Cuba's "native" Santeria religion have suggested divine reasons for my immediate emotional bond with their country. That's alright by me, especially since I find Cubans to be a very spiritual people, even after 35 years of theoretically non-religious socialist-communist endeavors. For one thing, their land is so fantastic that it's easy to get spiritually aroused just being there. In addition, Cuban people have the dynamic kind of Latin personality that seems to say, "There's more to all of us than just what your eyes behold."

That our own family life in Canada has strong native spiritual roots became the basis for many of our newfound friendships. Cubans are as fascinated by North American Indians as are the people of most nations, so we gave them much pleasure by sharing photos and stories from back home, where native culture is part of our everyday life. Although most Cubans seem fairly familiar with social, political and economic problems of North America's native people, their main visual images have come from pre-1959 Hollywood movies, which they've been told are inaccurate, yet they've seen them over and over for lack of newer and better film material. Considering the abundance of negative reports they'd received about native matters (in some ways like those that we get about Cuba), it's no wonder they were amazed to learn that most of my native friends have their own good homes, drive fairly new cars or trucks, and in general enjoy a level of comfort in life far beyond that of the average Cuban.

As a third generation photographer I put some working purpose to my Cuban visits with plans to document scenes of vintage transportation, a subject I've often written about and for which Cuba is becoming well-known. More than fifty of the country's 156 sugar mills operate with turn-of-the-century steam technology (the newer among them built in the late 1920's!). Some mills still receive their sugar cane from fields aboard narrow gauge steam-powered trains more ancient than those attacked by Indians in the old movies. What's more, Cuba's roads are host to an endless array of ox-teams, horse-drawn wagons, and carriages, while the streets of every city and town are cruised by numerous 1940's and 50's Detroit automobiles that make whole neighborhoods look like movie sets. Taking pictures of all this transportation machinery is a challenge that has brought us a lot of fun and resulted in a good historical investment, not to mention our new friendships with many of the interesting people who keep all these things running.

Besides taking a lot of pictures, I've also had a lifelong habit to make written records about things I consider to be interesting. But Cuba still looks with suspicion on visitors who take too many notes, especially if they also carry cameras and a lot of film. In fact, not long before our first visit a couple of acquaintances had gone to Cuba separately but with similar goals to mine in regard to photographing old cars and steam engines, only to have all their papers and films confiscated by ambitious security agents as they were leaving the country.

In an attempt to protect myself from such a mishap, these "Letters from Cuba" were my way of making notes that were not. At the same time they allow me to satisfy several requests made by friends and family who said, "Send us a card from Cuba." Here they are, folks - a little more thorough than cards, and they took a little longer than I expected. But you were each in my mind as I wrote these letters, which not only helped ease the loneliness of being so far from home, but also got me to focus better on the many interesting friends and experiences that we met with in Cuba.

Cubans are the friendliest people I've ever encountered, which may come as a surprise to many of you. I too had expected to find fiery-eyed, bearded revolutionaries quoting Marx and Engels on every street corner, or carrying machine guns and shouting, "Death to America." As it turned out, the few fellows we saw wearing uniforms and carrying AK-47's were mostly guards at military installations, same as you'd see in any country. Among the general populace there was neither the feeling of military fervor that I'd often seen attributed to them, nor any sense of real bitterness towards other nationalities, including the United States, next door. Of course, there is definite resentment against the policies of the U.S. government, which appears to continue giving Cuba and its people very harsh and unfair treatment.

Among recent major changes in the world's international relations, America has seen fit to expand ties with communist China, which is more totalitarian than Cuba. America has also lifted its embargo against Vietnam, which has American blood on its hands; Cuba does not. My desire is that this book will contribute in some small way to a better understanding by the rest of the world as to how much Cuba wants and needs everyone else's friendship, plus respect for its unique differences. In writing these "letters" I've been asked to change some of the names in order to "protect the innocent." Even my best Cuban friends got nervous when I started writing down things that they told me; most refused to let me record them on tape at all. Although personal freedoms in Cuba are slowly expanding, the people are still not sure just how much they will now be allowed to express their thoughts in public. My own wish is that it be so much that by the time this book is published I'll have no problem bringing a bunch of copies into the country as gifts for all my friends.

AHW 1996

It's rare to meet an ox driver in most countries nowadays, but in Cuba many are still to be found. This gentleman was bringing sugarcane to the mill of Central Pepito Tey, near Cienfuegos. When we stopped to say hello he gave us firm handshakes and asked how we like Cuba, smiling proudly when we told him "very much." Straw hat, cigar and machete are typical accessories for his line of work, with the legendary beasts of burden continuing to be a daily reality.

Hotel Herradura,
Varadero Beach, Cuba - March 14, 1994

Dear Iniskim

Your brother and I have arrived safely in Varadero and are back at the Hotel Herradura, just a few rooms over from where you and I stayed last year, that same sound of ocean waves pounding up against the courtyard walls below our balcony. Okan hasn't really seen anything of Cuba yet, since we didn't make that boring drive from the airport to here until after dark (due to flight delays), but he likes it already just for the way our hotel room looks out at palm trees and the open seas. Wonder what he'll think once he gets visually caressed by some of those friendly dark eyed women that tried to lure you last year....

We've already had our first encounter with the Cuban system in distress. Two of our three large duffel bags got off the Russian built Cubana Airways plane with us, but the third stayed on to Havana, and from there we're not sure yet. It *might* return on a different plane tomorrow, we were told by an apologetic travel bureau representative, or it might stay on and go back to Canada!

My fear is that some desperate soul will waylay it for its contents of clothing and extra shoes. Most serious item for us is our tripod, the heavy one with the fluid head, which helps to make Okan's videos look more professional and easier to watch. It would put a major dent in our efforts to suddenly be without this tool and have to hold the camera by hand instead.

Actually, the missing bag doesn't concern me too much because it turned out that a whole bunch of bags were not left, with several fellow travellers having lost everything they brought for their Cuba vacation. At least the two bags we do have contain our main clothing, films and personal gear. Maybe we can *build* a tripod out of sugar cane stalks or something. Seriously, we probably could have one cooked up in some shop, since in Cuba they seem to build everything else, from buggies and carriages to major pieces of turn-of-the-century steam engines. There's certainly no hope of *buying* a tripod in Cuba - haven't even seen a photo store, nor any Cuban with a camera, just tourists.

There's one particularly sour note though, regarding the missing bag. We packed so many extra clothes and things to give away, plus a couple hundred prints from last year's photos, that the ticket counter lady back home said she'd have to charge us extra. She seemed somewhat embarrassed to tell us this, saying that her own Canadian airline is not so fussy, but in this case she was representing Cubana, which is very concerned about weight, and wants the extra tariffs. She said the charge should have been $280, but she only asked for $180. It seemed ironic that the "people-owned" airline of Cuba should penalize me for bringing gifts that are for a bunch of Cuban people.

The fellow travellers who lost their luggage were part of a boisterous, loud-talking group that filled nearly half the very cramped plane, or so it seemed, with their inter-seat drinking and partying, all in some kind of Slavic language. They laughed a lot, but nobody else on the plane did. They got off the bus at one of the fancy new hotels, still grumbling about Cubans and the lost baggage. They were sure obnoxious, and I don't think they came to look for new friends among the Cuban people.

Last year we flew in the comfort of Canadian Airlines, with music, magazines and good food. This time, none of the above, which made this obnoxious group especially bad entertainment. After the flight got underway, the attendants brought trays of tiny-cut, olive-topped slices of sandwiches made with half-dried bread, which I assumed was the promised meal. I took a couple and laid them in our unwashed hands, trying to avoid crumbs on my seat, wondering how many hands and sleeves would brush against those last pieces still on the trays before they too got hungrily devoured. About an hour later we got a surprise when actual meal trays were brought, though it was no surprise that they were third rate. A big piece of very tough meat dominated the small tray, with mine and many others left so raw in the middle that most of us handed them back uneaten. A virtual crime, considering we were heading for a country whose ordinary people never get such chunks of meat at all these days.

One of our two arriving bags had an "8" chalked at both ends when it came down from the conveyor belt, which gave us the privilege of a personal inspection by one of the uniformed guards. He was young and clean shaven, but seemed somewhat pale and shaken, with fresh cuts on his arm and forehead, from which he kept mopping drops of blood with some stiff paper napkins. When I asked what happened he said something hit him coming off the airplane, but I couldn't make out what. His English was very limited and you already know what my Spanish is like.

I was concerned what he'd think about the large supply of film I was bringing - over 100 rolls - though some of it was in the missing bag. But instead of the fresh film, what caught his interest were my bundles of prints. I sensed that for a moment he thought he'd caught some new kind of smuggler, one intent on earning money by selling them to a photo-starved populace. His attitude changed somewhat when I explained that they were photos of friends that I was bringing for presents, and even more so when he found his home region represented by one of the sugar mills where we spent a bunch of our time last year. Putting the photos away, he noticed that there were numerous bars of soap in the bag as well. Sheepishly, I explained that they were also for our friends. With that he picked one bar up and motioned that he was a friend and would like to have it. When I nodded, he double checked, saying it all with the sign language that Cubans use so much. I called him "amigo" and said it was his, at which he cast a moment's glance around, then casually moved the bar of soap down into one of the shelves below the inspection counter. After that he gave both sides of the bag a quick feel with his hands then told me to close it up and have a nice stay in Cuba. I took this experience as my first sign that things have loosened up a lot more since our last visit, which proved to be quite right, both for the better and worse.

Incidentally, you'll enjoy this karma scene: About a half dozen of the most loud-mouthed revellers on the plane remained too long by the baggage carousel, arguing (fruitlessly) with the airport Cubans about their missing bags, as a result of which they had to *stand* during the half hour ride to the hotel, all seats on the bus having been taken in the meantime. These guys were pretty drunk too, which I guess is how they like to spend their vacation.

Another sign of the changing times was a handwritten note covering that part of our bus driver's sunshade that he had pulled down - about a third of it - making the following un-socialist request: "Don't forget to tip the driver if you enjoyed the service." The small, middle-aged, light-skinned man in charge of the wheel didn't even say hello when we got aboard, nor did he show the usually common Cuban smile. The others either felt more generous than I, or more forgiving, as I noticed a small pile of Canadian paper money on the dashboard after they got off. He followed us into the hotel and tried to trade his new wealth for the U.S. dollars that everybody wants. When we were here last year he would have been arrested and put in jail just for having the foreign cash - remember how secretively some of our friends acted when we gave them some? But we saw in the paper that for the last few months Fidel has said it's now okay to own *dollars,* which is why everybody is trying to get hold of some. The black market is even busier than when we were here, and of course it's always operated mainly with American dollars. That means the more ambitious among those kinds who last year begged us for gum and soap are now openly requesting "doh-lahrs." My biggest concern is this: can crime be far behind? Boy, what a challenge this is going to be for Cuba, "now that the cat's out of the bag," so to speak.

We already had a short visit with my tocayo Adolfo, who was working and didn't have much time. He says that he and his folks are doing good and to send you their greetings. They want Okan and I to have a meal at their apartment before we leave, so I told him it would be near the end of the month. He was dressed in a fancy new leather jacket, a bit warm for Varadero, with everyone else in T-shirts and such, but he was obviously proud of it, maybe scared to leave it anywhere other than on himself while in town. He said a friend from Europe gave it to him, which means probably a girlfriend, knowing what a smooth operator he can be.

"Amigo is friend, but tocayo is brother," Adolfo explained

when I asked him the difference. He assured me in several ways that he takes our relationship pretty seriously. I'm still baffled by our first meeting last year right after you and I arrived, having just read a book titled *Tocayo* and thus knowing something of its meaning, which regards our sharing the same first name (as we both also do with our fathers). It was strange having the first real Cuban I ever talked to become my tocayo.

The new rush for dollars is driving Adolfo crazy, he said, though he admits to being after them himself. A part of him hates it. "What can I do?" he complained, "the only way my parents can get food or anything else is with dollars, but they cannot get dollars where they work. Only *I* can get them, here from tourists." At about this point some chicas interrupted our street visit, asking Adolfo if Okan and I wanted their company. He told them no, then gave them some of his cigarettes, so they didn't come out completely empty handed. They were three fine looking mulatto ladies, but Adolfo forgot about them the moment they moved away, as he continued instead with his dollar woes. "When you want to buy a big chicken for your family you pay three American dollars. When I say 'I'll give you two hundred pesos' (the average Cuban monthly wage) they say, 'no, we want U.S. dollars.' In the same way, a bottle of rum for a visit with my friends costs about two U.S. dollars on the black market, but even for 400 pesos you can't get one." The day we arrived, the exchange rate went from 100 pesos per dollar to 115, though on the black market you can get offered 200. Not much good when you can't buy anything with them except maybe some rice and beans, which are not of much use to "touristas" like us.

....Well, by golly, a whole day has gone by since I wrote this far in my letter, so I'll go on from here. Just got too sleepy last night, and today we've been on the go since this morning. In fact, I woke up way too early, as usual, from the sounds of roosters crowing (in a tourist city?) and of buses stopping out front. That was around daylight, between five and six, after which I only dozed. You remember how I was last year - the wild mountain man from the peaceful Rockies waking up to every car, motorcycle, or faulty air conditioner in the neighborhood, not to mention the loud salsa music, which began here at about seven this morning from at least two huge speakers in the area. Okan is no more bothered by this than you were last year, so maybe it's just my age.

Last night we went for a fairly long walk up and down the main drag of Varadero. Man, did the chicas ever lay into us! Grabbing our braids, smacking their lips, whistling, saying things we didn't understand. It was like running a gauntlet in some strange sort of poorhouse. I had to explain to Okan that these young women are often just bored, having seen little of Cuba and never anything outside of it, thus they're eager to make contact with someone who has. Being a very passionate people, maybe they also yearn for a physical taste of a foreigner, but I don't think that's always the case. Some of those who've come up certainly gave me distinct romantic impressions, especially the two this evening who walked on each side of me and stroked my body gently while whispering words of uncertain meaning. My general policy is to pretend nothing is happening and to go on my way, but at times like those it's hard not to at least give back a smile. I've told Okan we needn't be too flattered by the attention of these usually good-looking women, since they do about the same for every prospect they pass. Still, such attention is hard *not* to notice by the average man's ego. Even an old guy like me can feel an inch or two taller for the next few blocks.

The first couple days of our month long schedule were left open for laying on the beach and adjusting to things - "getting over the culture shock," as Okan said worriedly before we left home. But there wasn't any, so by the middle of the first day we already had enough sand and sunburn to notice a certain well known desire to get moving that always comes when we get near intriguing train operations or photogenic old steam engines. Your tales had Okan primed and ready, knowing the nearest narrow gauge line is only ten minutes from the beach by rental car. This time we had to settle on a cheap white Nissan sedan instead of the robust little Daihatsu 4-WD "jeep" that you and I drove around. All the jeeps were either rented, wrecked or broken down, with some of the last two categories parked at the lot for

Standing near the walls of the Hotel Herradura, 22-year old son Okan contemplates the blizzards we just left back home in the Canadian Rockies. The white sandy beach and clear blue waters of Varadero can be seen behind him. It took some discipline for us to leave this place each morning for uncertain searches of old steam powered trains that we photographed further inland.

inspection. The most wrecked one immediately caught my eye, crushed from all sides, lots of the locally common red earth ground into its body. "Hit a cow," a Havanauto worker told us in rough English, making a slash across his throat with an index finger to indicate death, then adding, "Russians, two; drinky, drinky!" With that he put a thumb to his mouth with closed fist and shook his head in disgust. Russians are notorious among Cubans as heavy drinkers, along with Germans. Only difference they say is that Germans mind their own business and spend a lot of money, whereas Russians are tight, but eager to try bossing the Cubans around. It's easy to find resentment among the people, including some of those who spent time living in Russia while being schooled. The two that were killed were tourists, it turned out, coming back to Varadero from a weekend in Havana, drinking along the way. They and the cow met the same fate as the erstwhile jeep in the lot: totalled. And for us, only a new, little old lady's type of car, with a few thousand miles of rough roads laying ahead. Wish the three of us well, especially the car. It's only got 1,200 klicks on the odometer! Poor thing.

The latest blow to Cuba's struggling economy has been this year's sugar harvest, which worried me before we left home because rumor had it that half the sugar mills were closed and their railroads not operating. The oldest and most inefficient mills would be the first to close, which could include most of the photogenic ones that we're trying to document.

Sure enough, our ten-minute drive to Central Humberto Alvarez would have shown us the same rusty tracks you and I saw last year, and probably the same little rusty fleet of narrow gauge engines under that decaying shed, but we found out in advance that this mill was shut down again, so we skipped it and drove on for another ten minutes to Central Jose Smith Comas, with its beautiful shining standard gauge locomotives and its lively operation. Lo and behold, no smoke coming from their tall stack either, and more rusty rails. Talking to a local man plowing a garden with his single ox, we learned that sugar cane normally processed here is this year being brought a couple times a day by one of the beautiful engines over some forty miles of good tracks to neighboring Central Espana, which helps to keep that mill from clos-ing.

Meanwhile, I'm sleepy and it's bedtime again. So I'll write you more experiences later on the trip.

Lots of love from your dad and brother.

Varadero Beach, Cuba
March 16, 1994

Hi Star

Happy birthday (shortly) from your brother Okan and me. It's near bedtime for us after another busy day here in Cuba. Saw a bunch of colourful and interesting trains today, plus an old VW bug. We also met a couple of "entertainers" who tried hard to entertain us, and to practice their English for a while. You probably would have enjoyed them more than we did, a couple of pretty "cool" guys, knowing a fair bit of the latest talk picked up from young Canadians who like to come here and party in Cuba during school breaks. The Cuban government hires young guys (and girls) to "entertain" these carefree tourists and maybe help keep them out of trouble (they don't always succeed - a number of party go-ers have returned to Canada knowing what the inside of a Cuban jail looks like).

Anyhow, these two guys tried to persuade us to join their "seafood party" tonight. They made it sound like the event of the week, that guys and gals from hotels up and down the beach would be there to enjoy. I didn't have a chance to explain that we came to Cuba for much different reasons, nor that $20 each for more seafood than we could possibly eat is more than double our daily supper allowance. They said there'd be music and dancing and whatnot. But the thing was to start at 8 p.m. tonight and it's now nearly 11, yet the courtyard is still dead and quiet, with only the waves making loud noises. Thank heavens, since I've been at Cuban hotels with these parties underway, and they usually go on and on, with the ultra-loud salsa beat of some undecipherable band crashing through thin walls from several shoulder high speakers. Not the kind of sounds a mountain man like me can go to sleep by!

These particular "entertainers" were quite proud of their position. They just got hired as the first pair of their kind at this hotel, one of the less glamorous places that mainly offers clean rooms at good rates ($40 U.S. a night for the two of us). They're on probation, sort of, having to show how good they can entertain people before they get on full time. Hope tonight's seafood party is no indication of their overall success. I just looked down into the courtyard and saw them sitting together dejectedly near their expensive seafood buffet, with not a party-goer in sight. Imagine what an ordinary Cuban would do for a chance at some of that fancy grub?

These guys said they were school teachers until a few weeks ago, earning 160 pesos per month (one and a half U.S. dollars at the current exchange rate). Now they get 260 pesos, with chances at far more if they pass the required exam after their three months of probation. They didn't say, but the pay is actually not much better than teaching. However, by being around tourists they get a chance for some American dollars, which they don't get in classrooms. With the black market being Cuba's only source for most goods, dollars are the key to enriching one's life.

Whenever I think about the changes underway, and those still coming yet to Cuba, it makes me think of kids that have been locked up for years, suddenly getting turned loose to fend for themselves. Those with skills to hustle will probably hit the big time real fast, while the plain ordinary honest folks will stay about as poor as they are now, only their orderly society of the past 30-some years will decay quickly around them. Once Fidel starts loosening enough screws (and I think he just about has), I can't imagine how he'll hold his disciplined society together. A place like Varadero will be especially full of hustlers all seeking vulnerable tourists. I just hope weapons don't become readily available to them, since that could make the country quite dangerous compared to now.

By the way, we met an interesting black medicine man today! That's what he said he was, in the few words of English that he knew. A really dark black fellow, wearing no shirt and an orange hard hat, he came rushing up to us after we left the hotel and went down the beach a ways to swim. Said he'd seen us arrive earlier - he's a laborer working on plumbing and other repairs to our building - and wanted to meet us. He just came up and said hello, then real earnestly asked, "You - medicine man?" I wasn't sure what to answer, until he pointed to himself and said, "Me -

medicine man." We all three laughed, and I nodded my head figuring the answer is probably yes to the question he had in mind,
concerning native spiritual matters.

He's got a 15 year old daughter, too, though she's the oldest of
his kids, not the youngest like you. They only see each other
once in a *big* while. The kids and his wife live near Santiago de
Cuba, at the other end of the island. He says there's not enough
jobs down there, and that the pay is less. Here, he gets 250 pesos
a month, about like the entertainers, and again he's close to the
flow of dollars. But he looked indignant when I suggested American money had anything to do with his job, telling me, "I am a
laborer; who is going to give me dollars?" Us, for one, though
he'll have to wait till a little later on our trip, to make sure we
have enough to go around. Says he'll still be working here when
we come back for our last two days in Cuba. Same day that we
fly to Canada he leaves on a bus for back home. Otherwise, he's
here four months at a stretch. You think sometimes it's too much
having a dad around who works mostly at home, so imagine instead how it would be for us if I had to be gone one third of the
year at a time! He does get free housing with his job and pays
only 50 centavos a day for two meals, which is really cheap. Says
supper is mostly rice, one or two boiled vegetables, and sometimes maybe a sweet dessert made from sugar cane. Occasionally
they get chicken, more often fish, but never meat, nor any other
food treats. When I jokingly asked if the good looking women
of Varadero don't become tempting during those four months
away from home he said very seriously, "Todo solo," holding up
one finger, meaning he stays completely alone. When I looked
hard at him to determine what he meant, he added, "Mucho Sida,
mui peligro!" meaning much Aids, very dangerous. I was glad to
hear such talk, since several friends have told us, "the Cuban people are very promiscuous." When someone in Cuba tests positive
for HIV they're sent off to special sanatoriums, mostly former
military barracks, one in each province, and that's where they live
from then on.

A funny thing happened here at our room while we were gone
today. You'll appreciate this, especially after your stint last sum-

mer working at housekeeping in a tourist lodge. Here, they have to do impromptu repairs besides just fixing the beds, floors and bathrooms. Last night when we checked in we found the toilet hard to flush. A Russian model, with a plunger at the top that you pull upwards instead of using a handle. We had to jiggle the wire to make it work. But tonight it wouldn't work at all, so Okan took the lid off to find out why. Apparently the maid didn't like the sticking wire either, so she had replaced it with a new buckskin thong - one of those that I tie my braids with but had accidentally left laying around! I untied it and took it back, then we fixed the wire so that it finally worked right. Those soft thongs are too precious for that kind of service!

You're probably wanting to hear something about the Cuban guys, how they look and dress, and what they dance to. I've never been a great judge of men, but if they're equal to Cuba's women, then they must be a pretty fine looking bunch. It helps a whole lot that they have little to eat, especially in the way of fattening things, plus their overworked transportation system means they often walk, so fat people are hardly seen, and even the elderly appear quite sprightly.

Here in Varadero most of the young Cubans dress pretty sharp, mainly because they encounter a lot of foreigners either through their jobs or through being hustlers, and many tourists are thoughtful enough to give away most of their clothing before heading back home. That's why you'll see a couple of dudes riding together on a single old bicycle, maybe the only wheels they own, but they're wearing hundred dollar runners and fancy Italian pullovers that they could never hope to buy in Cuba for cash. It would be immensely challenging to walk around here with *you* instead of with Okan, because the men go "ssst, ssst" quite loudly to any women that catch their eye, and they pretty much look at them all. I guess expectedly so, since the women and girls do the same to us. People here are used to calling out to strangers as if they know them, which takes some getting used to, especially when they say suggestive things as well. "Hey, how's it going," someone will often shout in Spanish through our car window as we drive past. Since we don't know most of their varied local

*Afternoon traffic on downtown streets of old Cardenas looks
different from that seen on ocean-side boulevards of nearby
tourist-filled Varadero.*

expressions, they could just as well be telling us insults, thus we
never know for sure how to respond. Usually we settle for a duo
of loud "hayys's" and quick waves of our hands. And believe me,
we do that quite a lot as we drive around. That's probably what
you would notice most about the young crowd here - or the old
crowd too - an attitude almost as if they were all family, all members of the same fraternity or sorority. No atmosphere of gangs,
individual groups, or even much of arrogant show-offs. Wonder
how soon that'll change, with the opening up of their society.
The thought of it must be helping to turn Fidel's beard grey, as
he no doubt sees the inevitable crumbling of social morals he's
worked so hard to promote. Sure is something to see and partake
in - a society of people with such commitment to each other and
their land. Would that these were commodities, so we could trade
some of our food and comforts to them for some of their human
togetherness.

From what I hear, teenagers in Cuba don't do a lot of real dating, since they're in school much of the day and expected to do volunteer work during some of their free time. Yet there are always crowds of them at the beach and in the parks, standing around talking, flirting, hugging, same as anywhere else. Cars are too scarce for the young and too expensive to operate, though a few own mopeds and light motorcycles. Girls often ride sidesaddle on bikes with boys, as do husbands and wives. For a romantic date a guy can take his girl for a ride on a carriage drawn by horses, which costs only a few centavos and allows some bit of private cuddling - a rare thing in a country where housing shortages keep two and three generations together in small family apartments. The country is so crowded that it's hard to find anywhere without people. Privacy is scarce, though for tourists perhaps even more so, with everyone seemingly interested in everything done by us.

On a different note, Okan and I went "cruising" last night through the very aged town of Cardenas. It was after a long day of photographing trains, the sun had already set, and we were in no rush to get back to our beachfront hotel, just 20 minutes away. But what an amazing difference in that short distance! From modern and thriving tourist developments to a crowded and crumbling old city whose downtown is without any of the lights, action, stores, or entertainment places you'd expect in a city of this size anywhere else.

We drove along in silence for a while, then compared our thoughts, which perhaps showed the difference in our ages, along with our everyday outlook. I had been thinking of how life here would be utterly boring for me; looking at the buildings, I was intrigued by their many interesting details, carvings, posts and pillars, but I also noticed the well advanced decay in everything, the result of years of national poverty. Okan on the other hand said he was imagining the place after a streak of good luck, with all the neat old buildings fixed up and bustling, with lots of bright stores and activity. Cardenas does have great potential, thinking of the many old warehouses and tenements in cities back home that have become born-again shopping and social centers. On a rocky point jutting out into the ocean at the edge of Cardenas stands a tall pole where Cuba first flew its own flag, so the town has potential landmark status just on that basis alone.

There's also a "modern" part of town, virtually a whole city by itself, with street after potholed street of big ugly concrete and steel boxes, each of which serves as home for several dozen families. Typical Stalinist "worker's homes," in which everybody is supposed to be the same, although they don't really fit Cuban personalities any better than they enhance Cuban scenery, and besides that they're crumbling from poor construction. The task ahead for Cuba in repairing its housing seems nearly impossible to a guy like me, who can barely keep up with our own handful of cabins and cabooses at home. Seemingly every building I've looked at needs major repairs, and we regularly pass through whole towns and villages that look almost ready to be abandoned. Cuban economists will grapple with this one for generations to come.

Tomorrow we head for another part of the country, so who knows from where I'll write to you again. But you can be sure I'll be thinking about you and looking forward to telling you of our adventures in person.

The street-side face of a navy blue '48 Chevrolet, polished and well maintained.

March 20, 1994
Santa Clara Libre Hotel

Dear Wife

A big hello from hot and sensual Cuba, and from your husband who misses you a lot. So many good looking women in our surroundings all day long that it's hard not to wish for my own (you, that is!), that I could kiss and hug. People in this country kiss and hug a lot, and they do it openly, though generally not very much with tourists. A few of our friends from last year and some members of their families have greeted us in that way, and it sure feels special.

Could say 'I wish you were here', but it wouldn't be completely true. Don't think you'd care for our constant tracking down of train scenes, which means lots of dirt roads with stretches of rock that makes driving somewhat like playing chess on a badger hill during a strong prairie wind, with the other "players" trying to steer their bikes, oxcarts and tractors around the same big potholes and outcroppings. In other words, the traffic can be awful, and in addition it's hot and dusty all day long, with no place to stop for a soda or even just for plain ice water, unless we're around friends, which is fortunately a fair bit of the time. From the tap, all water in Cuba is lukewarm, since it generally comes out of shallow wells (and a lot of these are no doubt contaminated by today's standards). It's a wonder people don't get sick, especially visitors like us, but tourist brochures claim proudly that "water is drinkable everywhere in Cuba," and we've certainly had lots of it with no problem. A few of our friends (usually railroaders) drink directly from open streams, and *that* we sure wouldn't do.

Today is our baby's fifteenth birthday and I'm a bit sad not to be there to give her a big hug and eat some of her cake (and I sure do miss your desserts, Cuba's greatest shortcoming in hotel food, though I feel guilty saying anything about it, considering that ordinary Cubans get no dessert at all, unless you count the ever present sugar cane). Anyhow, I presume the young lady got the card I drew for her before I left and the two of you will no doubt entertain yourselves quite well even with us so far away. Speaking of babies, another one of ours is in the the bathroom washing trousers in the sink. He's used to changing his clothes daily at home and having somebody else eventually wash them (you, mainly) so this is kind of a good experience for him. He did leave a pile of laundry on his bed the other morning with a note in Spanish that said, "Wash, please," (we looked it up in our pocket dictionary) which was accompanied by all the spare change we had between us (about three U.S. dollars). We heard that some room cleaners make extra income by doing private laundry on the side, but ours must have a rich aunt in Miami, since she just made the bed and put the bag back over it, note, spare change and all. Otherwise, laundromats are not to be seen in this country, nor washing machines. Muchos clothes flapping on lines in the wind everywhere we go.

All the windows in our hotel room are open and the sounds of 1994 Cuba are almost overwhelming from down below. There are motorcycles and cars of all ages, nationalities and muffler quality constantly cruising the old plaza. Music is blaring from some of their radios, and from loudspeakers here and there throughout the city, which spreads out around us on all sides. Music with lots of rhythm and drums; salsa, calypso, rock, rap-rock; most of it in Spanish, but also some of the latest tunes from New York, Miami and L.A. Plus, a seeming addiction to Whitney Huston's "I'll Always Love You," which we hear loudly at least a couple times a day and sometimes from two different sources at once, making it an unbalanced monster stereo presentation. And there's lots of amplified d.j. type talking with and in between the music, plus a constant hubbub of Cuban voices everywhere on the streets and in the buildings; a very expressive people, not shy to be heard aloud in public. Mixed with all this is the honking of horns and the clip-clop of horse's hooves pulling the multitudes of wagons and carriages that bring people to the plaza and take them away again. They look neat at night, with flames flickering on their rear axles from small oil lamps. Wish the wagons out on the dark highways at nights would have these. It wouldn't be so dangerously easy to drive along and suddenly discover them by surprise. Several times we've had close calls, especially with wagons going in both directions at once and taking up the whole highway, yet lit only by our headlights.

Earlier this evening we went for supper downstairs, where Iniskim and I were entertained last year by those fabulous folk singers, "Trio Los Brillantes." But not only were they gone this time, we even got chased out of our old basement cafeteria which is now the nightly meeting and eating place for Communist Party block committee members, of which Santa Clara has a couple dozen, based on a quick glance I took at the long tables. We were told politely that the "tourist restaurant" is now on the top floor, one above our room. Interestingly, the downstairs staff was still the same from last year, whereas the upstairs place has mostly new people. We took the elevator up, admiring the dozen or so bullet holes in and around the basement door while we waited.

"Monument to Che," said the soft-spoken elevator operator when I asked him about them. "He captured this building for the Revolution," he explained; "big fight here, this place. That's why I like to work it." He's an engineering student, working at the hotel to earn his way through school and to learn other languages. "Especially English," he assured us with a shy smile. He only looks about 17 or 18, but that could be from the sparse eating conditions.

This is a somewhat notorious hotel, considering I dismissed it at first glance last year as an architectural derelict. A colour slide of its grey concrete and glass facade would make an auditorium audience yawn, at least until you pointed out several dozen conspicuous specks in the hotel face, and then explained that they are left over from when Che Guavara's forces had a troop of dictator Batista's secret police pinned down inside, trading shots with them from machine guns and whatever else. The regular army troops and other Batista men around Santa Clara had already surrendered or fled, but these guys had done some of the worst things to the people so they didn't want to give up. Trouble was, a bunch of tourists got stuck in the hotel with them. Since I've learned about this, it's been on my mind whenever we've gone up and down the stairs and corridors.

The tenth floor no longer shows signs of being the last stand of a dictator's despised secret police. Our table was beside an open window from which we could see other buildings around the open plaza, from the roofs of which Revolutionary sharpshooters tried unsuccessfully to pick off the police marksmen who were shooting from in here. To keep anyone from coming up after them, the cops had carted mattresses from rooms on the first floor and heaved them down the narrow stairwell until they formed an impenetrable plug. Actually, it was that factor which gave me some concern last year when we stayed here. The only way out of this big cement box is down that same narrow stairway, with no other fire escapes whatsoever (other than the windows). The revolutionaries couldn't set the place on fire because of the tourists inside. There was enough food and water in the hotel for them, and the Batista policemen, who happened in addition to be on the same floor as the hotel bar. What they didn't know was that downstairs among the tourists there was a hotel employee with a secret transmitter for talking to the revolutionaries outside. This guy eventually led all the tourists to a particular hotel room window that happened to be right next to a similar window in an adjacent building, just two feet away. A few faint hearted tourists had to be "coaxed" to make this high altitude transfer of buildings, but once they were all out, the mattress pile got set afire from below until the henchmen were smoked out. Surprisingly, they all managed to come out on foot, none having been shot during the long pitched battle. But when they got into the plaza with their hands up, a huge crowd surrounded them and before long those same policemen all lay dead on the street and sidewalk, never to carry out acts of repression against ordinary Cuban citizens again. So, that's the dramatic story of this hotel, where your husband and son are right now staying. Makes me appreciate all the more how you and I have gotten to raise our children in a land that has no hotels decorated with revolutionary bullet holes. Not yet, anyway!

Our dinner consisted of plain boiled chicken, bean soup, boiled yucca (sort of a potato), mixed salad of green tomato and cucumber, white rice, and a strange little bottle of Cuban cola that tasted alright, especially to my constantly-thirsty palate. The whole thing, doubled, cost us $16, which I considered more than fair. On the other hand, at current exchange rates that comes to 1600 Cuban pesos, and that sounds like a lot.

Instead of the pleasant folk-singing trio from last year, this penthouse restaurant offered sort of a jazz combo whose heavy percussion was more suited to the belting down of drinks than the relaxed enjoyment of my long-awaited meal. I was relieved when, after two lengthy numbers, they got ready to take a break. A band member named Mariano came to our table for a chat and said that he and his wife (the keyboard player) are very highly paid by Cuban standards, making together 1700 pesos per month. Keep in mind that the average wage is down around 250 pesos. But, like everyone else, he complained that they can't buy anything with the money. "You can only use so much beans and rice," he said with a smirk. "I have friends in other countries, and one of them from Germany sent me $150 for a present in December. Now it is almost April and I am still supporting my wife and daughter on that money." When I asked him how, he said, "From the black market, of course! Everything now comes from the black market." He said stores have practically nothing, not even the ration goods, a complaint we've heard over and over.

"It could be the biggest mistake Fidel has made," he went on, "allowing the people to have American dollars. We don't know where that will lead us. But I have no idea what Fidel could do instead, and I don't think anyone else has an idea. That is our economic problem right now - our country's biggest problem." He feels that the U.S. embargo, or "blocada" as it is constantly called, is in itself not such a big concern, but rather that it symbolizes the country's troubles, demoralizes the people, indicates the country's world standing and gives the government something to stand behind in explaining all sorts of problems, some not really involved with the embargo at all.

It surprised me that Mariano used Fidel's name so openly, since I've found it conspicuous that most people won't, even if I try to get them to. I first figured they wouldn't say it out of fear, but now I'm beginning to think it has as much to do with respect for the man. It may be that they're used to foreigners saying critical things about him so they'd rather avoid the subject than have that happen. At any rate, those who want to mention Fidel usually stroke their chins, signifying a beard, else they'll use some vague term like "the boss" or "the old one," and usually in English. Mariano was talking in good English, but the name Fidel still stood out, at least in my ears, though none of the dozen or so other people in the restaurant (mostly staff) seemed to notice.

Mariano wasn't even shy to talk aloud about the value in Cuba of having "connections," something that a classless society would seemingly not allow. He said, "Because of my music, I have friends in places who help me get things that others can't get so easily. For instance, if my wife and I want to eat in a tourist hotel like this one or go somewhere by train, we don't have to stand in lines for hours and hours, days ahead. I just ask one of my friends, and they arrange it. We really hate to use our friends in this way, but what choice do we have? With both of us practicing and playing all the time, when could we go stand in lines?"

His biggest complaint in life is the changing attitudes and morals among his fellow Cubans. He said, "We are a very proud people and it hurts us to see our children begging tourists for candy and gum, and especially now for dollars. We are different from the people in other Latin countries. There, the ones who beg often have nothing at all, no homes, no food, no shoes. But our children are not like that, none of them. Those who beg for gum are all wearing shoes, and often they are well dressed. They all have homes and families. Why do they go begging? What deep need are they craving? This is what we have to find out and cure, quickly, before it becomes a cancer within our society."

With all the heavy talking I sort of lost my appetite, though the food was good; there was still some left over when I felt finished. Then I remembered that we were going across the street to the park afterwards for a visit with Cristina, an old friend of mine from last year, who told me in a short conversation this evening when we arrived that she actually *lives* "on the street." For twenty centavos she gets one meal a day at the cafeteria nearby here, on the plaza (that's less than a nickel), but it consists mainly of a boiled egg and some bread, sometimes bean soup or a bit of rice, plus a drink. "They call the drink lemonade, but it's mainly sweet water," she sighed. No wonder she looks like she weighs less than a hundred pounds.

It took 10 minutes for me to get the waiter to understand that I wanted something to wrap the leftovers with (another student in his 20's, making first attempts at conversational English!). He finally brought me a single sheet of yesterday's mimeographed menu, at which point the musician joined in, berated the poor fellow for his incompetence, and got him to come back with two more menu sheets. At that he got told it was good, so our conversation went on while I scooped up one piece of wet chicken plus some bits of rice and green salad (Cristina says she never sees any salad here in town, and certainly not chicken). Once wrapped it quickly got soggy, so you can imagine I didn't waste much time getting to the elevator and out through the lobby to the intended diner, who was equally speedy in gulping the meal down. Her obvious hunger and gratitude were more than worth my eating only half of what is for us a normal supper. The couple dollar bills I gave her at the end of our visit got her even more excited, since at the least it would pay for a couple months of her meager cafeteria dining.

I told you about Cristina last year when we came back from Cuba, but you might have forgotten. Her light skin and smooth New Jersey dialect had me convinced she was a misguided tourist when she first came up and started talking in English to us. When I realized she was definitely a Cuban resident I wondered if she'd been so spaced out in the sixties that she got left behind when all those American "radicals" used to come down to help "struggling Communist Cuba" with its sugar harvests. She has kind of a bewildered look, besides being so frail, and she talks pretty slow, but after the long visit we had this evening I think it's more likely that she's a real deep thinker who feels very frustrated from years of being part of a very controlled society in which she's never quite found her place.

Cristina was eighteen at the time of the revolution ("Oh, I'm pretty old," she told me with a serious look, seeming to mean more in spirit than in years), and she was actually a resident of Cuba by choice. She was born here, but both her parents had foreign roots. In fact, they split up while she was young, at which time she moved with her mother to the U.S. (yes, New Jersey!) where she went to school and had many friends. But then her mother died, so she came back to Cuba to live with her mother's best friend. "When the revolution came I could have gone back to the U.S., but in my heart I've always been Cuban and most of us young people were pretty thrilled about the change; we really liked Fidel and what he was saying. Things have sure turned out different from the way we imagined back then, but there have been many good changes along with the bad." We were sitting on one of the dozens of benches along the winding walk-ways of the park, with lots of other people walking and sitting and carrying on their own conversations. Still, now and then Cristina would glance around before going on with her talking. She told me later that everyone has probably heard her thoughts by now and that it's been a long time since anybody bothered her about them. When I asked if they used to, she looked at me very knowingly and said, "I've seen the inside of jail more than once," then she laughed as though she bore no ill feelings.

"During the revolution I had relatives on both sides," she recalled. "I was living in Havana with my adopted auntie and I remember the bombs going off regularly, the occasional times of terror when we thought we'd all be killed. Part of the reason we were so thrilled when Fidel and his men arrived in Havana is because we knew the worst was over, or we figured it was. Actually, those first years were pretty tough until we all got used to the new system, but then we had a long time where things were pretty good and most everybody was satisfied. Now? We're into another bad period, but it's much, much worse than ever before."

"The young have no respect for this system, nor for their elders or their families, and that's an important reason why Cuba is changing. We've had too many years of nothing happening, so they don't believe in the revolution anymore. They can see through it - through all the slogans and posters. It's very obvious to everybody by now that the whole deal is a failure, so why should they believe in it? We're all looking for something to believe in, but for most of the young it's not Fidel and his revolution and so far I don't think anybody knows what it's going to be."

Our conversation had me so engrossed that I barely noticed a small crowd gathering around Okan, who started it all by responding to a couple of young fellows who had wanted somebody to practice their English with. Of course, he didn't bargain on being surrounded by a dozen practitioners, one of whom stood quite near us, straddling his bicycle. He seemed so intent on Okan's conversation that I never noticed his ears being turned towards us. But Cristina did, especially since she already recognized him as a member of the secret police. I did notice that she suddenly quit talking, then whispered, "let's go for a walk." When she told me later why, I recalled there had been something a little different about this fellow, but I hadn't bothered to dwell on it. By the time we circled the park once and got back, Okan still had most of his crowd, minus the guy on the bicycle.

Like you, Cristina has had four children, but the results for her have not been so happy and loving. Her oldest son married a girl from France and now lives there with her, but never writes or visits. Her oldest daughter is married in Havana and also has a life of her own. Two teenage children still live with their dad here in Santa Clara, but they argue with her every time she goes to see them, as does the husband (who she says abused her for many years). She's afraid of him - a house painter - but goes there and stays with them for a night or two, now and then. No doubt there's more to the story, but that's all she told me. You can see why I gave her a couple of dollars, after she hesitantly asked me if I could "possibly spare any change." When I gave her the bills she kind of winced with joy and said, "I'll be rich for a while." That's assuming she gets it spent, not lost or stolen. She told me that's happened to her on several occasions - a disaster, since she carries with her everything she owns. Twice she lost the whole works, other times just bits and pieces. The first total loss was worst because it included all her family pictures.

A sunny Sunday morning in the plaza of Santa Clara, with several goat-drawn carts on hand to take children for rides. This photo was taken just before private enterprise was again allowed, so these "goat drivers" must have belonged to some government department.

"This country knows itself very well - it has strong feelings of nationality," she said in its defense. "But we've never been free and independent. First we were a Spanish colony, then a U.S. colony, then a Soviet colony, and now? Our country has never been developed properly, just exploited. It will take money to develop it, and where will that come from? Our present system is not good for the land, else there would be food in the country for us right now. The system doesn't offer the right incentives for those who know how to improve things." She claims it is still very important *who* you know and how well you tip, not necessarily how good you are. "The grand revolutionary ideals were never fully put into practice," she feels sure, "they were just a good idea." She figures a whole new system is needed, but like everyone else she has no idea what kind.

"Japan is one example we are studying," Mariano had said earlier upstairs. "Like Cuba, it is also a small island nation with few resources, having to import all its oil, most of its food, and so forth. But the question is whether we have the skills and discipline needed to succeed in the way Japan has?" There is no doubt that the Japanese and Cubans are two very different kinds of people. Our entertainer friends say the Japanese are among the hardest tourists to talk with, never mind entertain. They prefer their own company and thoughts, which must appear to Cubans as haughty since their own life is very open and social.

"A year ago I wouldn't have spoken to you about our problems like this," Mariano assured me, "someone would have heard me and there would have been much trouble. But now, people are speaking out. I'm receiving magazines from friends in Canada that I could never have before. I'm also receiving books and records to help my work. In that sense the new revolution is already underway."

Cristina seems so pitiful when I listen to her tales of woe, yet she's not really looking for sympathy, just understanding. She readily admits that she lives on the street from her own choice. She's lost her will to care, which is as pitiful a statement coming from a nice little lady as I can imagine.

"During the Mariel boatlift I nearly got out of Cuba," she said, still angry with herself for not doing so. "I applied and everything, but I couldn't get anyone in the U.S. to sponsor me. At that time I still had little kids and didn't want to abandon them, else I could have gone over alone. I wish now I had just gone. I've known a much better life in the past, and I'm very tired of living this one. So many in this country don't even know a better life, they've never had anything else. For them there is even less hope than for me, often just a big yearning, though for what, we don't know. More and more I hear others speak of it." She then asked me to contact a cousin of hers in Miami, and a godmother in Kansas. She's hoping that maybe by hearing about her they'll sponsor her next time, or at least send her a few dollars in a letter. She claims I'm the first tourist who's given her money in many months, that usually when she goes up to talk with them they just leave. Could be in part because this hotel is used mainly by Latin travellers, while regular tourists stay outside of town at the motel. Else she just wants to make me feel more important.

By the way, before getting this far in my letter another whole day has passed. Fell asleep while writing last night, then got up pretty early this morning for a long drive to the Mal Tiempo sugar mill where we wanted to photograph some of the shop workers and their old engines in the morning light. When we came out of the hotel, Cristina and her friend Daniel were already sitting on the park bench nearest to our car. I cheerfully waved and said good morning, to which she replied kind of grumpily, "For *you* it's a good morning, but not for us." Wow, what a send-off; talk about a guilt trip. The damned rental car cost us more for this single day of chasing trains than poor Cristina sees in a whole year! Still, we managed to have a good time at trackside and to capture some poignant images. More on that in another letter. Bye for now.

Santa Clara Libre Hotel
March 20, 1994

Gruezi Heinz!

I'm picturing you reading this letter at your desk while my father's beloved Alps loom silently in the distance outside your
window. This letter goes from one small country to another, and
for very different reasons I really love them both. I'll try to give
you a few comparisons, though to start with I'll say that in most
ways they are not very much alike. From the clippings you've
sent me out of Swiss newspapers I gather you know enough
about Cuba and its situation to understand something of what I
mean about the differences. For instance, one is rich and very
successful, the other is very, very poor. Yet, whereas the Swiss
with their wealth seem often rushed in life and always very concerned about money, Cubans don't have much in the way of pos-
sessions, but they'll share what they do have, expecially their time
and warm friendship.

Santa Clara is a sprawling city with a crowded downtown that
boasts just this single hotel, whose 9th floor rooms provide the
highest beds in the whole area. For the next few nights Okan and
I will occupy a couple of those high beds. There is a "motel" outside of town where most of the tourists stay, *when* tourists stay in
Santa Clara (attractions here are severely limited). The motel is
just off the country's "autopista," or national freeway, which is
mostly just a wide but very empty road. The motel has rooms
scattered around a fenced-in park, with the location and architecture meant to imitate what Cubans guess ancient native villages
looked like. The natives were wiped out by Spaniards long ago,
though we've heard that there are still some areas of Cuba where
people claim distant Indian ancestry. In that way - and many
more - Cuba is totally different from the U.S. and Canada next
door.

Our hotel room is plain and cramped, painted in pale shades
of pink and green, containing two small, well-worn beds, each
with a rickety dresser. We also have a plug-in fan and an old
Russian made radio. The two big front windows open up to the

main attraction - a boom box of sounds playing the Cuban
Nightime Symphony of Santa Clara. And what a cacophony of
sounds it is: the buzzing of small motorcycles going around the
plaza with bad mufflers; the drumbeats and instrumental wailings
of Latin bands playing at nearby locations; the rattling, pound-

*Evening rush hour in downtown Santa Clara, with no throngs
of city shoppers, nor commuters hurrying home. Although this
view shows   part of the plaza in the very heart of town, you
see no shops along the street, nor rows of neon signs. The
only evidence of business are two horse-drawn taxis plus the
lone vendor in the foreground, quietly selling bouquets of
fresh flowers from the back of his yellow bicycle. This was the
first week the government had allowed such private enterprise,
in 1994. Since then the number of entrepreneurs have rapidly
grown.*

ing and honking of old cars and overworked trucks as they roar
up and down the pot-holed streets; many voices of people talking, laughing and shouting to each other; plus the constant passing of horses hauling carriages and wagons. For sure this place
sounds different from any downtown I've ever stayed in. This
makes me wonder if there are travellers who could identify some

of the world's cities just by hearing their sounds from a hotel room like this?

Okan and I spent a couple of interesting hours walking among all those people down there, winding our way past the open doors of small street side apartments, which were often crowded, and sometimes had very antique furniture. We also passed quite a few old stores, which were mostly empty. Our destination was the downtown train station, about a dozen blocks away, wanting to get out and walk after a long day of driving around the country-side in our rented car. At one street corner we came upon an old green beat-up 1928 Model A Ford sedan, which is so far the old-est of the many vintage American cars that have attracted our eyes, *and* cameras. Behind it was parked a 1960's Yugoslavian motorcycle with a sidecar, and while we stopped to get a shot of the Model A, a skinny horse clomped by pulling a small covered wagon filled with fresh bread, its reins in the hands of a little old man in straw hat and torn trousers who was chomping on an unlit cigar while continuously - and without mercy - flicking the poor creature on its boney rear end with the tip of his long handled whip. These are the kinds of experiences that make the docu-mentation of transportation so interesting here.

We passed by one store just as another horse-drawn wagon stopped out front, where a crowd of people with empty sacks stood waiting. A rugged looking fellow jumped down from the seat and hauled out two handfuls of freshly killed and still un-plucked chickens, tied together by their legs. In spite of this scarce sign of fresh meat, most of the crowd managed to find time to stare at us. Having their attention anyway, I decided that taking a picture wouldn't cause any more stir, so I grabbed the camera with a wide-angle lens from the black leather bag that Okan was carrying on his shoulder.

Well, lo and behold, at that same moment some ugly old black man came out of the crowd towards me in a threatening way, suddenly talking loudly in Spanish and saying things I couldn't understand. When he stuck his dirty hand out and demanded I give him a dollar I began to get the drift of his message. He was dressed in worn out army fatigues and reeked of alcohol, his

whole face having that puffy, dazed look that comes from too
many pints circulating through the blood system.

At first I tried to ignore him while taking my picture, but then
he got even louder and more insistent, shoving his hand right in
front of my face. The ridiculousness of it all finally made me
laugh out loud, then I took my hand and slapped his in the"high
five" so popular among American blacks, a move that Okan
thought was "pretty cool." I don't think the old guy did, though it
caught him off guard long enough so I could put away the camera and get us moved along. In the process we picked up the
company of a couple of schoolboys dressed in white shirts and
khaki shorts, wearing red scarves and carrying their schoolbags,
both of them eager to try out their limited bits of classroom English.

"You from? German? Italy? Russia?" When we told them Canada, they shouted with glee and smiled big. "Canada good
friend," they assured us, a comment we hear from many Cubans.
When I told them we were headed towards the railroad station
they immediately went ahead and said they'd guide us there. I
didn't bother explaining that I'd already walked there a few times
the year before.

These guys were so slim and small that it surprised us when
they said they were 13, though from the questions they kept asking it was apparent that they were beyond being little kids. They
got even more excited when they learned we were involved with
"Indios de Canada" and that our braids were in connection to
that. They looked up regularly at 6' 3" Okan with a gleam in
their eyes that said, for the moment, "he's our hero!" We showed
them a few of our back-home photos that no doubt furthered the
whole image, especially the one of Okan in his traditional dance
outfit, feathers, bells and all. We figured, why not help the poor
fellows with something exotic to talk about with their buddies for
the next few days?

Eventually we stopped along the narrow sidewalk at a place
where two main streets meet in a T, one side headed downtown,
another leading to the front of the busy train station, with the
longest part crossing all the station tracks before heading out of

town. A traffic hub for road and track, with lots of action and good late-afternoon lighting.

When a parked train began to pull away from the station and across the busy road, I'd already composed the photo in my mind, my wide angle lens letting me include a couple of local fellows lounging on their funky three-wheeled delivery bikes at the curb right in front of us.

In an instant I had the camera out of the bag and was just pressing down on the shutter when that same old ugly guy came slobbering up again, demanding loudly that photos cost "one dollar" and that he'd allow none to be taken until I paid. The picture turned out as planned, except for part of a black hand that shows in one upper corner, not enough to cover anything of importance but as a permanent memento of this challenging experience.

There was just time for one shot before the train was gone from view so I put the camera away, but decided to stand my ground while the old guy kept up his tirade at a fairly loud pitch. I actually agreed with some of what he said, about tourists who come to Cuba and spend a lot of money, thinking because of that they can take pictures of everything for free. Maybe I should have given him the dollar he wanted and gotten him off our backs. Actually, I'd have given him *two* dollars to pose for me, if he'd asked me to pay in a nice way. But on principle I decided to stay there and view the traffic scene and give no money at all.

At this point the two boys took up our defense and asked the man to move on, but he just told them to shut up. Then the two delivery guys joined in, still lounging on their three-wheelers but apparently annoyed, not with my camera but with his loud rantings. Okan turned to me and said, "I wonder what Heinz would do in a situation like this?" which at least put an interesting new perspective on the matter for us. I don't know if he asked because he considers you a great world traveller, or because he thinks you know the solution to any kind of problem, but it made me wonder in what ways our responses to negative people only make them more so, rather than calming things down. One of the two guys on the bikes finally got up and came over, put his arm around the old guy's shoulder and talked to him so softly that we couldn't really hear, then led him down the street a ways, from where he didn't return. The two small boys followed us back to our hotel in the other direction. So, what would you have done in our place, Heinz?

Not far from the hotel was a big pharmacy with several doors standing open, so I got up the nerve to peek inside, feeling immediately like a voyeur for doing so. There were a couple dozen old fashioned brown bottles of various sizes on display along wall shelves, though I don't know what if anything was inside them. I'm sure it wasn't aspirins, Rolaids or any other such common relief agents that we normally find in drugstores. The long glass counters were completely bare, and the two people in white coats standing behind them looked as if they had nothing to do. I waved and they nodded, then I walked on while trying to imagine what life would be like at home if our drugstores only had a bunch of brown bottles.

We also paused briefly at one of the downtown "youth hangouts," if communist Cuba can be said to have such a thing. A tea shop, the two boys told us, something like a Marxist A&W, where you stand in a long line and visit with your girlfriend or whoever, until you reach the counter, pay five centavos for a glass of tea (ten centavos for two, if its your girl friend), then you sit, *if* you can find room, and slowly drink your tea while visiting some more. In usual Cuban fashion, all this is dominated by music playing very loudly over the whole area from big speakers.

You'll be especially interested to know that the tune playing just then is a current Cuban hit among the young and it concerns the Swiss hero, Wilhelm Tell! In the international manner of rock and roll's social commentary, Tell's son is saying to his famous crossbow shooting father, "This time *I'll* shoot the apple from *your* head!" You'll understand the meaning better if you switch Wilhelm's bushy-bearded face for someone else who is more Cuban, and then think of the son as being Cuba's youth... What it means for the future I cannot imagine, and probably the tea-drinkers sitting inside can't either, nor can the folks on the crowded plaza, bombarded by the same tune through those huge loudspeakers. This country is definitely opening up and changing! I can't imagine a parody of Deng Xiao Ping being sung in downtown Beijing.

Speaking of youth, your adopted grandson Okan has been a pretty good partner so far on this trip, which makes me recall other long distance trips he and I have made, such as the time you brought us to the summit of the Alps aboard a glass-covered coach hauled by a turn-of-the-century steam locomotive. That train was spotless, but we tourists were kept away from any of its mechanical operations. Like most boys, Okan would have liked to stand by the engineer, or blow the whistle. So now we're here in Cuba, where he's already had a couple of turns running the whole train, whistle, throttle and all. And these are trains that Swiss inspectors would immediately condemn from ever running again. Old and nearly worn out, patched together and often leaking. But the main thing is that Okan has had a taste of *real* railroading, and he sure likes it. So well, in fact, that he's been daydreaming about coming back with his brother Iniskim to work on some of these trains full time for a few months, even without pay or money, he says. The crews at our favorite place said right away they'd have him, so there you go. I raise my sons around tipis in the mountains, only to see them grow up and move away to run dilapidated old sugar trains in Cuba! Of course, when I was 20 like Okan I might have talked about doing something like that, before getting settled down.

Switzerland is quite highly regarded by the Cubans I've talked to, by the way. Maybe the Swiss political system has some points to offer for Cuba's upcoming changes. Maybe they can get used to voting for all their leaders at the local level, as in the Swiss system. I think they'd do well with an honest and completely open democratic system, something they've never yet experienced in all their history. And I must add that they do elect local representatives to speak for them in Havana, which I never knew before I came here.

From your newspaper clippings I find the Swiss to have a more positive outlook on Cuba than a lot of media and people across North America. Some Swiss stories express optimism for the future, whereas most of what we get on this continent predicts the imminent downfall of Fidel and the total collapse of Cuba. In fact, one Pulitzer-prize winning author may have to wipe eggs from his face if "Castro's Final Hour," is not soon, as his 1993 book title predicts. Personally, I can see Fidel retiring as an elder statesman, leaving those who take his place to effect the major changes that will indeed improve things. Any man who can lead a nation for 35 years or more and still have most of his people's affections (if not direct approval) deserves to retire and share his wisdom in a more congenial manner.

Do you remember that time old Dan Weasel Moccasin gave you an Indian name during our medicine pipe ceremony and you shared your gratitude with the assembled crowd by passing out a whole sack full of Toblerone chocolate bars from Switzerland? That's already become a legend in the tribe, with friends and family regularly asking me when you're coming over with some more. Well, last year Iniskim managed to do some horse trading down at the beach in Varadero, giving cash and a couple of good printed T-shirts for two boxes of Cuba's finest Cohiba cigars - the brand that Fidel is said to favour (though he only chews on them nowadays, in keeping with health directives for everyone to quit smoking). This spring, when we had our ceremony everybody ended up with Cuban cigars instead of Swiss chocolates. Does this mean you and I are guilty of influencing a traditional culture, wherein the treats have generally been wild berry soup and the gifts have been horses and blankets? But then, as you know, tobacco smoking is an important part of every ceremony, so the hand-rolled cigars were quite well received, especially after I explained what they cost per piece (about the price of four big hamburgers at home).

We only had a couple offers last year to sell us contraband goods like cigars, but this year black market activity seems much more noticeable. Several people have approached us openly, right in front of hotels, offering cigars, liquor, even marijuana. Include the women, and you have the basic street economy of about any city or tourist spot in the world, though it could lead a

Cuban to a long jail term. That this is now done so openly is either a sign of despair, or it's become common knowledge that people are not being caught very much. Iniskim said when his cigar trade was arranged, the fellow went down to the beach and dug the two cartons up from the sand. The seller admitted that a relative walked out with them from the cigar factory where he works. One of the guys in front of the hotel this year showed us a couple of boxes right under his jacket, with plain clothes police at the hotel entrance less than twenty feet away. Hopefully, economic developments will soon provide more legitimate options for those who are eager to earn cash.

The Swiss presence here seems surprisingly low, considering Cuba is now eagerly looking for investment partners. There's lots of Spanish money, along with German and Canadian, but little Swiss and of course no U.S. One has to wonder who will fill the void left by the recently departed Russians and other East Europeans. Their mechanical presence is certainly everywhere, from

A sign of socialism with a symbol of capitalism. This old green Cadillac was parked outside a Santa Clara gas station. It would be interesting to hear what became of the car's original owner, and to learn how the present owner got hold of it. No doubt the two would have much different lives.

cars and buses to toilets and refrigerators. Maybe that's one reason the Swiss have held back, for fear of being asked to put their
precision skills to work trying to correct the hopelessly imprecise
East Bloc remainders. Also, it might be tough at this point training Cubans how to handle Swiss precision, after all the years
they've been beating the hell out of stubborn machines that often
need a whack or two before they run at all.

There are still a fair number of old Mercedes cars rolling
around, left behind by the better-off folks when they escaped after the revolution. Except for a few that are actually nice ones,
the rest are just varying degrees short of being total junk, with
parts missing or hanging off in ways that would make the Benz
executives cringe if they saw them. Locomotive engineers routinely yank the throttles wide open on their worn out old steam
engines, making the wheels spin wildly as they assault steep
grades with often way more cars of heavy sugar cane than the
old teapots should be trying to pull. How do you fit quality and
precision into the midst of a system like that? Maybe teach them
to make everything on their own, so that appreciation will come
right at the start. The country is certainly full of eager workers,
what with "100% employment" ever since the revolution, though
it looks to us like there are usually two or three workers around
each job where we would have one. Still, the example of Switzerland as a small but successful country maintaining its own pride
and neutrality in the midst of bigger neighbors should prove to
be of some useful inspiration to Cubans in the years ahead. I
hope they find this to be food for thought.

Looking forward to further talks of this sort when you next
visit our home in the Rockies.

Santa Clara Libre Hotel
March 24, 1994

Hey Dennis!

Lots of bicycles and good looking women in Cuba! I know that'll get your attention. You should be here, cruising the streets of this lovely town in one of your aerodynamic space age bikes, with your long golden locks flowing out behind. Believe me, you'd be a hit in every way, then even *you* wouldn't be able to handle all the romantic offers.

Day by day we see countless cyclists weaving all over everywhere, with almost total disregard for other traffic. It's no wonder they get involved in lots of accidents. We're wearing out the horn on our rented car just from honking at all these cycling maniacs, though hardly any of them pay attention. If there's two or three together, they don't mind holding up cars, trucks and buses while they pedal leisurely, probably discussing the weather and politics. Worst of all, they do the same thing at *night*, generally without any lights, or even reflectors. Deadly! Last night for the very first time I got two cyclists to move right off the road for me - an amazing response - but only because I jammed on my brakes so hard right behind them that the tires squealed, while I honked and they hit the ditch, all at about the same time. And I was serious too! A pair of bright lights from an old tractor coming towards us had me so blinded that I saw nothing at all of the unlit bicycles ahead in my narrow lane. Good thing the tractor *had* lights - most of them don't. Maybe I would have passed the bikers only to end up in some farmer's lap, or much worse.

So, you asked me to look into the Cuban world of bicycling and I've tried to learn a few things that might help you decide whether you'd want to invest in a business here. Keep in mind that the whole social system is so different from Canada that it's difficult to separate cycling from everything else that's peculiarly Cuban. At any rate, you'd have to come here and spend a while with the people before you make any serious decisions. I know you just asked me to look, but I want to warn you that it's easy in Cuba to get enthused over certain things while forgetting their context within reality. Such as the lack of money and the limited hopes for economic recovery.

Okay, the most common bikes are very plain Chinese models painted in pretty colours. "Flying Pigeon" is the most popular name; for some strange reason they have it lettered in plain old English on the frame, though neither the Chinese who make them nor the Cubans who ride them normally use that language. Maybe it's supposed to evoke memories of American bikes, which are now rare but highly valued. Ask any seasoned Cuban biker and you'll hear that old, used pre-1959 U.S. models are preferred over brand new Chinese ones. Come to think of it, the style of lettering used to write Flying Pigeon does bring to mind the name Schwinn. Last year at the sugar factory of Mal Tiempo an old, retired locomotive foreman named Pepe rode his baby-blue Schwinn down to the shops every evening to inspect his aging narrow gauge engines, while the young crew members called out warm greetings and made the sign for "very fine" towards his bicycle, kissing the tips of their fingers while flicking them in its direction. Spotless, with all the chrome polished, it brought Pepe to work since back when he was still just an ordinary locomotive engineer himself in the years before Fidel's revolution.

Bike shops would no doubt be near the top of any list of viable businesses, once they are allowed to operate fully in Cuba. I've seen a few fellows working with more than one bike, a pile of tools and parts nearby suggesting an unofficial home business, but nothing that could be called a real bike shop. No mountain bikes, either, though plenty of roads and terrain for which they'd be perfectly suited. Typically, a Cuban applies through the workplace for a new bike, which Cuba obtains by the hundreds of thousands from China in exchange for sugar. They're low in cost and paid for through deductions from wages, which otherwise don't buy much anyway. By contrast, *you're* talking about making *private* transactions, for machines that would cost three or four times what the average Cuban makes in a year. Until that changes, I don't think you'd be able to do business here at all, even if you were only a minor partner. A scary thought when you're talking about selling and servicing precision machines, since Cubans haven't had much experience with anything like that.

Do you remember our friend Ken, who said to look him up if we ever got to Havana? We didn't, but we found him nonetheless, standing outside the fence of a luxury hotel in Varadero, watching the lively danc'ng at a garden party in progress to the loud amplified music of a salsa band. Okan and I had stopped to watch for a moment ourselves when we saw him, grinning happily, to all appearances still blissed out with his recent discovery of 'paradise.' His used car exporting plans sound like they're stranded in bureaucracy, but he did drive off - when we finished visiting - in a red and white '56 Buick Roadmaster convertible, looking for all the world like one of those gangsters that used to come down and play in Cuba before Fidel took over. In a nickel and dime kind of way, I guess that's what our friend Ken is; Cuba is slowly allowing his kind to come back again. Too bad...

Not that life has been all peaches and cream for him, according to some of his tales. He says they only give him a three month tourist visa, so every ninety days he flies to Mexico or one of the other Caribbean countries for a night or two, then he comes back. In the past, that would not have been tolerated. In addition, he keeps renting private houses instead of staying at tourist hotels like he's supposed to (all tourist visas warn specifically that private accommodations are not permitted). Says he usually keeps the homeowner as a roommate and then finances a lot of parties, for which the roommate provides the women and other entertainment, while our friend lugs food and liquor from tourist shops. Both sides of the party seem to win, but not the neighbors, who regularly call the cops, who regularly figure out that our friend is behind all the trouble. In the past he'd either be in jail by now, or thrown out of the country for good, making it a noteworthy (if unpleasant) example of Cuba's recent liberalization. By the way, he says the Buick cost him $700 cash, U.S., but he had to have a friend buy it and put it in his own name, as foreigners cannot own Cuban property outright. Guess he trusts his friend pretty good. He says there would be plenty of vintage cars available if only he could ship them north cheap enough, *and* if he could conquer the Cuban red tape. They're so hard up for any running machinery they don't want to let it go out of the country - even a '56 Buick - or a 1928 LaSalle, which was being used in one small town as a taxi.

You asked me to check if there was a chance of buying vintage bikes and shipping them north. I would think so, especially once trade with Cuba becomes more normal. I haven't had time to inspect bikes for their brands, of course, but they *were* mostly American before 1959, same as the cars, so they must still exist today in somewhat corresponding numbers. I see antique looking furniture in many houses we've passed, usually just a piece or two, mind you, since everyone's living pretty sparse. I've also seen some old saddles on horses, though most look fairly new and funky. I bet you'd enjoy pulling into a typical small Cuban farming town on your shiny mountain bike and parking it next

The mechanical ingenuity of materially-poor Cuba often amazes visitors to the country. For instance, lack of wheelchairs and practical public transportation led this veteran of the Angola war to fashion his own rig, which provides good excercise in addition to reasonably independent travel.

to a hitching post and half a dozen horses. Back to the future, or some such thing.

This evening I had my first encounter with the Cuban telephone system, which is aged and can be difficult. When I explained to the hotel clerk that I wanted to make a long distance call home, he said that first I'd have to wait my turn, at the front desk. After a while we were led back to a little cubicle, which had one bright light bulb and two small desks, plus chairs, each with a telephone, looking like a police interrogation room. A stern-faced young lady was seated at one of the desks, telephone in hand, waiting for us expectantly. She was the operator, and we spent the next twenty minutes in her presence trying to explain in simple words where we wanted to call, then listening to her trying to explain it to others on down the line, several times over, and over. "Lots of operators," she said with a touch of apology, after about the fourth time that she'd told me to pick up our phone only to have the line go dead. When we finally got through to Beverly and Star, who were at the creek-side pay phone nearest our home, it was really difficult for us to communicate. Everything *they* said broke up in a strange electronic way, while everything I said came right back in an eerie echo. Meanwhile, other voices kept drifting in and out. A frustrating experience, since Okan and I were lonely for the news and sounds of home. The only consolation was that some fifteen minutes of this, *plus* two nights in our room, came to a total of only $60 in U.S. cash (though the clerk suggested it would be way more if I used a credit card, which I didn't). That's about the low end of the scale for tourist costs in 1994, from what we've experienced.

After the phone call we went out to the plaza for a stroll along the wide sidewalks in front of the classic old Spanish style buildings, passing through huge stone columns and arches, then over winding paths through the park where, as in parks universal, all manner of interesting looking persons had come to spend time. Many stared at us, not unfriendly, apparently just interested. More than a few hissed at us, which in Cuba means, "Hey! Over here!" Some were guys, some were girls, and no doubt they each had an interesting story to tell, else a scam they wanted to pull.

We sat down on an empty bench and within seconds the remaining space was occupied by a couple who had evidently been following us. Lo and behold, they were friends from last year - Iniskim and I met them at the same place, had a few good visits with them, thought they were unusually strange for Cuba, gave them a few presents, and never expected to see them again.

"Hey, my friend," said the fellow as he came up and shook my hand. I didn't recognize him at first with his beard and ponytail, unusual for a Cuban in his fifties - though many of Fidel's followers looked like that around the triumph of the revolution. It was Daniel, a friend from last year who speaks good English and says things are *not* getting any better in Cuba at all. Some rules are being relaxed, he admits, "but the people are nowhere near free," and this is the main theme in his life. Like Cristina, he lives in and around the park and loves to discuss life and its living.

"I don't know how many times I went to jail just for a talk with some tourists," he said defiantly, though not too loud. "We have a constitution that says we get free speech, but it's a lie. Even now, if the police heard this conversation we're having, I could go to jail, even for five years, if they decide. No, I don't see anything good coming for us too soon, the people won't fight for their freedom."

Daniel took a small blue plastic comb out of his pants pocket and shook it in the air, saying, "You cannot go into a store here in Santa Clara and buy *this*!" He continued to shake the comb as if he were controlling a deeper rage, then added, "Nor shoes, pants, underwear, radio, *nothing*!" Then suddenly he put the comb down and looked at me smiling. "I'm wrong," he said softly, "there *is* one single store in town where you *might* find such a thing - the commissary store! You go there, and you bring what you want to sell - maybe a blue comb, who knows. They look it over, then offer you a contract whereby they keep part of the income. *There* they are selling the things of a desperate people, selling them to those who are even perhaps more desperate."

Must close and go to sleep now. More rustic trains and interesting people early tomorrow.

Rancho Luna Hotel, Cienfuegos
March 23, 1994

Hello Elaine

Here's a greeting from the hot sunny shores of the Caribbean, close to the city of Cienfuegos and not far from the house where you stayed when you came to Cuba last year, at least until that night of the infamous police raid!

We're staying at the Rancho Luna Hotel, instead of taking your advice and tempting fate at a private residence. Sure, we could save money (this place is nearly fifty bucks U.S. a night, with two beds and a shower, plus a big window facing the beach), but during the week that we're staying here we want to concentrate on our work, not on whether we can outwit the Cuban system in its slowly-dying attempt to isolate foreign tourists from its own citizens. *That* law hasn't been eased yet, even with things getting more open otherwise. That is, according to Rene, the fellow who interpreted last year and got you off the hook. When I gave him your greetings he looked puzzled at first by your name, but when I mentioned the middle-of-night police raid he remembered and said, "Oh, what a nightmare." They apparently raided several houses that had private guests and rounded up a bunch of people, including a few local prostitutes.

As I recall, you did take a couple of bus tours, but didn't get out into the country with a rental car. Hope next time you get a chance to do that, as it sure feels different to be *among* the people, once you get off the main tourist routes. Probably 90% of the people visiting Cuba see the country only through tour bus windows - *if* they leave their tourist hotel at all (and a great many don't). Out in the country you could probably walk up to any door, tell them you want to be their friend, and they'd invite you inside for something - a coffee, or whatever bit of meager food stuff they might have.

You and Jack were talking about dismantling your Harleys and bringing them over here for transportation. That would sure get you guys in touch with the Cuban people fast, from the way they befriend us with just a plain rental car (which many inspect carefully, there being no such cars in common use where they live). I've never seen a chopper in Cuba, though so far I've identified two vintage Harleys, a couple of British Triumphs and one BMW. Lots of motor bikes in this country, as I'm sure you noticed, but they're mostly those noisy smokers from various East European communist factories, plus lightweight whiners that come from China, Korea and who knows where else. Modern Harleys would be only slightly less rare here than spaceships. Maybe you could even persude Fidel to take a ride on one. I hear he's always had an eye out for adventurous women!

We haven't stayed away from private homes totally. For instance, yesterday evening Okan and I had a memorable supper with a wonderful family. Yolanda is the sister of our retired locomotive shop foreman friend Efren Figueredo, with whom Iniskim and I already spent time last year. Okan and I have been using the pleasant, airy little home he and his wife have near the engine shops as our base of operations, eating meals with them each day during the breaks we take from riding with our friends. Yolanda stopped by and shared one of those meals with us then insisted we come to eat at her house when she learned we'd be passing by. She lives just two blocks from the highway that jogs through the middle of the pleasant little town of Palmira, her house being sort of a Cuban version of "middle-class suburbs," with a flat roof and walls of concrete blocks covered by stucco. The idea of a "middle" class would make her laugh, since everyone she knows is poor, except for tourists like us.

Yolanda's whole family was sitting in front of the house when we pulled up, as were other families in the neighborhood, all noticing the only automobile in sight (a brand new one at that). Beside the house stood a nicely painted carriage, the horse for which we met later in the back yard. Horse drawn rigs were also parked next to several other homes, though no animals were in sight. Some lowered '49 Fords or '57 Chevies would have fit right in here, with shades of southwest chicano scenes, but no one here has a car at all. Yolanda introduced us in rapid succession (and quick Spanish) to her son, his wife, their child-in-arm, another son (without a wife) and finally her husband Xavier, who has a thick mustache and is the stereotype of a handsome macho Cuban man. The slim sons were younger versions of their dad, with Yolanda herself very attractive, especially for a middle-aged grandmother, wearing a handwoven Central American style red blouse that gave her brown skin and black hair a further native accent.

The sparsely furnished front room had a decidedly homey feel, with a few vases, some pictures on the walls and other details. Very conspicuous was a pink telephone - extremely rare in the Cuban households we visited - located here because Xavier works as a medic for the nearby sugar mill. We passed through her kitchen of plain basic cupboards and counters plus a long dining table and a number of chairs. Beyond it was a sink with cold running water from which we drank and washed our hands. Xavier said the water comes from their own well outside, a shallow one, which caused me some concern since their back yard is not very big, yet it housed, in addition to the already mentioned horse, a big pig, a flock of chickens and several fighting cocks. A real suburban barnyard, evidence of family self-sufficiency that could be in the future for most people if world conditions become much worse.

The fighting cocks are a family specialty, raised and trained by the two sons. There was a big round wire cage, some ten feet across and very high topped, sitting at one side of the yard, waiting for the next fighting match and its attendant crowd. Skinny, hyper-looking little critters, those fighting cocks are balder and much uglier than regular roosters, their exposed skin being kind of a creepy pinkish red. One brother held his cock towards the regular barnyard rooster who made an instant charge at it with his feet, protecting his hens and their chicks to the delight of the young men. I was surprised to learn that if they'd let the fighting cock go, the regular rooster would demolish it. Apparently they're bigger and more ferocious, whereas the type trained for the ring are more "sporty" and entertaining. With our own fondness for animals we didn't mind missing out on a bout or two.

I'm often impressed by how resourceful Cubans are in carrying out their difficult life. The rest of the world could learn a lot,

Vaqueros y Caballeros - Cowboys and horsemen, rounding up cattle in the dry hills near Cienfuegos. Most of these fellows ride the range as in days of the old west, with nearby towns providing hitching racks instead of auto parking lots.

and I think exchanges could even be made. For instance, Yolanda said she was embarrassed because of her primitive stove that sat in the middle of the yard near the rooster arena. It was handmade of stone, brick and cement, with some scrap steel grating on top, fueled by bits of wood the family gathers wherever they can find it. A variation of this stove could be useful in many places where the environment still allows fires and where wood of some sort can be found more easily than oil or gas. After looking into solar box cooking back home lately, where the sun shines much less than in Cuba, I've wondered why Fidel's people don't develop solar box cookery, especially in view of the massive fuel shortages.

The setting sun shone through the leafy backyard trees while Yolanda stirred the contents of several pans and dishes and her sons kept us entertained with small talk. As usual our family photo album got a lot of attention, Yolanda having told everyone after seeing it at her brother's. Even while birds kept on singing, the evening got dark fast, at which point candles were lit, there being no other light in the house. "You are experiencing one of our everyday problems," she had told us when we first arrived. "Today we have had no electricity since morning, so we have no lights and I cannot even offer you a cold drink. All our ice has already melted." All the same, the home cooked meal was fabulous, maybe a bit plain by modern tourist standards, but helped by the pleasant mood of the candlelit household. There was a bit of meat, several vegetables, and bread. Cubans share the custom with North American Indians of feeding guests the best they have in the house, frequently sitting back without getting any of it themselves. In the past they may have done the same thing with lodging, as many Indian people still do, but the Cuban system no longer allows overnight visitors without special permission. We have been invited by several of our country friends to sleep in their homes, either because they don't know that it's against the law (notably, no one in a city has yet invited us), else they don't figure anyone around their neighborhood would care. Maybe one of these times I'll take somebody up on it, though I'm still thinking about your experience with the police last year.

Our meal included a bowl of black beans like the ones that you got so tired of, though we still like them, especially with rice and fresh tomatoes. Am learning to enjoy the latter in their green form, as well as the usual red. We just got started eating when the lights suddenly came on in our house and everywhere else in town, judging from the loud cheer that broke out in the whole neighborhood, followed by a round of applause. "Thanks God," said Yolanda in a most earnest tone, as if a small miracle had been done to help her in hosting the company. Preferring candlelight to a plain glaring electric bulb, I was pleased for her sake, but would have preferred to go without it. This event was literally a bright spot in her otherwise ordinary day.

Okan has been getting mauled by mosquitoes at our beach hotel; I keep telling him it's the fancy deodorant and other stuff he puts on himself. I don't use anything like that and have hardly any bites to show for it. Poor guy, one got him on the ball of his foot, since his six foot three frame hangs out way beyond the

short bed and sheets. Mosquitoes are buzzing around the room
right now, since we have our bedside lights on and a couple of
the windows wide open. I dislike air conditioning, so I'd rather
suffer the consequences of mosquitoes to get the fresh air. Besides, another fringe benefit of the open window is getting such a
clear rendition of tonight's cricket orchestra; there's a great many
of them, taking over the stage from birds that sang loudly all day
long outside in the big trees that grow by the edge of the sand
beach.

In the twilight we watched an oil tanker heading for the port at
Cienfuegos, maybe 15 kilometers away. Down at the hotel dock
there are two boats tied up - one looks like a 1920's wooden fishing vessel, the other is a vintage Chris Craft motor cruiser offering rides to hotel guests. A strange international mix there is here
too, although most of the bookings come through Toronto, this
being considered a "Canadian" hotel in the scheme of things. It
was originally built by Germans, consisting of several large glass
and steel two-story box-like hulks, built on various levels and
connected by terraced concrete walkways that lead from dry hillsides down to the beach. One huge building is part open-air lobby (with an indoor stream and a mini-jungle, plus resident cats to
catch any intruding critters); there's also a bar, a large buffet restaurant, rental car and tour bus tables, plus a fairly well stocked
tourist store that has clothes, food, liquor and even film. It's a
nice place to rest up from our long, hot days, but I keep having
the feeling that we're missing out on a lot by not staying with our
friends in the country overnight.

Soon we're off to another part of Cuba. so more on that later.

Rancho Luna Hotel
March 23, 1994

Hi Star

Today I'm going to give you a short little history lesson about Cuba. I'm sitting in the shade of a big blue umbrella down at the beach by our hotel near Cienfuegos. Your brother is walking around "looking at the sights," if you know what I mean! Anyway, consider this a chapter in your home schooling.

It's hard to imagine now, but before the time of Christopher Columbus an estimated half million Indians - as in North American natives - considered the island of Cuba their home and domain. Unfortunately Columbus "discovered" them in 1492. The next year he came back with boatloads of settlers who brought along sugar plants, and those two (settlers and sugar) took over Cuba like weeds in a garden. Within a few years Spaniards were building towns and taking control. Thirty years later they started bringing black Africans as slaves; by 1895 these numbered some 600,000, which was more than the original native population. Unfortunately, those original tribes had been wiped out just 60 years after meeting Columbus, mainly by murder, disease, and from the prevalent European attitude of destroying everything not Christian.

If Columbus were to arrive on Cuban shores today, chances are he'd think it was Africa. Lighter skinned Cubans of Spanish ancestry outnumbered and dominated blacks throughout much of the country's history, but Fidel decreed that under the new system everyone would be treated equal, and it generally seems to be that way today. Afro-Cubans have benefitted most from this decree, so they have tended to stay and support Fidel's system, while Spanish-Cubans more often felt that they lost, so more of them have left, causing a great change in Cuba's social demographics. Most of the slaves came from just a few African tribes, whose descendants have managed to retain some of their African heritage and spiritual ways which forms the basis of Cuba's most popular "native" religions. The largest is Santeria, whose strength neither slavery nor communism managed to destroy.

Sugar was originally just one of many crops planted by Spanish settlers when they got to Cuba. Not until the building of sugar mills in the 1700's did sugar growing become an industry, at first with an annual output of around 10,000 tons. A hundred years later Cuba was the world's leading producer of sugar, with one million tons being produced by 1894. The record amount since then was something over 8 million tons, but that happened only once, as the result of a controversial nationwide marathon during which Fidel urged all Cubans to show their worth to the world by working together and aiming at a 10 million ton goal. They failed to reach the target, though a record was set, while in the process many other parts of the system were neglected. As part of that record-setting effort the government cancelled Christmas as a holiday, and since then it's never been brought back.

In 1868 the island's population decided they wanted to be independent as Cubans, no longer as colonials of Spain. This resulted in ten years of revolution led by Maximo Gomez and Carlos Manuel de Cespedes, names that you see everywhere today in Cuba. Unfortunately, Spain won that first encounter. It wasn't until 1880 that slavery was abolished in Cuba, and for a long time afterwards many blacks continued to serve their former masters for low pay and poor conditions, mainly because they didn't know anything else. In 1895 Jose Marti led the second Cuban revolution, though he was killed before there were any results. Independence finally came in 1898, after the U.S. blamed Spain for blowing up its warship "Maine" in Havana harbor and thus entered the fight on the side of those seeking independence. Their side won, but what the Cubans got instead of independence was nearly five years of U.S. military rule, after which the Americans pulled out but warned that they'd be back if things didn't go right. Thus they came back in 1905, then again between 1917 and 1922. In the process they protected the interests of rich men who were investing in Cuban sugar, mining, transportation and so forth. Ordinary Cubans struggled through life in poverty, many growing resentful over the rich Americans and their habit of backing notorious Cuban dictators who helped plunder the country while caring little about conditions among the people at large.

The last of these American-backed dictators was Fulgencio Batista, who first started ruling Cuba in 1940. In 1953 a young lawyer and former student leader named Fidel Castro took a band of followers and brashly attacked one of Batista's military garrisons. They were overwhelmed and nearly slaughtered, with

Top: "Model of the communist Man. Model of the Revolutionary Man. Symbol of permanence and invincibility." Che Guevarra.

Bottom: "The Problems can be solved with Moral, with Honor, with Principles."

Fidel and other survivors receiving lengthy prison sentences. However, in 1955 they were freed under amnesty and the following year Fidel and Che Guevara began their guerrilla war in the mountains of Sierra Maestre against immense odds, eventually gaining victory over a much larger, better armed, American-backed force. This accomplishment has left Cubans with a rich folklore of heroes and true tales to help keep them alive the revolutionary spirit.

"Fatherland or Death" has been one of Cuba's main slogans since Fidel came to power. We see it on billboards and walls wherever we go. Others read "Cuba for Us," "Together we can Succeed", " Yes for Cuba," and the most popular of all, "Socialism or Death." Our cynical friend Cristina says, "They're just decorations these days - we all know what they say and for most of us the messages are meaningless. They sound good, but where are the results?" Time will tell I guess, or, as Fidel has long said, "History will absolve me." Could be. Meanwhile, my own favorite symbol here is the Cuban flag - an irony with its blue and white stripes topped by red and a white star, as if it were part of the stars and stripes family next door. Actually, it's been the Cuban flag since independence from Spain. That's it for my history lesson.

March 22, 1995
Rancho Luna Hotel,
Cienfuegos, Cuba

Hello Stuckey:
   Heaven for old railroaders like you must be here in Cuba, from what I've seen the last few days with Okan! Take this morning for instance, when we walked into a scene you knew well back in the old days on the Canadian Pacific. There was a locomotive shop with a pair of Consolidations steaming outside, three more inside, plus one stripped down to its very basics, with domes, pipes, bell, whistle and all other components neatly piled on the floor, as the locomotive is getting a complete rebuild. Just imagine, from your home in Manitoba this experience would be only about a four or five hour flight away! And the people are really friendly, even letting us run their engines, and *you* know as well as anyone what kind of satisfaction a man can get from pulling back that big lever, feeling the resulting lurch when the wheels start to turn, hearing a mighty chuff as the steaming machine responds. Okan has at last gotten to know this thrill himself through first-hand experience, though he's sure waited long enough. He got early lessons as a very young fireman aboard a little narrow gauge logging Shay on Vancouver Island, back when he was only seven. He spent several hours with an old guy about your age named Spike, who later gave him further lessons on a bigger engine at Fort Steele, near our home. But he *never* got to pull the throttle at those times, nor operate the brakes. Those trains always had tourist passengers aboard, while here in Cuba the cargo is only sugarcane. Besides that, he's quite a bit older now, so the Cuban fellows get a kick out of teaching this great big Canadian Indian with braids how to run their little antique steam engines.
   We have one problem that I bet you never faced while taking pictures back in your steam days - attracting crowds of kids, who gather around us as soon as we stop anywhere and bring out our cameras. Mostly they're just curious kids who want to be around strangers, of which they see relatively few out in the country

where most of the steam works. Also, they are no doubt hoping some tidbit or trinket will somehow come their way - as it frequently does, at least from us.

This morning before we entered the locomotive shops our friend Efren, the retired shop foreman, brought us to the community car wash - a pressurized hose and a concrete pad - where he got one of the local guys to give our rental car a cleaning. Unfortunately, this really attracted the kids - our white Nissan standing out from the trucks and government jeeps they mostly see around here - so the event became something like a carnival arriving in town. From there they all followed us into the shops,

Crazy time at Mal Tiempo, with local kids running all over the locomotive shop. Only a few are seen here by Okan, who is trying to shoot videos of the shop men hammering and welding parts for the empty boiler shell in back that will be the basis for a nearly new locomotive. These shops had been off limits to tourists for many years, so the kids couldn't resist following, with shop crews hesitant to complain and cause trouble with neighboring families. By the time of our next visit this problem had been solved, with police letting all children know that dangerous running around underfoot would no longer be tolerated.

where a large patch of steel was just being welded onto the boiler of the engine that is being rebuilt, a dangerous job - as you know. Also, I think such boiler patch repairs are now outlawed in our country as being unsafe. As we tried to get pictures of this interesting and archaic mechanical process, some thirty kids, several of them barefoot, crowded around us *and* around the workers. Hot sparks and bits of metal were flying about and there were several calls for the kids to leave, but when none paid attention the guys just shrugged their shoulders and kept on working. I felt guilty for us being the cause of this, but was apparently witnessing one of many distinctly Cuban traits whereby kids and wives can cruise in among the machinery to visit their men at work, or even ride with them aboard the engines and cabooses. There was an atmosphere something like this in railroading of the U.S. and Canada back in the early part of this century, but certainly not nowadays.

As an old union man you'll be interested to hear how labour is treated in the Cuban system. First of all, everyone is officially employed and it's pretty hard to get fired. Also it takes a lot of red tape to change jobs or relocate. There are always guys standing around visiting each other at any work site, including right in the middle of the shops. Seldom are they all busy on projects at once. If we show up and bring out our family photo album, all but the most essential work will be dropped and the workers will gather around us for however long we'll visit with them. An hour is nothing, especially if they decide to start showing us around the shop, too. Of course, the important thing to remember here is that Fidel has told them over and over, "It's *your* country - everything in it is *yours*." Slogans written on walls and toolboxes remind them that if they fool around on the job too much, output suffers, the country makes less money, things get a little worse for everyone. Trouble is, things are so bad right now that some people figure it couldn't get much worse anyway, so why try hard.

Don't know how much your union work concerned safety matters, but these are apparently not very important to the workers here. The number of dangerous items and practices that we see every day boggles the mind, though on asking around it sounds like accidents aren't particularly frequent. For a start, these railroaders climb up and down on *anything*, whether it's starting, moving, or standing. If they're in a hurry, they don't hesitate to jump - even from the cab of an engine - often to run ahead and change a switch right in the face of their oncoming train - then they jump back aboard, doing the whole thing without losing a beat or really coming to a stop once. As an experienced brake and throttle handler I don't need to tell you what might happen with one misstep. And these dangerous ballets seem to be repeated over and over wherever we visit.

Another thing your union wouldn't have liked is the easy way the workers move from one duty to another without care; engineers, firemen and brakemen switch back and forth as the mood suits them and the train rolls along. It's a standard crew alright, with an engineer, fireman, two brakemen and a conductor, but off duty workers frequently ride along, apparently for lack of anything better to do, and they pitch right in with the work while they're aboard.

In the stereotype of a communist country two guys going around taking pictures with lots of cameras and film would be hassled quite a bit, yet we've only had one run-in so far, and that was with an angry group of railfans from America! Got downright nasty with us too, though I guess you've been around enough of them to know how possessive *some* photographers get about their picture taking. We laugh about it now on hindsight, but the trip would have been better off without this experience. Here's what happened:

The narrow gauge railroad of Central Mal Tiempo has been a favourite of ours since last year when Iniskim and I were immediately welcomed by its locomotive foreman, Efren Figueredo, who later made his house our home and has become our good friend. We rode on their trains a couple times last year, this year even more, always being treated by the crews as special friends. Part of our luggage included a pile of shirts, gloves, caps and other things of use to them, plus a big handful of prints, the first photo many have had of themselves in years.

Yesterday we went to that railroad again, this time so Okan could shoot video footage of the train at some of the best spots along the scenic line, including a couple of wide curves and a high stone bridge, plus several grades where the little locomotives "get down on their knees," as old railroaders like to say, struggling to haul that heavy cane up and over the hills, sometimes stalling out near the top with a wild spinning of wheels and wicked belching of black smoke. Although Okan has been enthused about trains all his life, or at least since we brought our first caboose home when he was five, and although he's photographed many steam engines at work in many places, he was still totally spellbound by the Mal Tiempo trains, having never witnessed their kind of out and out railroading.

So, we were bouncing along over these rough oxcart and tractor trails, driving our rented Nissan to the guidance of our buddy Daisby, a young, happy-go-lucky, spunky little brakeman who helped us over these same roads last year. I'm sure I'd never find the way on my own, as they disappear into canefields, double around rock-strewn bends, sometimes heading far away from the tracks, but always coming back to them where good photo scenes present themselves. Daisby speaks not a word of English (though we've been trying to teach him) so I have to decipher his rapid Spanish while struggling to keep up with a train that constantly zips left and bounces right, my knuckles white from always having to look out for treacherous rocks, holes and numerous other obstacles lurking along the way.

We had caught up to the train at a place where the tracks and our road ran parallel, so I jockied for a position that would allow Okan to shoot good video footage of the train bucking wildly right next to us, emitting steam and smoke and thunderous noises. The crew was waving, equally excited by our match race, while Daisby was shouting directions. Suddenly we crested a curving hill and there, dead up ahead on a steeper hillside, I saw a couple of bright shiny rental cars - certainly a rare sight in this part of the country - and immediately thereafter I spotted a cluster of tourist looking guys in shorts and colourful clothes, their tripods and various camera lenses glinting in the bright light - as

*Cuban horse meets iron horse at Mal Tiempo, as our friend
Daisby shows off his precious mount during an after hours visit to the shop. Earlier he had helped bring in a train of sugarcane as fireman aboard No. 1355, a handsome little narrow
gauge Consolidation built by Baldwin in 1920.*

I mercilessly drove into the midst of their well-prepared photo and ruined the whole thing for them. Purposely, so they afterwards claimed! Never mind that we were in the midst of an exciting chase ourselves and that Okan was also shooting pictures. This I tried to tell them, and that I didn't see a hole big enough in the road to drive the Nissan into, in order to disappear. They sure wouldn't have liked my other alternative, coming to a dusty screeching halt in the midst of their scene. So I did the only thing that seemed right at the moment, which was to just keep alongside that swaying, steaming train. Out of one eye I did notice a single large Texan finger being flung high in the air, so I assumed right away that they didn't like our presence. The salute came from none other than my erstwhile pen pal from the big state, a six foot six buddy who gave me valuable advice for both of my trips, based on his own annual ones that go back over ten years of successfully foiling the U.S. government's attempts to keep him out of Cuba. In fact, he and I just met for the first time the other day, at our hotel, but this second meeting didn't go so well. He was guiding the fellow Americans, a couple of businessmen and steam engine owners, apparently nervous about being in Cuba illegally, but eager to check out future prospects for museum-type purchases.

At a little place called Potrelillo the empty cane cars get uncoupled and left near the reload machine, after which the filled cars are hauled back to the mill. While we were watching this exchange, our Texan friend drove up in his rental car, alone, still sounding pretty hot under the collar. "We had ourselves a good shot until you ruined it," he fumed, so I apologized. When he repeated the same thing, I apologized again, to which he just grumbled, "Well, jeezuz! didn't you see us?" We exchanged outlines of our visits to further sugar mills, since we are all headed in the same general direction over the next few days and don't want to keep running into each other.

One of the highlights of our visit to Cuba last year was a ride with an elderly Spanish gentleman named Obdulio Rubi in his black 1947 De Soto, the first kind of car my dad ever owned after we came from the old country in the '50s. I spotted this while strolling around the plaza of a church in Santa Clara. We had a very interesting talk with Senor Rubi while he was polishing the chrome on this classic, his wife watching through an open window from their apartment across the street. While we talked he suddenly tapped two fingers on his shoulder and glanced at a man coming slowly our way. The polishing got more ambitious, while I snapped a couple of close-ups with my wide angle lens, trying to accent the car's 1940's styling. "Neighborhood watch," he whispered afterwards; "peligro!" he added, meaning dangerous. Not wanting to cause any problem, I thanked him for the visit and we continued on our way. We had gone about a block when he pulled up from behind in the DeSoto and motioned for us to get in. He was going to have something checked on the car by his mechanic and said he figured we'd enjoy a ride. His previously quiet demeanor didn't prepare me for the way he constantly honked his horn and bore down on the rest of traffic, as if he were chauffeuring the maximo leader himself. To top it off, the car stalled several times - that's what he wanted to have the mechanic check - which was doubly embarrassing after he'd honked at someone a few times to get them out of the way. Strange that no one shouted back at his honking, or gave our Texan friend's kind of salute. Some looked at our driver rather coolly and obeyed, while most just ignored his honking and kept right on going, causing him to mutter things that we couldn't understand.

The mechanic said it was Sunday and that he wasn't working, though he only did so on his own time, as a black market operation, anyway. Our friend grumbled some more when we left, saying to himself, "Why is he suddenly so religious?" He drove us up and down a few more streets, then brought us to our hotel, apologizing that the shortage of gasoline didn't allow him to drive around any further. I put a five dollar bill on his seat, after he refused to take it from my hand. We had corresponded a couple of times after that, so I looked forward to this chance of giving Okan a taste of my dad's De Soto. But, lo and behold, when our friend pulled up outside the hotel at the agreed upon time, he was at the wheel of a little, ugly Russian Lada, a classless car by comparison (pun intended). We shook hands and I introduced Okan, then we sat down on a park bench and tried to visit, mainly in Spanish. Things went along haltingly until we were suddenly interrupted by a cheerful looking fellow saying, "Excuse me, my name is Roger - did I not meet you and your son here last year?" He looked familiar, so I said "Yes, but a different son." This led to a few more words, then Mr. Rubi suddenly suggested we could all visit better at his house, so he drove off in the Lada and we followed him in our car.

Through Roger we learned why Mr. Rubi no longer had his DeSoto. The mechanical troubles grew worse after our visit last year and the car finally quit altogether, so he sold it to his mechanic for 3,000 pesos, which is $30 U.S. at official rates, certainly not very much money. He said the Lada is worth $20,000 pesos ($200 U.S.), but he's just renting it from an old doctor who can no longer drive. Car parts keep getting harder to come by, but they can be "ordered" from "street mechanics" who work out of their homes and have a kind of network of their own involving old cars and parts.

The DeSoto had originally belonged to Mr. Rubi's father, who bought it new from the Dodge dealership in town. When I expressed surprise at the idea of such a capitalist venture in Santa Clara, he laughed and said that before the revolution he and his brother provided the competition, their own dealership down the road selling Buick and General Motors cars. After the revolution, this business was taken away from them without much compensation, forcing Mr. Rubi to take up work as an electrician. When I asked how he felt about the revolution because of this, he looked nervous, shook his head, and claimed he'd never given it too much thought. "I believe in God, not politics." was his only reply. Behind him on the wall hung a large, very old and heavy-framed painting of the Virgin Mary. From the front windows of his home where we sat there was an impressive view of the church and its plaza across the street, shaded by trees well-populated by noisy birds. The home also had some of the finest furniture I've seen in this country, with dark woods and fine cane work, handed down from his father, whose father had brought it from Spain.

Mrs. Rubi brought a small pot of hot coffee, thick and black, which we drank from tiny cups in the Cuban fashion, a potent brew for a guy like me who doesn't take strong drinks of any kind, preferring his own mountain water. Mr. Rubi apologized that they couldn't offer us more, but said that his pension of 76 pesos per month is not enough for even just the two of them to eat with. He said the only way to get more is on the black market, which deals only in U.S. dollars that old folks like him find hard to come by. Roger said he and his girlfriend buy most of their food on the black market, with dollars that they get from foreign friends. He's studying to be an "entertainer," a catch-all phrase in Fidel's Cuba for those who are musically inclined or can otherwise help keep tourists busy. Being an entertainer is today about the most lucrative job open to young people. It is essential to speak a foreign language or two, with English preferred. Unfortunaty, such jobs are far beyond the reach of older people like Mr. Rubi, who says he is watching a whole new society of Cubans emerging.

We asked him about the fellow who walked past us last year, the one for whom he gave the "stripes" sign with two fingers on his shoulder. He said back then you could still get into trouble simply for talking with foreigners, especially if it involved a money transaction, though this year they're apparently no longer so strict about that. I recalled that we had been talking about how much an old DeSoto was worth when the nosy fellow showed up. He said that now, "everybody is struggling to survive", even the local "eyes," so they don't interfere so much in people's lives anymore.

"But if the wrong *ears* hear certain talk there can still be trouble," he added, then got up quickly and moved to one of the open windows, standing so that he could look down to see if anyone was listening from below on the sidewalk.

"No one trusts the police and I don't think they ever have in this country," Roger explained quietly as a result of Mr. Rubi's secretive actions. "They exist to protect the system, so we don't know if anything can be done until the bearded one is dead and gone." He feels that only 5 to 10 percent of the population still favor Fidel's leadership, the rest "have had enough" and either want Fidel to retire, else to drop dead. So far all the people we've met who talked like that (not many) lived in a town or city.

The stretch of highway between Santa Clara and Cienfuegos only takes a couple of hours to drive if you go right on through, though I can't imagine doing that, since four of Cuba's best steam-powered sugar railroads are located in between, including our favorite, Mal Tiempo.

Another narrow gauge operation, called Espartaco, is located almost next door to Mal Tiempo, just a few minutes further down the highway, yet the atmosphere is very different at each of them. For instance, instead of open friendship, Espartaco sends an armed guard to chase you out the moment you show up on the mill grounds. No engine rides or offers of cold water or invitation for a shop visit. Still, we always stop at each of the four on our way down, since operations change from day to day, even hour to hour, so you never know what photos you might get. Today it was a dead diesel on a mainline freight train, for instance, blocking the exit of the sugar mill Ifrain Alfonso, whose husky black 1935 Baldwin Mikado is the heaviest and newest steam engine running in the land. When we got there it was cooling its heels, steaming impatiently at the junction where the diesel blocked the tracks. Like many sugar mills, Ifrain Alfonso's rail network requires that its trains travel over connecting segments of Cuba's federal railway system called Ferrocarilles de Cuba, or F.C.C. Perhaps not such a big deal with a fairly modern steam engine like this one, but in some cases mainline signals turn green for 19th century relics that wheeze and wobble as they hurry to get back out of the way.

On this day we finally arrived at Mal Tiempo in midafternoon and learned that one train was out on the line and that not much else was happening. Our retired friend Efren again brought us home for lunch, his wife having already prepared a varied selection of "guest" food. We had refried black beans, boiled white rice, boiled potatoes, even thin slices of hamburger meat, a real rarity in homes as simple as this one, plus some sliced green tomatoes, real orange juice and ice cold water from their fridge. Now, to you and I this would be a fairly ordinary meal, yet I knew this had to be a major effort on their part. Just the meat alone must have taken some doing to get. It was cooked on a smokey little oil stove in a kitchen without lights, where a few dishes and some silverware was about all I saw. Efren showed us silently the empty drawers and cupboards with only a shrug of his shoulders, same as when he opened the refrigerator to let us see that it contained five small items, with none of them being a major piece of food.

My friend Efren Figueredo Hernandez, retired Locomotive Shop Foreman at Central Mal Tiempo, former steam locomotive engineer, and onetime soldier for the revolutionary hero Camilo Cienfuegos. Also a fisherman and gentleman, Efren says little about the pain he suffers from seeing his beloved Cuba undergoing so many difficulties. Like others of his generation he sees great changes coming but is uncertain about them and feels powerless to do anything about it. His simple home and many friends suffice as major pleasures, along with his family, a transistor radio, and the strong coffee he regularly sips from an old Coke can. Peace and respect would rule the world if all men were like Efren.

When I commented on the unusually well-stocked table, Efren tried to put on a good face to make us think that they eat this way all the time. But when I asked him specifically, he finally admitted that they *never* eat meat themselves, and after still further pressing he agreed that they don't often eat *most* of this, except for the rice and beans. Yet, he also let me know that it would be an insult if we refused any of it, and he insisted we eat more, long after we assured him we'd had enough and that he should put the rest away. He and his wife sat and visited with us, but didn't eat anything themselves. They were even more hesitant to admit that a good part of the meal had been bought on the black market, though I'm not sure how they paid. I did learn that the food comes from campesinos through a friend and that this system operates mainly with U.S. dollars. He said, for example, that one dollar buys twenty tomatoes. Officially, there are no rations to obtain tomatoes. Each person gets five pounds of rice per month, at 15 pesos a pound, the same with beets, which cost 25. A hamburger patty is only 2 pesos, according to ration prices, but there hasn't been any in a long, long time. Two skinny little loaves of bread are 10 pesos. And still Efren is behind the revolution all the way, just as he was in the Escambray Mountains some thirty-five years ago. He says Fidel is a good leader with a good system, only the economy is bad. He doesn't have much, yet he barely complains. When I ask what will happen, he shrugs his shoulders and admits the future doesn't look good.

Our final stop of the day was at another of the four mills, an intriguing place called Pepito Tey, which Iniskim and I missed last year because their railroad wasn't operating then. It turns out to be just fifteen minutes from our beachside hotel, and at least as photogenic, even without the many tourists in tiny bathing suits. The tree-lined community of Pepito Tey is nestled in a pleasant green dale with the sugar mill itself at the bottom of the hill. It is a large rambling metal building from 1910, with a tall brick chimney belching black smoke. Near it are the locomotive and car shops, along with the railroad yard whose narrow gauge tracks climb steeply upgrade at both ends, forcing departing trains to barrel full blast out of town, throttle wide open, creating a symphony that reverberates off the adjoining buildings, then travels slowly up the sides of the whole dale. This is indeed a unique setting for such a railroad drama, which reaches its climax when the train's engineer pulls down on the cord that is connected to a melodious brass whistle whose dreamy wail then echoes far and wide.

According to the railfan network this is supposed to be one of the less friendly mills. One Brit wrote in a magazine that it was tough getting set up for good photos of trains leaving here because he could never find out ahead *when* that would be until he heard it starting the uphill assault, which left little time for photos since security guards ran him off whenever he tried to hang around with his cameras. Another example to show how things are changing, since we found just the opposite reception. On our first visit the other day we accidentally drove right into the middle of things at Pepito Tey before we realized it, since trees and community buildings kind of keep the little railroad hidden until the last moment. We got out and walked to an open gate where tracks were leading into the locomotive shop, figuring at least to have a quick look around before getting booted out. When no one bothered us, I took a chance, pulled out a camera and fired off a few shots showing a trio of fine looking Baldwin locomotives being prepared for work. Just about then it was lunch time, so within moments everyone laid their tools down and left. A smiling middle-aged fellow with a gold tooth came our way, wearing an orange hard hat and carrying a small gunny sack full of tomatoes. I asked him how many engines they have here, to which he said five, with three of them working. When I asked if it was possible to get permission for visiting the yard and shop area with a camera, he nodded and said yes. I then asked him with a chuckle, "Isn't the boss here bad to visitors?" He shook his head laughingly and said no, flashing his tooth in the sunlight. Having still some doubt because of that published article, I said again, "Are you sure it's no problem with the boss?" "No problem," he said, "*I'm* the boss!" We told him we'd be back when the lighting is better, to which we smiled again and nodded his head. Want to come there with us, Stuck? You could pretend some-

Fifteen minutes by rented car from beach-side resort hotels around the pleasant city of Cienfuegos is Central Pepito Tey and its 30-inch narrow gauge sugar railway, whose trains put on dramatic performances like this several times daily during the annual harvest. The handsome bridge with its red brick piers dates from just after the turn of the century, as does the Baldwin locomotive, still carrying its original oil burning headlight (though modified with an electric car lamp). Low grade fuel oil makes Cuban steam locomotives throw out a lot of black smoke, which may help photographers, but not the atmosphere. A skillful fireman can help minimalize this problem until a better solution is found.

body turned the clock back fifty years or so, then bring your gloves and overalls and get ready to head out on the road one more time.....

We'll be thinking of you!

Turning back the clock is part of Cuba's daily transportation reality, as seen here with a horse-drawn taxi, providing service in front of the arched doors of the 19th century Cardenas train station.

Cienfuegos Cuba,
March 24, 1994

Hello Jack Moon

What a surprise to hear from you after almost twenty years! How often I've wondered what you were up to, whether you were still alive or what? Got your letter the morning I left home with my son Okan for the trip I'm on right now; picked it up at the post office twelve miles down the road as we headed for the airport. I considered it a sign of good luck! You're the first guy that ever got me to thinking about Cuba, years ago, and believe it or not that's where I'm at right now!

Seems funny to think of you teaching school in Northern California, almost back to where I first met you, before you became a "radical revolutionary." Last time we saw each other you were driving your old pickup truck out of the Sun Dance camp in Southern Alberta, headed north to some other tribe where you said you had friends. You were sure that North America would have a big revolution within a few years. More than twenty have passed since then, what happened? Are you still involved with native issues, or did you drop that altogether? And did you ever succeed at getting yourself enrolled in your mother's tribe? Beverly lost her Indian status after we got legally married, but later they changed the rules and gave it back to her again. Here in Canada it used to be that a white woman could marry an Indian man and *gain* Indian status, whereas an Indian woman who married a white man lost hers. Too male-oriented for this day and age, so it was changed; now neither one gains or loses.

Such issues don't seem to be much of a problem here in Cuba, where the "native people" are sort of a Heinz 57 Varieties mixture of black, white, hispanic, Indian, latino and who knows what else, with all of them having about the same status, which is, to be dirt-poor and sometimes almost without hope. A long ways from the "society of the future" that you used to say Cuba was building, remember? Back then I thought you were crazy, making a hero out of Fidel and his Revolution, but afterwards I began to understand some of your points. My biggest problem is that I've just always been turned off by too many restrictions on human rights and personal freedoms.

As I recall you came to Cuba once to help with the 1965 sugar harvest, as part of some political movement. Wish I'd paid closer attention to your stories, since I can now appreciate what a challenge it must have been to work and live here as a foreigner back before there were such basic things as tourist hotels and rental cars. I'm very surprised at how simple the infrastructure of this country still is, as if we'd stepped back into the 1930's. Maybe it's part of our northern mentality that I should pay so much attention to infrastructure, when the really important result of Fidel's revolution has to do with the Cuban soul.

There's an unusual reason why I'm writing back to you so quickly, though I did plan to answer your letter at first chance anyway. This morning I met a guy here in Cuba who says he knew you once, and that gave me a real shock and surprise. He's not sure if you'll remember him, but here's the story:

My son and I had been out taking pictures of people in the countryside, especially of their steam-powered sugar trains. There's poor lighting for good photos at midday and it's also very hot, so we came back here to our hotel, changed into swim trunks, and went down to the sandy beach to lie along the Caribbean for a while. My son went for a swim and to have a look at some of the thinly clad scenery, so I just stayed in the shade of a big umbrella to study my maps and plot the next days of our journey around the country. We're headed for the other end of the island, on the opposite ocean, where a big sugar mill has an old time narrow gauge railroad that brings cane from an area similar to our mountains at home. By the way, we're here to make photo and video documentaries of Cuba's vintage railroading, a subject I often write about these days.

While I was engrossed on the beach, this well-tanned fellow in swim trunks came up and asked if I had a light. I didn't, but there was one in Okan's shirt pocket, since he carries the cigarettes that we offer to people we meet. I like this interesting Cuban custom, by the way, much like we have in native culture back home, which is to offer a smoke as a gesture of friendship. By his appearance I thought this guy might be an Italian tourist, of which there's many, so I made no effort to engage him in talk, wanting instead to figure out how many days we'd have at our next destination. But he stayed after getting his cigarette lit, then asked if we were Canadian Indians. Okan's shirt happened to have a big red maple leaf on it. He said he wondered because of our braids, so I just told him, "sort of," not wanting to bother giving a more complicated explanation about our family and tribal life to a stranger on a hot beach.

But this guy had more patience than me. He said he saw us on the plane coming down from Toronto and figured we might be on some kind of "mission." When I chuckled and said "no," he surprised me by asking if I knew anyone from Wounded Knee, South Dakota. A couple of people came to mind, including you, but again I figured it wasn't worth the effort to pursue, still seeing him as a foreign tourist. Wounded Knee is a pretty famous place among Europeans who are interested in native matters. The armed conflict of 1973 certainly brought world-wide public attention to the serious social issues that were raised. But the surprises were not over yet! Suddenly he asked me if I'd ever heard of Jack Moon. "Why yes," I told him, "there's a letter from Jack in my suitcase right now!" Somehow I knew right away he *had* to be talking about you!

He says his name is Mario, that he was born in Cuba, and that he was originally with Fidel in the revolution; he joined up in Santa Clara, was in the triumphant march to Havana, then was appointed assistant to the man in charge of all the sugar mills. His parents had owned such a mill, but wisely sold it a few years before 1959. He had the kind of experience that Fidel's new government needed. But when the country started befriending the Russians and veering toward communism he got disillusioned, joined an underground group that was working towards further revolution and more open democracy, then got caught operating an illegal radio in the attic of a friend's house. He says he was taken to the notorious prison on the Isle of Pines, tortured into confessions that got him sentenced to die, but somehow a family connection got him loose instead and sent off to Argentina, from where he made his way to the U.S., where the FBI drafted him to do undercover work. He thought the work would be in Florida's Cuban community, but in 1973 he found himself going to Wounded Knee instead. It appears the U.S. government thought Cuba was supplying weapons and training to the American Indian Movement and they wanted him to ferret out the details. You'll be interested to know that he says Cuba was *not* involved with AIM, though he figures they must have surely considered the idea. At any rate, Mario found no one with Cuban connections in the Indian camp.

But while he was there posing as a Cuban friend of the Indians he accidentally got forced into helping his FBI handlers make some arrests of people caught on the open prairie carrying gunpowder and dynamite towards the Indian camp! Maybe now you're starting to realize the connection, since apparently you were one of them. He says you thought he was one of you, another Indian from the camp, so you tried handing him part of your load when you saw that agents were heading your way. You told him to make a run with the stuff. Afterwards, you kept saying, "He's supposed to be one of us." Is that true, do you remember? He made it sound pretty real and I've never seen you since then, so I'm eager to hear if this all comes together.

Meanwhile, what do you think about the demise of world communism? As you recall, I never was a fan of that system, though you may be surprised to learn that I now feel convinced the world's future lies with some as-yet-untried variation of socialism and democracy, combined with international respect for all different people's customs and personal freedoms. Back in the sixties I thought such an international system was just around the corner, even while you were insisting there would first be a big social upheaval. So far, looks like we're both wrong, though it seems like the world keeps moving in a direction that could end up making us both right. Here in Cuba it also feels like they're moving towards a more user-friendly, open democracy - only they're approaching it from the opposite end as us. We've had maybe *too many* freedoms these past 25 years, while they've had *too few*!

Mario says he stays completely out of politics these days; he just wants to make money! No more high ideals of helping his countrymen, just a personal desire to capitalize on an unfortunate situation, wherein Cuba desperately needs dollars and he's got connections who'll provide them. Says he's here at this hotel having a vacation while assessing the potential climate for business in nearby Cienfuegos, where he was born. He'll have to be pretty imaginative, I think. After driving up and down the streets of Cienfuegos a number of times, we're still left with the feeling that we were seeing a spread out country village rather than the downtown of a port city. Hardly any shops, offices, restaurants or tourist places. Then again, what an ideal site for a clever merchant, once the folks on the streets have money to spend. So far they have mostly just Cuban pesos, but he needs them to have dollars in order to profit from his goods. He's also talking about setting up an assembly plant for furniture and electronic products, which will maybe earn him quicker profits. Sad for Cuba that after all these years of trying to make everyone equal, the one hope of saving their economy now is to let capitalists profit from low dollar wages, thus setting the stage for discontent among the masses of poor folk all over again. What's that about history repeating itself?

Better quit here for now and get some sleep. I'll write again.

Never will surrender

Cienfuegos Province
March 24, 1994

Hey Paul -

I thought of you and your green beret today while visiting a Cuban warrior! This guy could easily tell the four brave coups always required at our tribal ceremonies; he's gone through dangers for sure. Strange thing is, he looks somewhat native, though officially Cuba's native tribes are long gone. When I first saw him he was washing rental cars out behind our hotel and I thought he was just another skinny old man, his wrinkled face and dark sad eyes making him seem about sixty or seventy. But he says that he's only around fifty, like me, so he must have had a pretty tough life, yet sometimes when he talked the sad look was replaced by one of wisdom and experience.

I had driven our car around back to the paved lot where he was working, then parked in the shade of a big tree while waiting for the rental car manager to arrive so I could get a flat tire exchanged. He was overdue from his daily morning session at another hotel near Cienfuegos, where he was supposed to meet renters wanting to pick up their cars. Having learned this from the old man, who spoke fairly understandable English, I offered him a smoke as a sign of friendship. He shut off the leaking hose, took the cigarette and some matches, then sat down at the curb in front of me.

For a while we made small talk, he of course wanting to know where we're from and where we're going, the usual introductory questions. He lives in Cienfuegos with his father, who must be truly an old man. They'd both been collecting their pension, but weren't getting enough to eat and his dad could no longer get some important heart medicine. So a friend arranged this job for him with Havanautos, where he's able to get a few U.S. dollars from tourists who give him tips for preparing their rental cars. I asked how much he makes, but all he would say was, "Enough so that now my father can get his medicine and we can eat some real food."

He wanted to know if we were going down to Giron, the

Cuban name for the Bay of Pigs, one of the main tourist attractions in this part of Cuba, about an hour away. I told him no, since I hadn't even thought about it, then asked him if he'd ever gone there, which resulted in a strange smile and an answer of yes. I then asked if he knew anyone who'd been there during the famous invasion, to which he again smiled and said yes. Suddenly I got this peculiar hunch, so I asked if he'd had any part in the battle, to which he again nodded, then smiled and said softly, "Si!" That was my introduction to Julio Carerra, sort of a little old Cuban warrior.

When the "Bay of Pigs" became a headline in 1961 I was still going to high school in California. The way I learned about it in the news, a "secret army" of Cuban exiles had arrived on the island by boat and plane to join forces with some of their dissatisfied countrymen. Together they were going to drive out the new dictator Fidel Castro, who had joined communist Russia. That made him sound pretty bad to me, while the invaders were considered "good guys" in my neighborhood, where most people didn't otherwise really care.

Julio said he was a young teenage fellow in the Cuban militia at that time, as were most able men. His assignment was to guard the entrance to a farming cooperative somewhere near the infamous Bay. I took a few notes after he told me the story, so I'll quote from them:

I had a long night of guard duty and I was really sleepy, ready to go home when it got near daylight. All of a sudden the farm manager came driving up real fast in his big Buick and shouted for me to jump in. The back seat was full of guys with guns, and on the front seat was the boss' bazooka, along with a bunch of shells. He told me to put the stuff in my lap and we roared off. He said invaders had landed in the swamps down by the ocean and that Fidel himself had called and asked us to rush there and help fight off the attackers. This woke me up good, so good that I remembered having only six bullets for my gun, an old British Enfield rifle. Two of the guys in the back seat had automatic rifles, the others just had regular guns. I wasn't sure what the boss was going to do with the bazooka, since we saw him one time fire it and he completely missed the fence he was using for a target. I was glad to see that he also carried his holster and a pistol.

Julio said they must have been driving at over a hundred miles an hour down the country roads and that several times they almost didn't make the curves. At the town of Colon there were men running in all directions with weapons, getting aboard buses and trucks. Somebody there told them it was a major invasion. Until then he'd thought they were racing down to catch just a small boat load or two. As it turned out, there were several large ships carrying troops equipped with trucks and tanks, and there were airplanes providing overhead cover.

Fidel was on his way down to take charge of the defense himself, the estimated size of invading forces growing larger every time someone asked. By then it was daylight and there were reports of American planes and ships as well, so it appeared that Cuba was facing a major attack. It wasn't known yet by the Cubans that President Kennedy had gotten last minute cold feet about supporting this supposed secret invasion, so the U.S. planes and ships that they saw were forbidden to fire within Cuba or to lend any kind of actual military support to the invaders. At the other end of the news reports, listeners like myself heard U.S. government spokesmen claiming the Cuban exiles had launched this attack totally on their own - that American forces had been notified only at the last moment and were there just as observers. This became a scandal later when the public learned that the President had been in on the planning right from the start.   In fact, the plans were already being formed under the previous administration with the guidance of President Eisenhower. All the planes, ships, weapons and money used in attacking Cuba had been supplied through the CIA, which did a boy scout job of covering up the evidence.

At Covadonga we met a crowd of local men with guns, so we left our car and continued on foot. We could hear steady shooting and some of the men said they'd seen invaders not far away. I was still thinking about the six bullets and my old gun, wishing I had the automatic rifle that was kept at my militia barracks.

Our boss took the lead with his bazooka, while the rest of us stayed behind and kind of spread out. My boss fought with Fidel in the Sierra Maestra, so I felt confident following him. When we heard loud motors coming our way, the boss told us to take cover along a curve in the road and said not to fire until he shot first.

The enemy approached our position with two trucks, while we waited for our leader to fire. They were really close when he finally did, but the shot was too short. Luckily, the bazooka shell didn't explode when it hit the ground, but instead bounced back up and right into the lead truck, then it blew up. At that point we all opened fire with our weapons, aiming especially at the men who jumped out of the second truck. I couldn't say if I hit anyone, though there was a lot of blood in the area where I shot.

The enemy ran away, but we captured both trucks which were filled with weapons and supplies. There was a lot of ammunition but none of it fit our rifles. There were also a couple of machine guns, but others found them first. I myself got a Colt pistol with many bullets. We then went back to Covadonga to get help in moving the trucks and their contents, so the enemy couldn't get them back. About that time a whole militia battalion showed up, so we now had an army instead of just a bunch of poor farmers with a few old guns. These guys brought some of the new Russian artillery given to Cuba not long before, and they were ready for anything. We returned to the two trucks with some of these men and from there my boss still kept the lead as we went on towards the swamps where we could hear a lot of fighting taking place.

We cheered when a B-26 bomber with Cuban air force markings flew low overhead, though I wondered why he was coming right back without taking part in the fighting, until his guns opened up on us and we realized we'd been fooled. I don't know how much damage he did up the line, since we must have been a pretty long convoy, but three guys were killed right near me when the bullets hit the fuel truck they were driving. We had no radio to find out what was going on up ahead, nor to tell any others what had happened to us.

"Our leader wanted to reach San Blas before dark, so we

moved quickly along the road while keeping our ears open for more planes and watching the trees and bushes for enemy soldiers. Near San Blas we encountered a bunch of invaders who killed several of our men before we could return fire. We finally ran out of ammunition for our rifles and the big guns, so the boss sent a jeep back for more, but when it got to us an enemy shell hit it and blew it up. It was getting hard to advance, since we were exposed on the open road, with swamps on both sides, while the enemy already had all the hidden positions. Eventually we did reach the outskirts of San Blas, but by then it was dark and too dangerous to go on. Our leader sent word for us to hide and try to get some sleep.

In the militia we were trained to look after ourselves anywhere, so I wasn't too concerned. Still, I wanted to find a comfortable place because I hadn't slept yet from the night before. In the distance I could barely see the outline of a big building in the dark; I thought it was a storehouse, so I went over to have a better look. Suddenly a bunch of shots came my way, though luckily none hit me before I dropped to the ground. When the shooting stopped I raised up for a moment, aimed my rifle towards the noise and fired. A man screamed - I never heard such a sound before - and I could hear him thumping on the ground. Then a door opened up next to him and the bright beam of a flashlight raced my way, but I already had another bullet in my rifle so I fired again. We had been trained to shoot good. The flashlight fell to the ground and stayed there, but I heard no other sound and wasn't sure if I made a hit, so I just laid still for a long time. There were no sounds whatsoever, but I was scared of a trap.

Perhaps I let two hours go by, maybe more. I'm surprised nobody else showed up from either side. I kept dozing, then I'd wake up and see that the flashlight was getting dimmer, so finally I decided I'd better get up there to it and have a look before it died out altogether and things turned completely dark. My heart was in my mouth; I moved very slowly and quietly. When I got close, there was enough light left to show the first guy I shot at, a dark Cuban in camouflage clothes. I nearly had a heart attack, thinking for a minute that I'd shot my own kind. Then I noticed a second body just beyond the flashlight, dressed about the same, and I realized they weren't wearing Cuban military issue. Also, I didn't recognize their weapons, though I was glad to notice that they were semi-automatic rifles with big clips, and I could see more clips in their belts. I was still being cautious in case there were more of them waiting in ambush, but finally I jumped for the light and went right on through the door. All I saw was a big empty barn with nothing much in it and no place to hide. Still, I preferred to sleep in there to being out in the open, so I pulled the two bodies around the corner and then went in and closed to door to lay down. Crazy as it sounds, even after all that I was still able to fall asleep immediately.

Before daybreak I got up, wanting to look for my friends so they wouldn't shoot me by mistake. I had slept with both my new rifles and also my old one, but I still wanted the clips that those men carried. I didn't like having to go up to them again, but I needed the ammunition. I got four thirty-shot clips, all loaded, plus a good belt with knife, food and first-aid kit. These invaders were better equipped than we were while defending our land. It looked like American stuff, though both men seemed to be Cubans. This place was close to the ocean and I wondered if we were already surrounded. There was no more shooting nearby, but quite a lot in the distance. It was hard to walk quietly with three guns, two hanging from my shoulders and one in my hands, and it was tough getting through some of the narrow places in the trail. Finally I reached the highway, but I saw no one around. I didn't want to get caught up there in the open by myself, so I headed back down towards the building where I had spent the night, figuring the rest of my group must have moved past me in the dark. By this time it was getting daylight and it seemed that the shooting was moving closer. I could hear bombs and cannons too, plus several kinds of airplanes including U.S. jets.

On the other side of that building I was surprised to find a jeep. It could have been from the Cuban army, since there was no identification. But when I looked inside and saw a bunch of radio equipment I knew what those two had been up to. The building was apparently going to serve as a communication post. That made me wonder just how close the rest of the enemy were. Without thinking much of the risks, I jumped into this jeep and drove off, going down one of the dirt roads leading to San Blas. Somehow I missed the village altogether and as I came out to a field there were two tanks and several trucks that I knew were not Cuban. They already saw me by this time and I was pretty close so there was no use in turning back. For a few moments I thought I was dead, but it so happened that I was wearing my army T-shirt and pants, so I guess these invaders thought I was one of them. They waved to me and I waved back and kept right on driving, thinking surely they'd open up and shoot me from the back. I nearly wet my pants with fear, until they were out of sight in my mirror, and then I felt very happy and couldn't believe my luck.

Still I had a big problem, since I was now on the wrong side of the line in this battle. I followed roads that I thought would lead me back towards our own side without getting me near the group I just passed. Then suddenly I heard bombs go off nearby - the same bunch getting hit, I later found out - and moments later one of our own Cuban Sea Fury's dived down and opened fire on me, thinking I was an invader. Thank heavens the first shots missed and his guns got stuck after that. I found this out later, when I met the pilot in Santa Clara and we had a good laugh about it. I thought I should get out and walk, so I wouldn't be attacked again, but I also didn't want to be stranded on foot in the midst of enemies.

Suddenly I saw a group of men in the road ahead. Two were wearing camouflage and carrying guns, which they immediately aimed at me. The rest looked like Cuban workers with their hands tied behind their backs. Realizing what was happening, I decided the best thing to do was again just to keep rolling. But in passing them I saw that a couple of the prisoners were friends who had been with me the day before, so I suddenly stopped the jeep and backed up, moving the rifle quickly across my lap so it was ready to fire. The two guys in charge looked confused as I got nearer but they didn't lift their guns fast enough. I managed to shoot them both right where they stood together. It all went so quickly that the prisoners were still diving for cover after I was already finished, which made me laugh out loud. It's crazy what happens to a man when he kills somebody - I felt strong for days afterwards, but later I came to feel very bad about it. You're never the same after you've killed. Those guys could have been my distant cousins.

There were planes flying all over, so I thought it was best for us to get away from that jeep. I used my new knife to cut loose some of the men, then the rest untied each other. We had five guns between us, with me keeping one of the automatic rifles and two extra clips. My friends said that our boss was on the other side of San Blas, so I had just missed him by a few streets when I first got the jeep. We were then about five or six kilometers from there, but the men said all the crossroads were in control of the invading mercenaries. However, some in our group were local campesinos, and they knew all the trails, so we took off with them in the lead.

What we didn't know was that by this time the invaders were being overpowered by our side. They were alone; the Americans didn't come in with them after all. The enemy had already left the area we were in, though we could still hear a lot of shooting and bombing not too far away. We walked for a long time before we finally ran into others from our side who told us what was actually going on. Then I got a ride in a truck back to my home, where I finally got some good sleep and something to eat. Later on I was called to Havana and given some medals and other honors for what I did, but I'm still surprised at how it happened. I served in our army when I was quite young, but I never imagined having to take part in a real battle, or that I would kill other men. I hate the thought, but it was the reality, and now it's history.

For Okan and I, meeting this old guy made us wonder how many others have exciting stories to tell. Sort of reminds me of hearing tales from the last old buffalo hunters and tipi dwellers back in the 1960's, when I first started making written records of other people's adventures and accomplishments.

Got some fresh raw tobacco today, direct from a poor old farmer and his wife who are growing it by their thatched hut along the highway. They were pleased to hear that it would be given out at a gathering of "Indios de Canada," though I'm sure they don't have anything in their experience that would let them really imagine what happens at our tipi ceremonies. See you there in a few weeks, partner.

Light traffic on the cobblestone streets of Trinidad, a famous colonial-era town not far from Cienfuegos. Fascinating architecture draws many tourists, who stay in beach-front hotels along the nearby Caribbean.

Rancho Luna Hotel, on the Caribbean
March 26, 1994

Hello again, Stuckey;

Just couldn't resist writing a few more lines to tell you about the fantastic train trip Okan and I had today, each of us spending a couple of exciting hours at the throttle of an old narrow gauge Consolidation during a run from the sugar mill at Mal Tiempo through rolling cane fields to deliver empties and pick up loads of cane at three reload points along the twenty mile line. We left the mill in mid-afternoon while the sun was still hot. Our friend Fabio, the shop foreman, took the right hand seat as engineer, while I stood behind, watching closely his careful play between brake lever and throttle, plus his regular tugs on a third brass handle that allowed sand for extra traction to fall between wheels and rails. We made this same trip the other day with the regular crew, who usually handle the engine more roughly and run it faster than he does. Makes sense, since he's in charge back at the shop where they have to repair whatever damage is done to these old rigs.

We again had young Orelvis as fireman and he again brought along his pretty girlfriend. To our relief she opted this time to sit back behind the first tender, thus not getting in the way of our pictures like last time when she shared the fireman's seat with her boyfriend, wearing a bright red blouse and spoiling the authentic hardworking look of our train scenes. However, she was nearly as distracting this time by the fact that she sat in a conspicuous place where her partly-see-through blouse made it hard not to look, especially when we all bounced up and down from the rough tracks. What a beautiful highlight to an already memorable trip.

She was a good sport about it too, allowing a lot of teasing and banter from everyone without taking offense. It started this morning at the shop when the foreman told us, using some common Cuban hand signs, that he considered her "extra pretty" and wanted to take her from the "ugly guy" that she was with. We all laughed, including her boyfriend, who is noticeably proud of his handsome Spanish features and his stout, wooly chest. His father is normally the engineer on this run, but out of deference to the shop foreman he gave up the throttle and rode instead on the tender, often jumping down to line switches, which is actually the job of a brakeman. The way they alternate is interesting, and it was this relaxed and shared attitude that made it feel so normal for Okan and I each to have a turn at the throttle too, quite long turns at that.

The funniest member of our crew was "Buckwheat," a skinny young black guy whose real name is Frank, but who was given the nickname last year by Iniskim for his hero in the old "Spanky and the Gang" movies. Both Buckwheats share a silly boyish exuberance that's almost contagious, the Cuban one often keeping the whole train crew laughing. At one point he signed with his hands that the fireman's girlfriend is pretty, doing it plainly so both she and her boyfriend could see. I signed back, "yes" and added that my son would bring her back home to Canada. Buckwheat laughed uproariously and slapped his thigh real hard once, while the rest of us watched him bemused. Our old teakettle was meanwhile rattling and rolling down the narrow gauge tracks in charge of Okan. The girlfriend then signed to Orelvis, who was sitting on the fireman's seat beside her, that she was going to "get rid of him" (with a brushing motion of her hand and a pouting look on her lips) and then "fly off" with the "engineer" (by flapping her hands, then pointing at Okan and imitating his hand on the throttle). At that point Okan, who was quite concentrated on the business of running this whole train, caught the smiles and some of the signs across the engine cab, but only enough to know that he was the subject of something, especially when he looked over his shoulder for a moment at the rest of us back up on the tender, where Buckwheat was still looking at him and cracking up.

The boyfriend's bare furry chest suddenly looked a little sunk as he took his hands from the fuel controls and held them up to his girlfriend as if praying, then signing to her, "no, no - me!" This went back and forth several times, Buckwheat constantly getting more excited, until I began to worry that he might tumble from the tender in one of his laughing fits. Okan continued to have a tight grip on the throttle, causing black clouds to billow out of the stack as we worked our way upgrade. Finally the boy-friend signed that he would push Okan overboard, jokingly of course, to which I immediately replied with signs, "he's much bigger than you." He jumped up from his seat and pretended to hide behind a corner where the cab comes inward, covering his eyes with one hand since only part of himself was not showing. At this point Buckwheat exploded, first backwards, then forwards, his mouth of large white teeth spread far apart towards the sky, bulby eyes looking ready to pop out, with the sounds of a happy hyena ringing so loud that even with all the din and rattle of our train and the loudly barking smoke stack, Okan spun around to see what had happened. The rest of us laughed out loud as well, since it all seemed so ridiculous as we barrelled along. Someday I hope that pretty young lady tells this story to her grandkids.

Strangely enough, on the same trip we also got to see Buck-wheat turn angry. He's really dark black, which seems to give more power to his pronounced teeth and eyes, and he tops this off with a funky curled-up straw hat. When he gets mad in a crowd it's almost as noticeable as when he's laughing.

Our destination was the little village of Potrelillo, where a chain and motor driven reload system takes fresh sugar cane from trucks and trailers and dumps it into empty railroad cars that look like open-topped shoe boxes with rusty chain link fences around the sides. When we got the empty cars exchanged for our loads, the crew led Okan and I to a nearby white shack with a big open window, through which a slim dark woman la-dled water and lemonade into "sort of washed between drinkers" glasses. She also had a pile of semi-ripe little oranges, for which the crew paid a few centavos (less than an American penny). There were about a dozen cane workers gathered around, taking a break and having drinks, their system being pretty liberal about "labouring" on the job. They all looked curiously at the two of us but were pretty friendly, especially after we smiled and waved a general hello. One guy among them was sipping from a brown bottle of what the crew later said was home-made cane liquor -

rotgut stuff - and by his actions he'd obviously been at it for a while. He came right over and offered us a drink, but when we shook our heads he only became more insistent. In a flash Buckwheat stood between us, vigorously shaking his finger as a "no." Then when the guy tried once more, Buckwheat's eyes suddenly got big and round while his sinewy body started flexing, making him look like a jungle tiger ready to pounce. Luckily, the other guy backed down and stalked away with his bottle, at which point Buckwheat broke out in a grin that defused the tension in the rest of us. Definitely a dynamite little character.

Coming back from Portrelillo we had to stop and pick up the fireman and his girlfriend, who had unloaded themselves on our way down in order to do "a little swimming." At the time I told them in signs, "no loving, no, no!" and got lots of giggles and chuckles in response, even from the crew who seemed quite familiar with the game. Can you imagine a fireman back home getting off to swim with his girlfriend along the route of his run? But heck, we had an extra brakeman aboard, our little friend Daisby, who came to be with us, so he did the firing work while Okan had by now taken over fully as engineer. Thus, for a while I got to take pictures of the train without a red blouse getting in my way! When they got back aboard later and she saw my camera, she said right away, "no photos!" at which point I noticed that she only *carried* the blouse, all wet and crumpled, wearing instead her boyfriend's thin T-shirt, which left only the colouring underneath to one's imagination. I took no photos, to be sure, but it wasn't my fault that she sat right in my line of vision as we continued to bounce our way homeward...

By the way, the place where we picked up this romantic couple was one of the most dramatic spots we've seen anywhere on a railroad in Cuba, with a tall handsome stone bridge crossing a narrow green canyon in which flowed a stream too wide to jump

Opposite: Satisfied crew at the end of another run over the narrow gauge at Mal Tiempo. Brakemen Frank (Buckwheat) and Daisby, are left and centre, standing with fireman Orelvis. In the gangway is shop foreman Fabio, while beaming proudly from the engineer's window is Okan, who will never forget that sunset when he was in charge of handling the throttle.

and deep enough to swim in, the bridge piers solidly anchored among huge boulders. The site was also a water-stop for the locomotive, with a gasoline pump at trackside fired up to suck water from the stream through a canvas hose. Only an oxcart trail leads to this rare spot, and even then you have to go up on the tracks and walk a ways before you can see the bridge. It was such an ideal scene that the crew willingly gave us time to climb down and set up our cameras, than ran the whole train back and forth twice so we could take photos and video footage, though as usual in these cases, they all came to our side of the engine when it passed, posing proudly the whole way, rather than giving us a shot of them at work as they would normally look. Even so, their pride didn't detract from the spectacular scene, especially with black smoke and white steam billowing forth.

Buckwheat's dangerous antics up on the tender are typical for these crews. Another example was our smiling friend Daisby, who for a start wore shoes with soles nearly coming off, held on only with stitchings and wrappings of thin copper wire. At a place where we left the mainline and went a couple of miles down a wobbly branch to another reload, Daisby dropped off and got out his big aluminum-handled sheath knife. By the time we came back up this branch with the loads he had three bundles of head-high green grass cut, tied and piled beside the tracks, ready to throw on the cowcatcher. Feed for the single horse that provides work and transportation for his family at Mal Tiempo. He stood track side and watched our approach while at the same time trimming the last of ten sugar cane stalks that he'd also cut during our absence. These he handed around to everyone, then busied himself with one of his own by chopping it slowly with the knife. Only trouble was, our train rocked and rolled along as he did this, and for some reason he was too restless to sit down, so he kept jumping from engine cab to the front tender, then to the second tender, walking and hopping in his flimsy shoes over moving surfaces thoroughly coated, even floating, in gooey oil, all the while working on that piece of cane with his sharp knife. He seemed oblivious to the danger for himself and others, yet never came close to having a mishap.

Efren's predecessor as locomotive shop foreman at Mal Tiempo was Jose Perez, better known to everyone as Pepe, the resident old timer, whose home is nearby. Here he is seen outside the shop building at sunset, posing proudly with his baby blue pre-revolutionary, American-made Schwinn, which looks like it just rolled off the showroom floor, even though he's been riding it on rough roads and around greasy tracks all these years. At home he keeps it indoors, near his bed.

Pepe is also Mal Tiempo's most dedicated fisherman, going out nearly every day to the stream that feeds the local millpond, where he catches telapia, an imported fish that thrives in Cuba's warm fresh water. One time he asked Okan and I if we could bring him a few hooks on our next visit. His gear consists of hook and line, along with homemade sinker, spun overhead by hand and then tossed out into the water. Like most other things, hooks are hard to come by, especially out in the country, where actual fishing equipment is almost nonexistent. So, we brought him a couple packages of hooks and leaders, gathering the whole shop crew around as we pulled the packages from a little canvas bag. Lo and behold, one of the hooks had a longer line attached, which surprised old Pepe greatly. I encouraged him to keep pulling as it slowly came out of the bag, until suddenly there was a solid tug, as if he'd hooked a fish. He paused to look at me questioningly for a moment, a shy toothless grin trying to take over from doubt, as if he dared not let himself think there was anything more than those treasured hooks. But in another moment he was crooning with glee, then muttering to himself in Spanish, as he pulled forth a brand new collapsible rod and spinning reel. It was a prize he'd hardly dreamed about, causing all the workers to clap and cheer, then go up one at a time to shake his hand and add to his pleasure. He seemed like a little boy when he got up on his Schwinn and pedalled away, the presents tucked safely under his arm.

Too bad we have to come home to a tourist hotel each night afterwards, such an abrupt change that it makes me wonder if we're still in the same country. But I laugh when I think about those party-going beach dwellers telling their friends back home that they spent a week or two in Cuba. About like a Cuban going to Disneyland for a few days and saying he went to America.

Tonight when we came into the hotel we felt pretty conspicuous in our grubby train-running jeans and caps, walking through the lobby full of tourists in fancy Hawaiian shirts, shorts, wild hats and designer glasses. This place has a spacious dining room with four long tables full of buffet foods, including piles of meat and other things that the Cuban servers never see in their own homes. Worst of all is the amount of stuff people leave behind on their plates which is surely noticed by those who work here, even if they never say a word about it as they clean the tables and pile the plates on their carts. I hear they get to keep any leftover food they want and are glad to get it.

This morning we took our time heading out to the sugar railroads, having already missed the best early morning light for photos, which comes at about six or seven around here. So we drove the long way, through downtown Cienfuegos, to experience this seaside city at its busiest. On the outskirts we passed through several blocks of old villas, fancy places with big overgrown yards, lots of stone decorations, tall elaborate fences and impressive gates. I wondered what became of the people who built them, and how it is that among all of today's Cuban poor only a few are lucky enough to live in these hillside mansions. After the revolution the policy was to let families keep their homes - unless they abandoned them, in which case they were often turned over for low prices to nearby poor families, or - if the place was large enough - turned into group homes for disadvantaged or disabled children.

We passed through the opposite extremes in housing just a few minutes later, in a dusty, dirty neighborhood of rough looking hovels along the far end of a peninsula that juts out into the harbor. Fidel's Cuba is basically raceless these days, even our various black friends agree, but this poor neighborhood was noticeably more African in origin than most, yet the people were still just as friendly. Anytime we feel like strangers while passing through a place, all we have to do is smile and start waving, and instantly we have lots of friends.

We stopped for gas at the only station serving tourists in that part of town, not far from the four-star Jagua Hotel, an imposing structure near the tip of another peninsula, priced about three times the rate of our "ordinary" tourist digs twenty minutes out of town. The gas attendant spoke good English and was obviously interested in meeting his customers, so I got out and we talked. But when I asked if he thought change was coming soon to the country he became quite evasive. I suggested that maybe it's time the "big boss" retires, which he pretended not to understand. When I repeated the idea he said, "I like him very much." Maybe, I thought to myself, realizing that he wouldn't dare say otherwise to a stranger, an unknown tourist. It could be that *I* like Fidel very much and am just checking up on workers. Cuba may be changing and getting more open, but it still has a secret police working to instill fear in the people, which keeps most of them from expressing their true feelings and thoughts.

By the way, from tales I've heard about you and Mavis roaring all over the country on your big motorcycle while chasing trains and photographing them in the forties and fifties, you might feel right at home along these Cuban back roads, where you never know what will come rolling around the next sharp bend. Night driving is especially nerve-wracking, with less than half the assorted bikes, tractors, ox teams and other rigs having any kind of lights or reflectors. I think the Cuban government would do well to invest some of its very precious money in red and white glowing strips to let everyone who rolls along at night at least get themselves a little bit marked out.

Last night I got daring with the risky night-time driving system. Normally I go about 25 mph after dark, even slower when I know there's unlit traffic ahead, or when we're rolling through a town. An ambulance roared past us just after we got out on the highway from our last sugar mill, where we'd taken some good shots at sunset and twilight. The ambulance had no flashing red lights but it was really moving. Figuring he'd clear the road for us, I stepped on the gas pedal and kept right behind him, thus making a quick dash of some thirty-five miles into town. Instead of taking two nervous hours for the trip, we made it in 30 minutes, him still rolling fast even after I chickened out near downtown Cienfuegos. I don't know how he did it, except apparently to trust his sheer force and fortitude. There were actually some close calls, mainly for him, although a couple of times I did hit our brakes hard enough to squeal the tires.

The Havanautos representative at our hotel showed us two rental cars that were lately totalled by tourists. One had been driven by a couple of Russians up near Santa Clara, two empty vodka bottles being found near their carcasses. The other wrecked car had carried four Angolans when it hit the side of a train that was crossing the autopista, Cuba's only attempt at a freeway, in the dark of night! We've driven that six-lane route without seeing another car for half an hour, passing only ox teams and bicycles, never expecting to meeet a train. Guess they didn't either.

Keep your fingers crossed for us!

A farmer heads for town on the highway between Trinidad and Cienfuegos, with a part of the Escambray range looming in the background.

Santa Clara, Cuba
March 27, 1994

Hi Brian:

Help! Our video camera broke down today and we're pretty upset about it, since there's lots of exciting and colourful action that we wanted to record here in Cuba. You warned me to buy Sony instead of Hitachi, but our local dealer offered me a good price and I was running short of money, so I believed him when he said, "What's the difference, it's like the old Ford versus Chevy debate." Maybe so, but at the moment it looks like you're right and we've got a lemon. Only the second week into a four week trip, with no repair shops in the country, nor tools in our baggage, though we'd probably need a degree in physics to decipher that modern little machine, even if we were better prepared. It broke down just as Okan was catching the final few feet of a struggling, then failing steam locomotive trying to haul a loaded train up a very steep grade. In fact, he was just inches from the track as the engine passed by him at a snail's pace, though it was making enough racket for a herd of elephants. He's been fiddling around with the many buttons on the camera ever since, trying to make the case open up, which it won't. He can get motor sounds, yes; but action, no; solution not in sight. The repeated sounds of it jamming up are becoming annoying since each time it reminds me of all that Okan will miss filming in the coming weeks. We're just now headed for the most colourful part of the trip.

You suggested I use my still camera to find signs of communism that might soon be gone. Unfortunately, I'm finding them less photogenic than I expected, with no great hammer and sickle statues looming into blue Caribbean skies, nor armed motorcades roaring through the jungles. Billboards and slogans on walls are about the most visual expressions of the continuing "revolution." "Cuba for Us," "Yes for Cuba," "Patriotism or Death." Said one good friend, "We've been seeing slogans all through the years, but where are the results to make the people want to believe in them?"

This morning I had an interesting visit with an elderly campesino who was coming home from his fields alongside the Central Marcelo Salado railroad yards. In the background were two steam engines moving cane cars about, nicely painted engines, huffing and puffing. Our campesino friend wore tall, black rubber boots and a battered straw hat while carrying a big machete so that its blade rested on the sweat soaked shoulder of his very worn yellow shirt. I understood him to say to me in a friendly tone the word "montana" a couple of times, so I thought he was asking about our home in the "montanas," or Rocky Mountains, which is part of our basic introduction to everyone we meet. I nodded and said "Si, montana!" even as I wondered how he knew about this, since we hadn't been around his particular area before. He motioned for me to wait, then went through the gate of a pole-fenced yard and into a shack-like house, from which he soon returned with two red and green pear-looking fruits that he presented with a big gold-toothed smile, saying "manzanas." I made note of the word - he hadn't said montana - and we thanked him, then we talked while he fussed with a big cow that he'd led from his fields by a rope, her calf trailing behind. He said his father used to own all the land we could see beside the railroad yard. He'd built it up as a finca, or plantation. But after the revolution the government took it away and left the family with just a small part of it for farming, plus the house in which he'd grown up, which was the shack behind us.

When I asked this old farmer the size of land that was left he motioned "tiny" with his fingers and said "not enough for all my family." After a pause he added "I could grow more, but they would only take it away from me. They would not let me sell it." I told him jokingly "If you get too hungry you can always eat the cow or calf." His expression turned grim and he shook his head, at the same time clasping his opposite wrists to show me where such activity would land him, handcuffed in prison. "She is only for work," he said earnestly, motioning to the content looking beast; "it is forbidden to eat them." Five years and more is the punishment for violating this law.

At that point another farmer came walking our way from the

nearby cane fields, this guy looking better dressed but also carrying a machete. Our new friend right away signalled on his shoulder with two fingers, meaning someone connected to a uniform, which always affects conversations. Replying to his hint I asked loudly and earnestly, "So, how much milk do you produce with this cow?" He answered with equal facetiousness, "Oh, not very much, I can't keep the calf away from her and he gets most of it." He then said two of her sons work as draft animals on his farm, which he shares with his son. With a sad look he added, "But now I can't work anymore, because my heart is too weak. I just go there and help a little bit, then my son sends me home.

After the official was gone, the old farmer said he's a member of the neighborhood watch committee checking to see why a tourist was visiting. He certainly gave me a cool greeting, eyeing me carefully on his way past. By way of explaining his caution, our friend said he once spent eight years in prison for talking too freely, touching the tip of his tongue to indicate that a neighborhood informer had turned him in. A more investigative writer might have pressed him for further details, but I could tell that he was uneasy with the subject and I generally prefer pleasant friendships to ambitious interrogations.

While we were thus visiting, Okan shot some video footage nearby of a neat little tank engine chuffing up and down the yard, sometimes pushing cars so hard that black smoke billowed while its tiny drivers slipped and spun wildly. The farmer invited me into his simple, rustic shack, which had the atmosphere of a good home. As soon as I stepped through the loose fitting doorway, he pointed proudly to seven bulging gunny sacks piled on top of a metal-legged table in the middle of an open room, covered by a scrap of plastic sheeting. "Rice," he said in Spanish, "enough to last my family all year." Grown and harvested by him and his son, he explained, now protected from mice and rain. An impressive and important stock among a people so chronically short of food. Next, he untied a string to open a well worn fridge, which contained only a few bottles of home made sauces, a big hunk of rough cheese, one last slice of some homemade cheesecake, plus the skinned and frozen carcass of a baby pig that a

This is how your great-grandparents might have travelled 100 and more years ago, but hard times in Cuba have made ox-teams quite important for transportation today. These eight oxen had just dropped off their load of hand cut sugarcane at the Pepito Tey reload, where a narrow gauge steam engine would soon arrive to take the filled cars for grinding at the mill.

friend gave him as a present and which he's saving "for a special occasion."

Out behind the shack he kept a good sized pig for raising little ones, plus a rooster and two hens that came running to the door when he called for them, followed soon after by a flock of chicks and their mom who had been in the bushes. From a rusty can he gave them all a bit of a snack, talking at the same time and showing more feeling towards his animals than most Cubans we've met so far. By contrast, the worst treatment of animals was done by an angry carriage driver, standing up in his seat, whipping his horses from behind with all his might, then jerking back on the reins so hard that the pain from the bits in their mouths made the poor creatures rear up on their hind legs, at which he whipped them down again, endangering not only his three passengers, but also the passerby. "Beast of burden," is an ancient expression that comes to mind often when I watch Cubans with their animals. Their harsh treatment is perhaps learned from experience, but for myself it is painful to witness.

We passed an abandoned military base on our way north from Santa Clara; the country's financial problems are forcing a downsizing in everything, we've been told, including the armed forces, whose hardware used to be supplied free of charge by the Soviets, perhaps more to annoy the Americans than for the Russians' publicly-professed love of their fellow communists. Much of that stuff will likely be useless in a few more years, when newer and better quality becomes available from closer sources, or when large changes in the system reduces even further any remaining threats from outside intervention. If military action were taken against Cuba now it would probably come from former Cubans willing to use weapons in order to force their own way around.

We've passed a lot of abandoned factories, big expensive looking hulks that don't seem very old. These were also built by the Soviets, in a misguided effort to rapidly industrialize Cuba. We heard about one that was supposed to make plastic shoes to help overcome a chronic shortage of footwear. But in this hot climate people preferred to go without shoes rather than wear hot plastic ones, so the factory experiment failed. A government by trial and error, critics have said about Fidel's 35-year era. Probably the biggest error in hindsight was to hook his country so firmly to the Soviet red star, which was then rising, but has now gone into a freefall, taking most everything with it. For instance, until a couple of years ago all of Cuba's fuel needs were supplied by the Soviets at half the world market price. To come up with that half, Cuba got to sell its sugar to them at three or four times the regular market price, so Cuba got super good deals in both directions. Now they have to pay for their fuel in cash at the regular rates, while a world glut of sugar means Cuba is lucky to get anything at all for the meager crops they've lately managed to produce. Bad weather, lack of fuel and parts for harvesting machinery, plus a diminishing enthusiasm among the workers, not to mention their physical slowing from lack of good food - have all combined to slow Cuba's No. 1 industry.

A few of our Cuban friends have also mentioned the negative impact they think Cuba's venture into Angola has had in the long run, somewhat in the way many Americans look back on Vietnam. There was a large amount of money, material and manpower wasted in Angola - fighting what turned out to be an idealistic battle among a people who weren't that idealistic themselves. It would certainly have made things a bit easier in Cuba now if those same resources had been allocated at home instead. This goes for Cuba's revolutionary efforts throughout Latin America, which have by and large borne little fruit, while the resulting ill will has done much to place Cuba in its present isolated situation.

My Cuban friends would perhaps be upset with me for even mentioning this thought, but in some ways the best thing they could do is apply for statehood in the U.S.A. Their own country's whole infrastructure is now so old and worthless that it will take an awfully rich uncle to pay for even the most basic replacements, such as those needed in the field of transportation and communication. The rich uncle lives next door, offers his member states some pretty good subsidy programs, allows a reasonable amount of personal expression and liberty, and would probably even be willing to give a lifetime pension and retirement home to old Fidel, if he could bring himself to accept such a dramatic change in relationships.

More realistically, it seems that Fidel should encourage private enterprise all he can, with the first signs of that encouragment already showing. The other day we saw a guy parked along the downtown plaza in Santa Clara during the evening rush, selling bouquets of fresh flowers from the back of a three-wheeled bicycle. Big deal, you say; yet he was the *only* private entrepreneur we saw on the whole plaza, which had several thousand people passing through. At our hotel in Varadero last week, a young fellow sold belts and leather purses of his own make, in his case only for U.S. dollars, while the flowers could be had for pesos as well. From what everybody says here, the black market is so pervasive that Fidel's best bet is to legalize it and try to catch some taxes....

Hello again, I was falling asleep last night when I wrote those final lines so I gave up. Now we're about three hundred kilometers away, having travelled Cuba's only "freeway" to reach a completely different part of Cuba. Our video situation has taken a surprising turn for the better, but I'll tell you about that later.

It's always a strange feeling for me to enter a town for the first time after reading its name and plotting its location on maps long ahead. So it was today with our drive eastward from the city of Santa Clara. That's as far as we got last year due to lack of time, but even then I studied what lay beyond. First came Ciego de Avila, a rather plain, unremarkable, sprawling city made up of the usual decaying buildings and crowded streets. Next was Camaguey, where the desire to have a momentary glimpse of the railroad station led us into such a heavy mid-day rush of traffic, that we made two complete loops around several curved and crowded downtown streets, in the process losing over twenty minutes from our schedule, yet we never did see either the station or its trains. After that came Las Tunas, where our fuel gauge was getting pretty low, but even after stopping at half a dozen gas stations and getting numerous directions we never did find the town's single establishment that would have filled our tourist tank for cash. Instead, we made a leap of faith and drove on "empty" to the next big town, Holguin, where it took us another fifteen minutes of searching before locating what seemed like a deserted 1950's petrol place, located right in the fork of a busy traffic Y. Lacking signs, the only reason we recognized this as a working gas station was that another car with tourist plates pulled in just ahead of us and immediately got serviced. You can imagine our relief, since options for fuel were quickly running out.

Now we're at the Hotel Guardelavaca, an ocean-side resort located in a beach town of the same name. When we pulled up to this place we began wondering if we'd gone in the wrong direction and were somehow back at the Rancho Luna, near Cienfuegos. Construction of both places was obviously based on the same blueprints, with the results equally ugly and humongous, though otherwise functional. From the earlier hotel I had sent a fax back to Canada telling the guy we bought our video camera from what went wrong with it and asking his suggestions. Told him to fax us back at this place, but when we checked in I found out they have no fax machine. That should have been the final strike against us, *except* that our friend and fellow train photographer from Texas just happens to be here tonight as well. This is his tenth trip to Cuba, so he is well experienced at solving problems. When the camera first broke down I had told Okan that he was the one guy in Cuba who *might* know what to do about it, *if* we could only find him. So it was quite convenient of him to make an appearance at this hotel.

He begged for time to have a swim and cool off after chasing trains all day, but agreed to have a look at our machine afterwards. When we met again in his room he brought out a travelling tool kit of which any camera mechanic would be proud. We stood and watched while he first tried the more obvious tricks (more obvious to him than to us, since he quickly managed to get the cartridge window open the rest of the way, so we could at least pull out our tape and make sure that it wasn't jammed and causing the problem). "I was afraid it would be more complicated than that," he said with a smirk, "and it is." You know those signs on electronic equipment that say only authorized mechanics should enter? Well, our friend asked if we wanted him to proceed, warning us that it might spoil our warranty. What choice did we have? When I told him to go ahead he said it would take him a while and excused us to make a rush for the restaurant, beating its closing time by less than five minutes. Having not eaten all day, that would have been a disaster, since in Cuba you can't just go down the street to an all-night cafe, deli, or snack shop.

We were shocked by the sight that greeted our eyes upon returning to our friend's room, for there in the midst of all his own clutter lay our new and valuable instrument, taken completely to pieces. He was just starting to put it back together, saying bluntly "you're dead in the water." Some kind of chip malfunction that won't allow the machine to proceed beyond closing up its case. "He showed us the monster camera that he carries, the kind you see on the six o' clock news being handled by two fellows. Mind you, this Texan is nearly the size of such a pair. He said, "Have a look at my back-up camera, that's the one you *should* have bought." Sure enough, his was a hand-sized machine of the Hi-8 type like we were using, a dirty, beat-up looking thing, but he said it had never failed him. Kind of made us feel ashamed of the flashy new Hitachi he was carefully reassembling for us.

Then I recalled that he was heading back home tomorrow, flying out of Havana (via Mexico, since there are no direct flights from the U.S. to Cuba). With one last hope for salvaging Okan's video career on this trip, I said to our friend, "Why don't you rent or sell us your little back-up, here?" Without hesitating he replied, "Make me an offer I can't refuse" (he runs a hobby shop back home), at which point both Okan and I knew we were saved. We were at his mercy, but he said $200 would be enough, plus a written promise that we'd return the machine to his home in the same condition (and we did, not even wiping off the countless miles of dust and grime in the process). If we'd shown up here just one day later we would have missed this last chance.

Here's my pick for finest vintage American car in Cuba, a royal blue 1933 Model A Ford that we spotted by the side of the road in the small town of Calimete, Matanzas province. Owner Guillermo Arguelles Vilar said the car had almost all original parts (obtained mostly on Cuba's word-of-mouth used car parts market), and that he wouldn't mind selling it for a good price.

Hotel Guardelavaca
March 29, 1994

Hi Mom:

Here's a letter from your son, travelling in Cuba with your grandson, letting you know we're doing fine and that the communists haven't got us in prison, nor working on rock piles. Guess that's not really a joke for you, after being separated from your family in Hungary all those years by the communist system. But believe me, this place doesn't feel anything like the police states you and I always imagined. For one thing, here in Cuba everyone goes out of their way to welcome visitors and tourists. This is especially true now, since the collapse of the East Bloc, which cost Cuba its main financial support and makes its government desperate for cash to keep the country going. Tourists provide millions of dollars and are fairly popular, so as a visitor you have to really *look* for trouble, it doesn't just come after you for being a curious capitalist any more.

Today we made the longest drive of our journey, some 300 kilometers on several kinds of roads, travelling from the middle of this island to the northeast coast, passing through endless flat scenery that finally turned to low mountains around here, like the ones where we lived when I was a boy. My father could have made good use of the bicycle racing skills he learned as a young man, although Cuban roads are in much worse condition than those in Switzerland, even back in his time.

Speaking of roads, we sure had a few exciting moments while rolling on the country's nearly empty freeway. Travelling at 90 km/h in our little rented Nissan car, the pavement in our lane suddenly turned into a twenty foot stretch of loose gravel with no warning whatsoever. Deadly! I think we survived only because we were going so fast that we reached the other side and got back to asphalt before we could start sliding out of control. Things got even worse a few miles later, when our side of the freeway suddenly ended altogether, again without warning, the road beyond being only in various rough stages of construction, which appears to have ended along with the demise of Soviet financial

support. No clear signs telling us where we should go next,
though many tire tracks headed across the dirt divider, showing
that others had continued their journey in the opposing lanes,
which were in good shape. There was certainly a great risk in
heading the wrong way on an unknown and unmarked freeway,
but we saw no other choice.

We kept rolling along pretty good for a while without seeing
another car or person, then I began to notice tire tracks crossing
back to the other side, which was now also paved again. Without
signs or flag persons, I wasn't sure what to do, until we passed two
guys on an old motorcycle going the other way, on our *right*,
waving their arms frantically for us to move over there. I slowed
down out of confusion, which turned out to be just moments before our part of the freeway ended completely in a strip of heavy
rocks.   By doing some deft maneuvering while sliding off
through dirt and across some more gravel we ended up on a narrow side street that took us through a small town, with still absolutely no signs telling us where we were or where we should be
going. Obviously we mis-guessed, since several sharp turns and
long streets only brought us back to part of the unbuilt freeway.
A wide strip of coarse gravel cut a strange swath through an otherwise peaceful looking neighborhood of older stucco houses,
whose residents were all gleefully watching us dumb tourists having to turn back around in the tight space. At that point I felt so
frustrated that I wanted to jump out and ask why they hadn't got
their government to provide strangers like us with a couple of
signs to save us a lot of extra hassle. We've entered other small
towns on main highways only to be led into circular plazas with
no signs telling which of many side streets to take, so this was not
our first such experience. After a couple hundred miles of driving in the blazing sun, I'm usually not too thrilled at having to
play guessing games in these crowded old Spanish mazes, especially not with lots of people looking at us, some calling out their
own comments and directions.

We find gas is sure much easier to get this year than last, when
only a few stations in the whole country served tourist cars and
we had to buy fuel coupons in advance at the place where we

rented the car. This year they take cash at stations displaying red and green "Cupet" signs, for Cuba Petroleum. Most of these stations also sell cold pop, snacks, and a few typical tourist items like canned foodstuff, film, batteries, even video tapes, all for U.S. dollars. Like cheese to mice, these hard cash transactions attract beggars, mostly young boys who swarm across to our car the moment we pull in, even though the attendants usually try to chase them away.

Incidentally, your grandson is much more patient and generous with these little beggars than I am, though even *he* gets mad when they start reaching in through our windows, which the hot weather forces us to keep open. It's annoying to sit, hot and sweaty, in a small car waiting for the tank to be filled, at the same time being stared at by a dozen or more pairs of eager eyes. We try to keep our camera bags and food items covered on the back seat and floor, everything in the car being quickly assessed by all the eyes, with food and shiny things getting the most attention. Kind of makes me feel guilty afterwards when we munch on some of our dried fruit and mixed nuts while rolling down the road, or coming back from the cashier's office with a couple of cold colas in my hand, I feel bad knowing those staring eyes have no hope of getting such treats, which cost the equivalent of half a month's Cuban wages. Okan and I have daydreamed a few times about winning big in some lottery, then bringing a chunk of it down here to share with a crowd of our Cuban friends. A one hundred dollar bill would probably bring as much ecstasy to a typical country family here as a million bucks would bring for most of us back home.

Our long drive today had some other rough spots before we got here to our hotel. After the freeway ended we travelled Cuba's Number 1 highway, which was in quality about like a number 24 at home. For one thing it was quite narrow for such a busy two-laner, with all sorts of big potholes showing up often when we least expected them. At times there were so many holes in the road that it was impossible to steer around them. In addition, there's the constant risk of hitting horses, bikes and other vehicles. Several times we came speeding up to find repair crews in the road with no warning of their presence, nor of what they had already torn up. They must have strong nerves, or they're in a rush to get to heaven. Considering the overall run-down condition of most motor vehicles in Cuba, plus the lack of money and spare parts, I'd be way more hesitant to rely on anyone's safe driving and braking, especially where the highway goes through the middle of towns that have many small side streets. From my first day of driving in Cuba I quickly picked up the local practice of keeping rhythm with my horn, honking freely and often.

Well mom, I'm getting sleepy, so I'll wait to tell you more of this adventure some other time.

A pink Nash Ambassador recalls the "futuristic" look of 1950's automobile styling, parked outside of a colonial-era house in Santiago de Cuba.

April 3, 1994
Don Lino Resort

Hello Monique

At last, here's a few lines from your old dad, written while travelling around in Cuba with your brother Okan. We're in a beautiful spot at the edge of a rocky cove overlooking the Atlantic Ocean, whose clear blue waters are cool and refreshing in the tropical sun, especially after a few hours of travelling dusty hill roads to find the scenes we want to photograph, stopping to meet interesting people along the way. Considering the extreme poverty these people live in, it's a sin for us to drive away from them to this den of comparative luxury, beyond a guarded gate where Cubans themselves are rarely allowed (except of course the resort workers). While Cubans have to stand in long lines for a few items of food, then work long hours for practically nothing, we can choose from well stocked buffet tables in air-conditioned comfort then afterwards lay on fancy mats to enjoy the sunshine and sandy beach.

So how's the food industry in Oregon these days? Still enjoying your job, looking for unique edibles, potables and so forth? You'd go crazy trying to do business with Cubans, from what I've seen of their food labelling, not to mention the limited quality. Strange tasting desserts of various sorts, none that seem familiar, plus odd-looking fruits that are mostly bland and hardly sweet. Ironic for a country whose main industry is sugar. I hear they grow some good coffee, which would probably make a hit on your deli shelves for its uniqueness if nothing else; for 30 years it's been illegal to bring Cuban goods, including coffee, into the U.S. (I won't explain this ridiculous embargo, to spare you a political discourse, but I have to mention that I find it an outdated and spiteful policy that mainly hurts the people, being applied by the U.S. for a number of reasons including Cold War sins the Cuban government was accused of ages ago). Cigars are great too - changing the subject - but I guess smokes aren't part of your store menu, so you won't be tempted by fine Cohibas.

Speaking of menus, you can sure get some interesting hints

about a foreign people by the way they address their English speaking customers, as in Asian-made instruction sheets. Cuban menus blend English and Spanish so that sometimes we've had to do "blind date" ordering. Our breakfast offering the other morning included a "cheegagi omblet," which turned out to be an omelet of cheese and egg. Can you imagine what means "Jaminex?" (Its not a misspelling of the common Jimenez family name, though that's close). If you just 'ha" your j's you'll quickly realize how some Cuban first year English student came up with yesterday's lunch offerings of "jot dog" and "jam sandwich" though real jam is as scarce in Cuba as ham, with the ordinary folks generally seeing neither one. Got that?

The same menu offered us just one single dessert item, described only as a "mixed fresh." It turned out to consist of a half dozen assorted slices from some kind of unidentifiable but bittersweet tasting fruits, which were certainly mixed, and seemed fairly fresh. Last week at a sidewalk cafe we daringly indulged in a treat called "ice fresh," which turned out to mean fresh fruit with ice cream, also tasting pretty good. Last time I had anything like it was in 1964, a couple years before you were born, when I was travelling by train through Guatemala and bought a similar concoction from some old man with a cart at a small train station. Ended up spending the next couple of days with deep regret, getting to know "Montezuma's revenge." Thank heavens Montezuma lived on the mainland, not here in Cuba; so far we've caught no bugs or interesting ailments. Actually, this is a testimonial to general Cuban hygiene, which is quite good, especially when you consider the people haven't been able to get their ration of soap for several months (they're supposed to get one bar every three months, though that got cut in half two years ago). On the black market it costs half a month's wage for plain soap, never mind the fancy ones made by Ivory, of which we brought a couple dozen, scattered throughout our luggage (so as not to make us look like soap salesmen), which we give to our friends as we meet them.

One of your Trader Joe stores would probably do good in the fancy tourist areas of Cuba, especially Havana or Varadero, where foreigners come to eat, drink and lay in the sun. But for the ordinary Cuban, your stores would seem like the height of decadence, or at the very least an Aladdin's lamp of dining possibilities, with a whole array of items most people here don't even bother to wish for, since delicatessen foods are virtually unknown. At the end of last year's trip Iniskim and I jettisoned our granola, chocolate bars and other munchies, getting great pleasure out of watching the recipients acting like kids in a candy store - especially since they were mostly older adults.

Service in communist countries has generally been considered poor in public establishments like restaurants, there being no tipping or other profit motivation, yet a virtual guarantee of lifelong employment. Actually, tipping has only lately been allowed again, and this year Cuban employees can even keep the American dollars (last year they had to hand them over to the government in exchange for coupons good at government stores where peso earners cannot shop). There is a new government program underway to teach tourist sector employees how to be friendly and efficient, so as to encourage more tourism. Training and testing are now required of all newcomers, who are usually young Cubans excited by the opportunities that this work gives them. Elderly workers, by contrast, tend to be quiet, sometimes surly, seldom able to speak English or even interested in trying. At this point in history everyone wants tourist money if they can get it, but these older folks regularly make me feel that they resent having to take it, and I almost feel that they resent my audacity to leave it for them. Funny thing is, deep inside I agree, I've never liked having to tempt someone to be nice to me with a gift of money, when they're already being paid to do their work. As a former restaurant waitress *you* probably won't agree with me, but don't forget that I spent a couple of my teenage years in a restaurant too, treasuring those tinkling coins in my pocket at the end of a shift.

By the way, today is Easter yet there's no sign of any festival or holiday, not even an Easter bunny. Most of the church buildings we've seen in Cuba are quite old and generally abandoned, some even falling down. Further back on our trip we went inside a Catholic Church in the city of Santa Clara, the only church we've seen with doors open and a priest inside, though I know there are others. Cubans are like cowboys and Indians in wearing their hats all the time, a custom I also practice, especially in this hot and sunny place (or on the Canadian prairies in winter!). But the priest inside the church gave me a dirty look and a verbal correction in Spanish, and darn if he didn't make me feel a bit like a sinner for it, even though I'm not really involved in his kind of organized religion. Most of the spiritual minded Cubans I've met express their faith through Santeria, or one of the other native practices that combine Christian-style prayer books with rituals brought from Africa, all of it developed here in Cuba. There is a distant similarity between Santeria altars and those used in our Blackfoot ceremonials back home. Both are made up of natural things: earth, plants, rocks, shells and so forth. Both groups use drums and rattles to accent songs whose few words have many deep meanings. Fidel has allowed Cuba's "native" faiths to prosper, even while he encouraged the decline of more formal religions. We see symbols of these native faiths everywhere and it's obvious there are many "native" practitioners. They frequently wear necklaces and bracelets of small beads, same as in North American native cultures, with different colours symbolizing important things. That Okan and I wear beads from our culture gets us a lot of attention, especially from the Santa Maria cult, who favour the particular red and white beads that we use.

We had a visit with an old farmer today who told us about fighting cocks, of which he's an expert. We saw this old guy standing with a muscular young fellow inside a fenced pasture as we drove by. We were going slow so as not to spook a horse and cart parked to one side of the dirt road, nor a pair of oxen standing patiently on the other. The pleasant early evening light was giving everything an orange glow, so I figured the two men would make a nice photo and whipped the car around, causing them to stop talking and look at us instead. We jumped out with camera bags in hand, something these two would hardly understand living so far out in the country. They must have wondered what the heck we were up to. But when we smiled and waved they did the same, which works in Cuba almost every time.

While walking past the two big oxen, I noticed that the brutes were not actually tied up as I had thought, but instead were just tied together through big steel nose rings with a heavy rope that lay dragging behind them on the ground. Perhaps they learned early on that if they walk away and one hoof steps on that rope, there'll be a nasty tug on the old proboscis. Anyhow, there followed a half hour visit between us four men, and throughout that time the two oxen never moved. Nor did the lone horse and its two wheeled cart for that matter, as if someone had turned off their keys and put on the parking brakes.

We walked up and made our introductions, explaining as usual where we come from and what we're doing, that we like taking pictures of Cuban people and transportation and so forth, so they agreed right away to let us take a couple of shots. When we were finished I shook their hands, called them amigos, and gave them each an American dollar. They gave the usual response of great pleasure and satisfaction, the old man asking if we also wanted to take a picture of him with his dog. Why not, I said, so he led us through an old wrought iron gate (literally *through* - they had just wired it shut, thinking to leave, and this time around they simply crawled through one of the larger gaps between the bars). The dog didn't turn out to be much to write home about, nor were the dilapidated structures particularly photogenic, but as we got back to the gate a bunch of "cool dudes" showed up, wearing runners, shorts, bracelets and sunglasses, a couple of them carrying bulky bags, all of them obviously familiar with our two new friends and especially respectful towards the old man. One of them reached into his bag and brought out a fighting cock, of all things, apparently freshly fought from the looks of his scratched and bloody body, one eye swollen shut and a lot of feathers missing. He looked pretty spaced-out, as the old man gently and skillfully took him and felt him all over with his hands and fingers. His prognosis was that the cock would survive, which made the young guys glad, since he'd apparently won the battle and had others on offer. What a life for a poor, ugly creature.

We came to this rather remote part of Cuba in order to visit a little narrow gauge railroad, probably the most interesting line in the whole country, definitely the most scenic. Mountains, canyons and lots of luscious farmland, with the base of operations less than ten minutes by car from the romantic seaside resort where Okan and I have rented a cabin! We're so close, in fact, that the boss of these trains has expressed an interest in hearing about tourist-oriented steam railroads in the U.S. and Canada, where they're quite successful. He says they've got an especially old engine that might be just the thing for such a run, and heavens knows there's already a steady stream of tourists looking for memorable adventures. Even our beautiful beach, with its bathing-tops-optional policy, can only bring so much pleasure. No-

This beach side restaurant at the Don Lino Resort served delicious varieties of buffet foods that my nearby farmer friends never dream of, much less ever see on their tables. Dozens of cabins like those at the left provide rustic but unforgettable accommodations along this unspoiled Atlantic beach and its inviting warm waters. Ten minutes from here is the narrow gauge railroad of Central Rafael Freyre, which has future plans of providing scenic steam train rides for groups of tourists.

tices at the check-in desk tell about excursion trips to offshore is-
lands aboard old Russian army helicopters, visits to the homes of
country farmers, special meals, wagon rides, and more. A narrow
gauge train trip would fit right in, and the railroad has tracks that
reach the end of a narrow peninsula jutting way out into the
ocean waters, about two miles from here, which would make a
perfect destination.

....I'm back, though you didn't know I left. Was writing the
previous lines in our cabin yesterday afternoon, resting on my
bed and waiting for Okan to come back from the beach, where
he had his eyes on a sexy young German girl in a tiny bikini
(her parents were on watch nearby!). When he finally showed up
I put my writing away, grabbed our camera gear, locked the cabin, then we drove off for another satisfying afternoon of photographing trains, railroad workers and other Cubans out in the
scenic ountryside where everybody seems to become friends.

This morning I was down at the beach, sitting under an umbrella, watching the people and the water. A guy walked up
whom I'd met earlier at the front desk. His name is Rene and he
lives in Canada but originally came from Cuba. I wanted to hear
more about this, so I was glad when he came by.

"It seems pretty crazy for me to come back here, with Fidel
still around," Rene told me with a vigorous shake of his bearded
face. "At one time he would have had me shot!" Raising his glass
of rum as if in salute, he said he never imagined he'd come back
as a tourist, after what he experienced back in 1961, when he and
a boatload of others got lost at sea while making their escape
from Cuba. "There were endless hours when I wished for any-
place on land, even back here. But I never imagined to return
first class, with a nice home in Canada and money in my pocket."
Here's the way he told me the story.

*I was 17 when my mother died. Fidel got us enthused with his
dramatic speeches about socialism, but what I really wanted to
do was join the New York Yankees. So, Cuba and I parted company. I swore I'd never come back, and I kept that promise for
30 years. But now I'm getting old, so it's time to see the people
and places once more.*

"As a boy I worked for an old neighbour of ours who fished with nets. One day he told me, 'I've got an offer for you. Help me to run this boat and we'll deliver two families to Miami. They're going to pay good and we'll split the money.' Miami, I thought to myself. Boy, if I can get over there I'm sure not coming back!

Those were big families that we took - a couple of doctors and their wives and children. We were 15 altogether on the boat, including the old man and I. The usual crew was two, or at most three, but there were empty holds for the fish, so that's where these people put their bedding. They brought a lot of food and water, which was lucky for us. In the dark night we left behind the lights of Caibarien. We didn't know our small compass was no good, so we headed way more west than we should have. By daylight there was no sign of land, nor by that next night. The old man said there was more than enough fuel to reach Florida, but it turned out we weren't headed for Florida so the fuel gave out. After that we drifted with the currents for many days and nights. The food and water got rationed, so we never quite ran out, but the crowded conditions were awful. We all got seasick, then food sick, and the sun shined down hot most of the days. Once we had a storm that nearly swamped us, and often we saw the grey tails of big sharks following along. I started getting delirious and thought the boat was our coffin, so I wanted to get out. They had to hold me down and give me a tranquilizer. Our skin was swelling up from the salt water, then cracking open from the hot, dry air, and finally getting infected. One doctor got so weak he could no longer walk around, though there really wasn't much room for walking. Several of us took turns watching for help on the water or in the sky, and finally on the seventh day it came in the form of a big fishing trawler. That's what we thought it was, but when it pulled alongside to pick us up the men spoke Spanish and were obviously Cuban, so we thought we'd been caught, and the women started crying and so forth. But the men talked friendly to us, then I saw that one of them had a bloody arm and that there was an American with a swollen face, so I got even more scared and thought maybe they were pirates. Instead, they were with the CIA and had just come back from staging a raid on Cuba. We wanted freedom in the U.S., but not exactly in this way.

Those Cubans turned out to be pretty friendly to us, giving us food, blankets and drinks, congratulating us for escaping from Fidel. They were fighters of communism, they told us, and as they passed around a bottle of rum they bragged about having brought over some commandos for a sabotage mission. This was pretty scary stuff; I was young and I feared for the worst. But we were out of Cuban waters, and without their help we might have drifted into the open Atlantic to perish, as many other Cubans have done. I later found out that the American with the swollen face had gotten that way by taking some part in the attack. They said there were four attack boats but only one came back to them before they found us. There was another trawler like theirs and it was going back to look for the rest.

After that it was nothing to reach Florida, and there my life changed very much. I lost track of the old man, but I still picture the way his boat looked floating alone on the water when we left it behind. After we reached the U.S. they took the old man away in an ambulance, but I heard he was alright. We got job offers from other Cuban Americans, and through my job I met a Canadian lady and with her I ended up owning an accounting firm in Calgary. I never wanted to come back here, and it feels like a big dream, but I think I'm looking at the final days of Fidel Castro, and who knows - maybe I can do some business here after that. Then again, maybe Fidel will stay around for a few more years, who knows? I bear no grudge, since he never did me any real harm; in fact, I thank him for inspiring me to leave Cuba and go where I am now. I'd never want to move back here, but the visit is interesting. I had forgotten how really poor us Cubans could be.

Stories like these are sure making Okan and I appreciate the freedom and prosperity we have at home all the more. And may *your* home be full of peace and satisfaction right now as well.

April 3, 1994
Don Lino Resort

Hi Star

   You would have enjoyed watching our special friend Adolfo
acting "Cuban cool" the other day.

   He showed up at our beach front hotel in a sporty flowered
shirt and a fancy pair of trousers, shook our hands, then walked
over to a nearby Coke machine and bought himself a bottle with
a crisp U.S. dollar bill taken from his pocket. No big deal, you
say? Here it is quite daring and illegal for an ordinary Cuban. He
strutted back over to our lobby couch, sat down with us, then
proceeded to openly enjoy the Coke, realizing he was being
watched by the desk clerks, porters, doormen, and especially the
plainclothes cop (there's one of these by every hotel door at all
hours). Adolfo didn't seem to care that he'd just spent the equivalent of a weeks' Cuban wages on this hint of rebellion. What's
more, he then sent Iniskim into the hotel's little grocery store for
a can of ham to bring home, which cost $5.40 U.S. It was his tip
money from the cafe where he works, and he can't legally spend
it anywhere himself. He's supposed to trade it to the government
(and he does with most of it) getting coupons good for special
purchases not available to others. He said that in a few weeks he'd
have enough of these coupons to get his mother a new replace-
ment for the broken Russian TV in their apartment.

   We then took Adolfo to the nearby city of Matanzas, where I
asked him to bring us to the house where he was born, so he directed me to drive down several narrow streets lined with intriguing old houses and other buildings where numerous people
walked, worked, talked and watched as we slowly drove by. The
many colours of paint were everywhere faded and showed the
country's lack of funds, yet there was a sense of order and an attempt at cleanliness that spoke well of the people. We parked behind a horse and carriage on a street that was raised in the middle
and left little room for sidewalks. Adolfo whistled a signal at a
huge wooden door that had wrought iron grips and fittings,
which his aunt unlocked from inside, bidding us to enter.

The home had the feeling of former splendor, much different from the thatched roof huts of campesinos we've visited out in the country. The high ceilings were painted white, along with all windows, which created lots of light, reflected from the shiny tile floor. We sat on old family furniture brought generations ago from Spain, perhaps by one of the serious gentlemen whose oil portraits hung in antique frames nearby.

Adolfo introduced us to his very aged grandmother, though she and the aunt both looked somewhat askance at Okan and I, two tall strangers with hair in braids. I don't think they understood Adolfo's enthusiastic explanation of our Canadian mountain lifestyle, either, and I was relieved when, after a bit, he told them that we were going to visit nearby friends. He brought us across the street and down just a few buildings, but what a change! In about the same amount of space as the home we had just left there was a low wooden bungalow partitioned into three dwellings, housing several families with a total population of 16. Among them were two old black ladies whose adult granddaughter was staying there along with her two small kids, making five in that unit alone.

But these crowded places were just as clean and homey as the fancier one, both sharing the sad feeling of poverty. Vines were growing along the walls, laundry was hanging from lines along the shared walkway. Adolfo introduced me to several of what he called his "religious brothers," all of whom lived there. These were wiry looking African-Cubans, friendly, but also somewhat shy. He later said that as a boy growing up in the house nearby, he was not allowed to play with the black kids on the street, but that nowadays hardly anybody cares anymore what colour of skin someone else has, with everyone mixing. Of the two women he's loved and lived with, both were African Cubans and both practiced the Santeria faith with him. Most of his best friends also happen to be black, for the same reason. He said his parents are reconciled to this, although it took them a while to get used to it. I told him that it took my parents a while too, before they got used to their only son putting aside college degrees in order to pursue a multi-racial and multi-spiritual life among another people. A new Cuba will probably see much more growth in multi-racial spiritual endeavors, partly to replace some of the old Marxist rhetoric that has been promoted like a religion for the past 35 years.

A common joke making the rounds in Cuba says, "Doctor, I think I'm going blind - when I open the refrigerator I don't see anything." Certainly when Adolfo untied the cord that closes his family's Russian-made fridge, there wasn't much to see: a nearly empty bottle of milk (a scarce commodity among adults; only young kids and some of the elderly receive official rations of it); a couple of fist-sized chunks of fat laying on pieces of newspaper; three pots of left over food; a couple of brown jars filled with tomatoe puree or other homemade sauces. Nothing there that we would consider the makings of a real meal. Still, the refrigerator stood in a prominent part of the living room rather than in the kitchen, indicating its status in their family life.

Adolfo's dad was getting ready for work on the afternoon shift, repairing electric lines. The electricity was off right then, as is usual in the daytime, so he couldn't even cook a quick meal or make himself coffee. He apologized for being unable to serve us anything, expressing genuine shame, even though I assured him we had no hunger. He brought us out to the kitchen, a plain, narrow, green painted room with hardly anything in it, its two windows looking out from the fourth floor at a sea of similar block buildings. He showed us the rough chunks of charcoal they cook meals with, *when* they have the food and the time. Handmade charcoal, from out in the country, provides Adolfo's family with their only dependable cooking fuel in the city.

There was a plastic barrel full of water standing near the sink, with several smaller plastic jugs filled on the counter. There was also a faucet, but when Adolfo turned it on only a few drops appeared. Bare light bulbs hung from the ceilings, but each room also had a kerosene lamp like we use back home. In fact, a lot of our daily lifestyle is similar to what we've seen in Cuba, though most Cubans yearn for more, whereas we prefer to keep the simplicity. On the other hand, it's much easier to haul water from a pump and use lamps in the evening like we do when you're in a peaceful cabin in the Canadian Rockies than if you're a working family living in a dilapidated fourth floor apartment, standing in long lines for every little thing you need just to survive on. Adolfo senior earns 171 pesos a month, working regular shifts Monday to Friday plus every other Saturday. Junior gets about the same, working longer shifts, though only every second or third day. The big difference between their jobs is that junior also gets tips from tourists, mostly in U.S. dollars, five to 10 dollars a day. His tips in one night are worth more than his dad's month-long wages. That's an important generation gap in Cuba today, with increasing numbers of young making much more money than their parents and other elders. Adolfo's dad said that in some ways things were better in the country back when he was young, before the revolution. He was 20 in 1959 and knows the differences between communism and colonial capitalism very well. He feels it was important for Cuba's society to go through all the difficulties and sacrifices in order to improve their morality and self esteem, and I get the feeling that a majority of people would agree with that, even those who may now think Fidel has outlived his usefulness, which junior does and senior doesn't.

The father was using a rag to wipe down his bike, a nice Chinese model that he keeps in the living room and carries up and down four flights of broken concrete stairs every day, often at night coming home in the dark. Kind, friendly and plain people, just trying to stay alive. There was nothing much else in the living room besides the bike, a TV, the string-tied fridge and a well worn chair with matching couch. Just the essentials, even with all three family members working full time. No car, no video, no upholstered rocking chair, hardly even any food to eat!

Junior went to his room for a while, then came back out wearing a white shirt, white shorts, white runners and a white baker's hat - his Santeria ritual outfit, with white representing peace. He asked us to come back into his room, where he offered us seats on plastic fold-up chairs and said he would show us something of his religion. First he asked us to thumb through a black book, written in Spanish, rather plainly printed, which he studies in order to learn the many numbers and signs that relate to various

The old Babalawo and his student. Necklaces of specifically coloured beads and the pure white cap identify this kindly gentleman as a spiritual leader in the Cuban religion of Santeria, widely practiced even in those years when regular churches were under pressure from the government. A new spiritual awakening in Cuba has brought out many young people, including the smiling fellow here whose Spanish forefathers looked down on Santeria as a primitive African faith brought over by black slaves. The warm relationship between these two symbolizes the change Cuban society has undergone with race relations in the years since the revolution.

factors in life, the combinations of which help Adolfo to determine whether an applicant should do certain things, go certain places, and so forth. When he has studied these teachings long enough to inspire confidence, Santeria followers will begin to seek his guidance. He said that some of his "brothers" specialize in the study of herbs and use them to doctor people's ailments.

He had several altars which he kept in sort of a closet, each one covered by a white cloth and identified by a different coloured bead necklace, which he put on one after the other as he took the cloths off. Among the things he uncovered were some native clay pots, the contents of one representing the "goddess of waters" and another the "goddess of fire." There were about six altogether, including one that looked like a mud face, with cowrie shells making mouth and eyes.

At the start of his ritual Adolfo mixed himself a drink from several different bottles - a tiny drink in a special cup - which he said included a white wine, honey and some rum soaked with bark and herbs. He prayed for us and our people, along with himself and his, sprinkling a few drops out first. I saw a similar offering custom once in the 1960's being performed with a drink of brandy by old Last Gun, who was then over 100 years old and said to have been the last buffalo hunter and scalp taker among the Blackfeet. After Adolfo took a few sips, he prayed for us, this time alternating between Spanish and the sing-song of Afro-Cuban phrases he's learned. He said other Santeria leaders, or Babalaos, also practice bilingual praying, which is interesting since Blackfoot ceremonies are slowly developing this compromise as well, now that the last tribal members are gone who spoke nothing but Blackfoot. Santeria's Afro tongue has survived generations of slavery and politics, which says something of its strength and spiritual value.

During his ritual Adolfo paused and asked earnestly if we and our "religious brothers" would pray for him and his religious brothers to gain freedom and to live in peace. We actually did so back at home, a few weeks later, when our family sponsored the ritual for a medicine bundle handed down from long ago, celebrating the return of thunder and all the goodness of spring, during which in place of the usual tobacco I gave out Cuban cigars. Each member of the large crowd gathered inside our tipi held aloft a tiny pinch of tobacco while making a prayer, not only for the freedom of Adolfo and his friends, but for all Cubans, along with suffering people around the world, giving as well our thanks for the blessings enjoyed, in particular by the friends and family of those who were gathered with us. There are some 15 to 20 of these ceremonies every year among the 25,000 or more Blackfoot people, but that was probably the first time Cubans have been mentioned at one of them, or that Cuban cigars were used for making the sacred tobacco offering.

Later, after changing back to his street clothes, Adolfo guided us on another drive around his old city, mainly to visit more friends, or "religious brothers." He spotted them wherever we went, calling them loudly through our windows from where he was perched in the middle of the back seat. While still several house lengths away his friends recognized him, shouting back and usually setting off a noisy banter that continued until we were out of earshot. Now and then he would ask me to stop so we could visit them. At a couple of Afro-Cuban homes he made us wait in the car while he went in alone, then at others we went in together. The people were friendly as usual and all the homes were tidy, even though materially these people were worse off than most of those who live in North American ghettos. We sensed here an air of pride and social unity instead of crime and moral decay. The question is, who will be the leaders of the future that can blend the best of these poverty lifestyles for the betterment of their people?

One particular section of the city is known for its black market, though just by driving through its streets you wouldn't realize it. Adolfo said you can buy most anything if you know someone and have the money, mainly U.S. dollars. We stopped near one intersection while he disappeared into a house, as neighbors with little else to do stood around in the heat and looked at our white rental car. Soon he came back, carrying a little cardboard box that contained freshly cooked rice and bits of pork. It looked good and homemade, though that's partly why I turned it down when Adolfo asked if we'd like to share it. Iniskim being more daring *and* liking the adventure of having an illegal meal, downed the whole thing and pronounced it the best pork dinner he's ever had, while Adolfo went back to get himself another one. They cost 25 pesos each, made by a widow woman who has six children. She buys the hard-to find meat from a relative who lives on a farm in the country. I told Iniskim that at least one of us better remain a "designated driver," though I'm happy to report that the meal and his stomach got along fine. Definitely not recommended for your average tourist, though.

Adolfo said Santeria followers appreciate that Fidel has allowed them to practice their faith all along, but most are not great fans of his. It is well known that there are government spies among the Santeria people; just like everywhere else; one or two are even said to be Babalaos. In Havana there is one so well liked by the government that journalists and other interested foreigners are routinely directed his way with the help of his own business cards! "Where *I* go, it's just among friends," Adolfo claimed in a low tone, "so we trust each other."

With that, I'll close this tale.

Sitting in the shade of an old doorway, Adolfo clowns with some of his "religious" brothers.

Santa Lucia, Cuba
April 4, 1994

Hey Jack!

How's my old school friend, at the mid-stage of life? Still sailing the seven seas? Haven't heard from you in ages, not since you sent that nice article about your family's boating adventures. I guess in our separate ways we've both found life in harmony with nature.

Lots of interesting boats here in Cuba, though I don't know enough about the subject to tell the good ones from the bad. Many look to me as though they belong in Jack London stories, or ones by Ernest Hemingway. Old time wooden boats, often painted in bright pastel colours, photogenic in the harbor, though probably not during storms out at sea.

You must have cruised Cuba's shores a few times during your submarine days in the U.S. Navy? I guess back then there was still a pretty serious Soviet military presence on this island, though I hear it's all gone now. Back in school together we thought that the bearded revolutionary Fidel Castro had done dirty tricks to bring communism at America's doorstep. I cheered for our side during the missile crisis and thought it was too bad we didn't come to blows and give them a good pummeling.

Boy, I sure see things differently now, after some lengthy immersions into Cuban life. To my surprise, 35 years of serious U.S. blockade hasn't destroyed a sense of respect and admiration that most Cuban people seem to have toward America, an attitude that they hardly have towards the Russians, who have been here helping them through that time. If the U.S. government had made more effort to work with Fidel and his people, a friendly relationship between the two countries could have easily been maintained all along, which would have greatly lessened the sufferings and heartaches of millions.

That suffering is pretty bad at this point in Cuba's history, especially when compared to our part of the world. While the communist system may have failed the Cuban economy, its people nevertheless all have homes and receive at least minimal food, schooling and medical care. Sadly, at this point that's about the extent of their immediate prospects, nothing much beyond the basics.

"Cuba has three main problems: breakfast, lunch and dinner," says my friend Ramon, whom I met in Matanzas while walking along a row of boat stalls, taking pictures and waving to some of the fellows and their families as they were cleaning and painting the various craft, each boat obviously the pride and joy of its owner's life. Ramon lives on one of them and says he has no place else; everything he owns is stashed aboard, except for whatever he keeps in a small locked shed up on shore, where the boat is beached. Like many others, Ramon is growing tired and frustrated of getting nowhere particular in life. Unlike most though, he's got a slim chance to escape, if he wants to leave it all behind: he's got his own boat!

"One of these days," Ramon assured me in fairly good English, "Enough gasoline, the courage, then I'll be gone!" He signalled a fast takeoff with his hand and looked towards the open sea, though the boat looked awfully small to a mountain man like me, thinking about those frequent tropical storms that churn up the shark-infested waters.

"My neighbor Enrico left last week and made six thousand U.S. dollars for taking a family from Santiago," he said. "He got to bring his own wife and two children and I'm sure they made it, because we had good weather then." He admitted other friends escaped by boat, but were never heard from again. "I'm looking for a family with money, to help pay the way, like those people Enrico took. They got a note from their relatives in New Jersey. There's a lot of rich Cubans in New Jersey, and they pay good to have their families brought out. Florida is the same. The government boats don't even try to stop us anymore, unless it's too obvious. Why should Fidel want to keep us here when he can't feed us? Those who go don't have to be fed."

Ramon spends his time repairing the boat between fishing trips. He says it's over 50 years old and always leaking. The motor is from a small Russian tractor, though it originally had an

American motor which gave out years ago for lack of parts. He doesn't fish far from the harbor of Matanzas because fuel is so hard to get, but he goes out to sea when he can, sleeping and eating in the small cabin. There's probably room for six people to ride his boat comfortably, with two in the cabin and the rest out back, at least while there's no storm! He brings another man along for the fishing, mainly to help with crab nets and lobster traps, trying to catch whatever he can.

"When I see the slogan 'Socialism or Death' I want to ask Fidel, "What is the answer?" said Ramon, after he asked me some things about Canada. "It looks to me like it should say instead, 'Socialism *and* Death.' Of course, what we have had these last 30 years is communism, not just socialism. That's where Fidel fooled us, me included. I was a teenager in school when he took power, and I thought it sounded pretty good that we should take over the big, rich, foreign companies and control everything ourselves. I didn't realize that would mean we are also controlled in everything we do and say, just like the factories. There was no indication of that when we got behind Fidel and Che and Camilo in driving the tyrant Batista out. So now we've ended up with another tyrant who has overstayed his time in office. He says we have a true democracy, but I say that Cuba has never had a true democracy, or even anything very close to it."

This seemed like pretty heavy talk for an unshaven little fisherman who has nothing but a small wooden boat, until he told me that he used to be the manager of a big factory in Havana. It was given to Cuba by the Russians and set up to make building materials, which are always in short supply. At first things went well, then it became harder to obtain supplies and raw materials. Finally, when the machinery broke down and there were no funds for replacements, the factory was closed and he was out of work. As a boy he fished this same bay with his father, so now he's back to his roots. Must be a humbling experience for a former factory manager, but when I asked him he just shrugged his shoulders and said, "It doesn't matter anymore - even factory managers have nothing nowadays. At least I can eat some of my work, even though I have to bring most of it to the cannery dock, where the government takes it and I just get a salary. Besides, this boat gives me more freedom than I ever had as a factory manager. People used to come to my house all day and night with problems. Now I just go out in the water a few meters and put out a line and no one disturbs me." He offered to take me for a ride on the boat, or even for a fishing trip, but my time was too short. He said there would be no cost, though he added that those he has taken "give whatever they want." Sort of like the chica ladies on the streets, who are not prostitutes because they charge no price, but they'll gladly accept gifts. I gave him some money and wished him well, momentarily transposing the image of him and his little boat to a dock in Miami, wishing I could help him in such a way that he wouldn't have to go.

Makes me think of a frequent comment about Cubans that I've read in the North American media, that *all* those who leave the island do so because they *hate* Fidel Castro. The feeling I get in talking to the people here is that they're sorry some of Fidel's ideas didn't work out, that the grand "revolutionary" dreams all didn't come true, but that if they did leave it would be to go where they can *have* something and *be* somebody, not because of the leader. Many feel their country is so far run down now that it will take a long time for things to get anywhere near normal, as in the world you and I know, or the one in nearby Florida. Of course, by leaving Cuba they lose the feeling of belonging to a big national family, a very tangible feeling found everywhere in Cuba, but much more seldom anywhere else. In place of the many conflicting and challenging political and social sectors that most other countries have to deal with, Cuba has basically one sector and everyone is a part of it. This aspect of Cuba seems to appeal to many of its foreign friends and visitors, though often with mixed emotions.

Not far from Ramon's boat I spotted a larger craft being worked on by three black fellows. They made an evocative picture, so I stopped the car and walked up to the locked gate at their fence. At the same moment a cute little girl from a nearby house came close and studied my face carefully, saying nothing but obviously intrigued. When the men looked up I called out a greeting, then asked if I could come in and take a picture of their boat. They said yes by nodding, though unfortunately they also gave up work and went into their shack, apparently figuring I wanted the boat alone. I called them back but it was too late, for they were now camera shy and, although I still got a very nice portrait of them standing by their boat, it lacked the authentic everyday repair work look that the scene had when I first pulled up. Another one of the many challenges in making photographic records of human life.

When I asked about their work they said they were tuning up the motor and patching the cabin roof, so I jokingly told them, "You must be getting ready to head for Miami." They laughed a bit nervously, looked at each other, sort of shook their heads in the negative, but said nothing. Surely the idea must have crossed their minds a few times; no doubt they would deny it to a stranger, though Ramon didn't. In the wrong ears such comments could lead to jail and perhaps a confiscated boat.

After thanking this trio for their time I walked back to the car, with the little girl still trailing me. I didn't give the men any money since there were three of them and they weren't nearly as friendly as Ramon. But I felt sorry for the girl, who had on a dirty, raggedy dress and no shoes, so I reached in my pocket and gave her all the loose change. One of the boatmen happened to see me doing this, so within seconds all three were headed my way, one of them saying in a rather mean tone that they should be the ones getting money for letting me take their picture. They had a point, but I didn't want to argue it, so I hopped into the car and drove off, looking back in the rear view mirror to see them surrounding the girl, presumably relieving her of the coins.

Wish I could tell you that I'd been a hero, but the coins weren't worth it. There'll be more little raggedy kids to give money to, so I'll just roll along. Look forward to your long-overdue reply!

Sunday, April 3, 1994
Don Lino Resort, near Santa Lucia

Hello Dave,

Happy anniversary of sorts! Do you remember what we were doing together exactly 30 years ago this summer? Kissing our girlfriends goodbye at L.A. International and flying off to the unknown for a couple weeks of train riding through the remote mountains and jungles of Mexico and Guatemala. Guess it must have been as great an adventure for you as for me - no doubt your kids are near boredom from hearing your tales, as are mine. Soldiers surrounding us with machine guns does give the journey a romantic air, though as I recall they were mainly suspicious because of our big camera bags. Remember the pretty girl in the berth next to mine, aboard our southbound sleeper from Veracruz? Or the mother and daughter who brought us to their stall-like rental room after we got off the train in the middle of the night in a village with no other accommodations. Do you regret missing out on that final day I spent alone with big mainline steam engines running out of Mexico City, while you were with that cute little Senorita in some park.

It's hard to believe that three full decades have gone by since we went down there to photograph and experience what we thought then was "the last of steam." Yet, here I am, again photographing and riding "the last of steam," though this time it *really* is the very last of it. Amazing, that there'd be any left this far into the 20th century, when it's so representative of the 19th. Unfortunately, now that you're an employee of the U.S. government you may have to wait a while to come here, or else settle for my stories and pictures. A benefit of being Canadian is that this country has remained steadfast friends with Cuba through these past 35 years, while the U.S. has been mostly antagonistic, creating bad feelings and lots of personal sufferings with its endless blockade.

It's somewhat interesting that both my trips in search of "the last of steam" has led me to countries with military dictatorships. Ironically, they've been on opposite wings, so to speak, with

Guatemala way over on the right and Cuba on the left. Is there some kind of odd connection between such regimes and the reliance on antique mechanical operations like old railroads with steam engines?

Before I came to Cuba the first time last year with Iniskim, I imagined the Latin people and tropical geography to be similar to Guatemala, but that wasn't the case. The two peoples look different, act different, and even speak their Spanish differently. There's a heavy aboriginal cast to Guatemalan society that is completely lacking in Cuba, where "native people" are descendants of Spanish colonizers and African slaves. There's almost no trace of the Caribe Indians who originally inhabited Cuba with an estimated half million population. Another difference is that Cubans are far more carefree and openly friendly than Guatemalans, without the unspoken mysteries of a local primitive past nor the fear of ruling class oppression that we found in 1960's Central America. Sure, Cubans avoid talking about subjects they know could get them into trouble, but we heard hardly anything about human rights abuses, and this in a country that the U.S. claims has too many, ignoring at the same time the mass killings of innocents back when the U.S. staunchly supported the regime in Guatemala.

Do you remember being called "gringos" wherever we went? I was amazed to find in Cuba that the word doesn't even exist; in fact, hardly anyone refers to our backgrounds in anything but positive tones, calling us "Amigos Canadiense," their Canadian friends. What a pleasure to be among a people like this, even though I can't talk to them a whole lot better than I could to the Central Americans when I was supposedly our interpreter. Cubans come in all colors, from deepest black to lightest white, with red, blonde and brown hair even among some of the brown skinned folks, and black curly hair on many light skinned ones. 300 years of intermarriage, topped by Fidel's 35 years of stressing equality seems to have sired a couple of generations who are not very racially prejudiced. An unheralded yet very valuable social experiment with positive results of a kind that is often in such short supply around today's world.

Latin women have been able to distract me on both trips, though 30 years ago I was an eager and single young fellow, whereas now I'm a vintage grandpa, happily married, no longer interested in "friendly" ladies beyond the joy and humor of their attention. They're called "chicas" here and they're way more forward than the girls we met in Mexico. As I recall, Guatemalan girls were so proper that we never did get to spend time with any of them. On some Cuban streets we're approached half a dozen times in an hour, with girls going so far as to squeeze the privates (mine) to get across their "friendly" message. Not necessarily prostitutes, these chicas look for boyfriends as their main pastime; eager for friendship, hoping perhaps to meet donors of unobtainable goods, or even an offer of marriage, which with a foreigner could mean a new life in a more prosperous land.

Our initiation to chicas came during the very first night we spent in Cuba, when Iniskim and I walked down the street from our beachfront hotel to have some fresh orange juice at a near-by sidewalk cafe. A little group of good looking black ladies strolled slowly past our table, looking intently at us while we quietly returned the favor. Sparks were flying - or readily could have - especially with a shapely tall one in a tight yellow outfit, wearing long, straight hair of the kind that always catches my eye (never mind the outfit!). Letting my gaze follow her a bit too long evidently signalled interest, so she sent one of the others over to ask for my company.

"Now see what you've done," said Iniskim in an annoyed tone, so I pretended ignorance when I got asked in Spanish if we'd like to go with them. She was insistent, so I finally replied in Spanish, "This is my son," thinking it would get rid of her. But all she said was, "That's not important," then went over to her group and came back with a real young one, who immediately tried to get friendly with Iniskim. They knew we were Canadians from the pins in our caps, but couldn't figure out which language we speak, trying alternately Spanish, French and German without eliciting any response from us. But we both broke out in a grin when the main talker finally said in a quiet but desperate voice, "You-wann fockie? Fockie?" Our reaction to that told her that we speak English, so she said the same thing again more seductively, at which point Iniskim put his foot down and replied with a firm, "No!" The young one next to him immediately turned and walked away.

But the older one was not so easily put off, telling me in quiet Spanish, "Your son is good looking! I will take him for a walk; my friend over there in the yellow wants to take you." So I told her, "That sounds very good, but you are about 25 years too late." When I showed her my wedding ring and clarified my meaning she shrugged, then went back to join her friends and together they all walked away. No meetings afterwards in each other's hotel rooms, nor in the darkened berths of a sleeping car. However, I've learned since then that there is, sadly, a growing segment of the tourist traffic coming to Cuba specifically for these friendly types of chicas, which is a shame for such a proud people, after 35 sheltered years.

Tonight at the supper table we had for neighbors a couple of Canadian investors from Toronto, plus their Cuban guide and interpreter, a friendly, light skinned fellow named Estevan. He's about the first Cuban I've heard claiming the U.S. embargo has actually had a positive effect on Cuba. "It has made us very self-sufficient," he explained proudly. "How many other countries of the world supply most of their own needs, even if we are very poor? Not very many, from what I know." It's true, Fidel has long stressed Cuban self reliance, so Estevan's testimonial would no doubt please him.

"For instance, we needed sports equipment, but couldn't get any," Estevan went on. "Sports are very important to us in Cuba, but we could no longer afford to buy the equipment. So instead we built what we call Sports Industries, where we sew baseballs by hand and make fine wooden bats. Last year we made over 50,000 bats and many were sold for cash to neighboring Latin countries, since we all like baseball. When the embargo is lifted, we expect the U.S. will become our biggest customer. So far our business efforts are still small, still in training, but we hope soon to have more money and a greater market.

The two Canadians with him were mainly interested in Cuba's minerals, not sports, plus "having a little good time." They put away several drinks in rapid succession, after which the older and more heavy-set of the two got very talkative. They own a couple of silver mines in Ontario, he bragged, and now they want to invest some of the profits in similar ventures down here in Cuba. Whenever he mentioned Cubans as a people, he lowered his voice and glanced at Estevan, who sat at the other side of the table enjoying his food and pretending not to hear. There was disdain in the businessman's voice as he told of delays and frustrations in trying to deal with the Cuban system, which he thinks is rotten and doomed. He said he and his partner plan to make "a quick killing," then get out while the going is good. His thick, ruddy cheeks shook with laughter when he said this, seeming much like the old stereotype "Ugly American," even though he was from Canada. He said the timing for investments is perfect right now, with things just starting to open up and so far no competition from the Americans. He expects to be bought out by them within a couple of years after the embargo is lifted.

Thankfully, the two excused themselves and left as soon as they were done eating, leaving Estevan to visit with us. He was obviously taking full advantage of his chance at an all-you-can-eat tourist meal. He said he just had to bury his only brother a couple of weeks ago. Drowned at sea, along with two cousins, trying to reach Florida in an old rowboat. From what I've heard about these crossings, they're sure no Sunday school picnic, but rather a pretty dangerous challenge.

First of all, there's over 100 kms of unpredictable ocean between the "island of frustration" and the "coast of great hopes." Frequent storms blow up, often quite suddenly, and the water currents are always changing. Most of the boats leave Cuba with very few provisions, since so little is available. If the boat blows off course it might drift for days, weeks or months, with fatal results for the occupants. Also, few Cubans have boating experience in open waters, nor are there many boats fit to handle them. To top it off, although Cuba is surrounded by water, statistics show that many Cubans can't swim. That may be just as well, since swimming between Cuba and Florida is sure to attract deadly attention from some of the numerous sharks. No wonder many would-be escapees say, "I'll wait for a plane," or more likely, "I'll stay here and wait for things to change." Certainly that's how most of our friends seem to look at it.

This whole issue however is the cause of a lot of stress among Cubans. The young often wonder if they'll eventually have to escape in order to make anything out of life, while the old get older faster by worrying about the escaping youth - especially when they hear nothing back from them for months. Then there are those too old to leave, or the many who love Cuba far too much at any rate, though even they are now questioning the future. Wherever we go, everybody has comments on Cuba's situation, no one seems afraid to talk about it, and no one has good answers or solutions.

Five years ago (even less), talking openly to others about such things would have led to prison, or at least to some serious "counselling." But now, even the most loyal of Fidel's faithful citizens appear to have painful second thoughts about all their years of self-sacrifice. The long heralded "we" of Cuba is slowly being pushed aside by individual needs and desires, the results of which will probably bring as much bad as good.

To give you some idea of what causes so much dismay, here's the current ration list our friend Estevan showed us. He says each person is entitled to receive, with a ration booklet, the following each month: 6 lbs. rice, 1 lb. beans, 6 eggs, 5 lbs. sugar. In addition, each person can go to the neighborhood bakery for one fresh (but very small) loaf of bread, daily. All this sounds like the basic ingredients for a couple of big family meals back home, but not food for a whole month. For anything more to eat the people have to scrounge on the black market, where prices are something like 30 pesos for a pound of rice, 25 for a liter of milk and on rare occasions when some low-grade meat is available, it costs over 100 pesos a pound. Keep in mind that the average state-paid wage in Cuba is about 275 pesos a month!

Coming back sweaty and tired from a long day of photographing and train chasing, I found myself getting energized to-

day in an unexpected manner. Okan and I had walked into our
hotel's open-air lobby wearing our grubby clothes and lugging
all our camera gear, wanting to ask on the way about making a
phone call to Canada later tonight. Suddenly a couple of musicians started playing their instruments at a pretty fast tempo, then
a pretty young lady came over and chose me for a partner in a
lively dance. Having shaken a leg or two in my time, I instantly
caught the rhythm and took this to be just another wonderful example of Cuban friendliness.

"We're the animation team," she told me afterwards, referring
to herself and a similarly pretty friend. "It's our job to make *you*
feel welcome, to have a good time, to give you animation!" Animation? I wondered to myself. I noticed that she danced and
flirted with most of the men at the resort over the next few days
and nights, though I never saw any indiscretions or had the feeling there was any serious hanky panky going on. Just Cuba's
way of trying to get those stodgy Germans and Dutch to loosen
up a bit during their Caribbean vacation. It sure did the trick for
me at the end of that long day. I even went to the resort's entertainment area that night to watch the two ladies lead various
group games and dances to the backing of a live band, until the
power suddenly went out and the beautiful little seaside resort
turned back into a dark ampitheatre of trees, crickets, huts and
breaking ocean surf.

In that same lobby I read through the guest book and noted
that most people liked their stay and said they'd come back.
Many mentioned the friendliness of Cuban people, one German
summing it up by saying, "The rich countries have a lot to learn
from Cuba, how to live happy with so little, while we have everything but are always unhappy." There were many good comments about Cuba and about the Cuban people made by sensitive
tourists, but there were also some lame-brain writers who showed
that they couldn't see beyond their own noses, like the German
who wrote, "The food is much too plain and ordinary," or another who snidely claimed, "The lack of meat at meals has driv-
en us nearly to eat one another."

A Canadian with a Hamilton, Ontario address wrote, "I'm

probably the first and last Newfie to come to Cuba, and I won't be back. I wrecked one jeep, rolled a moped, wore out a horse and could have used more variety of drinks at the bar." The next writer said, "I'm from Canada too, but please believe me that most of us are not like the guy above, who should have stayed home." One writer expressed my feelings best by saying, "Those who complain about this place should be staying at a luxury resort where they would be paying luxury prices." No kidding, for under 50 bucks you get good food, good beach and good sleep, yet people come this far just to complain. A "them and us" attitude - tourists and Cubans - will be one of the side effects of Cuba's burgeoning tourism. It remains to be seen how deep the Cuban psyche has been wounded by America's strong-arm tactics, and how this gets publicly expressed once the blockade is lifted and lots of Americans come around. "Them and us" may well get much more noticeable and important then.

By the way, the place where we're staying is a great attraction in itself, beside the fact that our favorite narrow gauge railroad begins just ten minutes away in the village of Santa Lucia. We're in a cozy little stone hut at the edge of a rocky bluff against which the ocean waves make their pounding and sloshing music day and night. The stone walls have windows and a palm thatched roof, while inside are two narrow beds, some easy chairs, plus a shower and toilet that work most of the time. To top it off, the room rate includes buffet supper for two in the rounded glass restaurant that sits out on a point of this bluff, with a fine sandy beach tucked under its long right wing for daytime sun worshippers. Since this resort caters mainly to German tourist groups, the food in this pleasant restaurant leans in that direction, making it more varied than at most other places we've stayed. Lots of fresh salads and vegetable dishes, plus a choice of tender roast, breaded local fish or fried chicken.

An interesting feature of this particular resort is that one end is a fenced compound of modern apartment style buildings reserved strictly for Cuban vacationers, who have their own beach, so that they and the foreigners only mix in the restaurant, where I found this out last night from a professor of economics at some higher school of learning in the nearby city of Holguin. At first I thought he was one of the restaurant's Cuban musicians - as with all tourist places, this one has a state-paid group playing good folk music - but he surprised me by saying, "No, I'm also a guest here, like you." When he saw my surprise he added, "But I am a Cuban." So we quickly got to talking about Cuba today, and Cuba in the future, and about how certain Cubans like himself are lucky enough to enjoy vacations at resorts like Don Lino.

I accepted the young professor's offer to visit him in his Cuban apartments, where the rooms are bigger and more homey than our huts, mainly because they're meant to serve whole vacationing families. In this case there were two long time friends and their wives, the professor's buddy being an athletic looking black fellow who is the manager of Holguin's main bottling plant, producing Cuban beer, cola and rum. His plant sends 12 million bottles of beer around Cuba annually, of which about two million get sold to tourists. For a Cuban, such a bottle costs from one to two pesos (more in a city and less in the country), while a tourist pays one U.S. dollar for the same thing. It takes about 120 pesos to make up that dollar, so you can see that the profit difference is immense.

The manager was keen to hear about business methods in Canada, then disappointed to find out that I don't know much about them. He thought all people in capitalist countries take direct personal interest in business and financial matters, probably dismissing me as naive for saying that money is not one of my life's goals. He thinks it is for *all* Cubans, especially at this time. He said there would soon have to be a lot more of it. "We will industrialize very quickly," he assured me, "once the blockade is lifted and U.S. financing arrives." But he wonders about the prospect of workers being exploited. "History may be coming back to haunt us again." His biggest concern is that, "for 20 years the people of Cuba have not had to work hard, so now it will be difficult to teach them, and only if they learn to work hard can we compete on the world's labour market." Pretty revolutionary thinking for a place like Cuba - from the manager of a state-run industry, at that.

They said it was a big deal for them to go on vacation so near to foreign tourists, even though they stay separated from us by a large wrought iron gate (for whose lock they both had keys, so that I couldn't figure out exactly who or what was being locked in or out). The professor said his worker's union arranges vacations for him and his family. When I asked how often, he said that three months ago they'd stayed for a week at nearby Playa Blanca, while last year at this time they stayed together at another beach place. When I asked how he got here he said simply, "my car," which turned out to be a little white Lada parked outside.

The professor got a bit evasive when I asked if other Cubans have the same vacation and travel opportunities, but finally admitted somewhat sheepishly that they don't, especially not the campesinos and other people of the land, who seem everywhere around here to be in the majority. In fact, we spent part of yesterday and today with a campesino family, and let me tell you that their conversations compared like day and night with what I heard from the professor.

For one thing, most of this farming family were barefooted, whereas the professor had on a fancy pair of European leather shoes. He also wore slacks and a good sport shirt, whereas our farmer friend and his brother wore rough homemade trousers and shirts that had holes in every sleeve. Their mother had on a thin white dress, while the young wife wore shorts and a large scarf that was tied to serve as sort of a halter top, convenient for nursing the naked toddler, which she did while studying the pages of our family photo album. The photos nearly got baptized, as the little kid's faucet suddenly opened, the mama instantly pulling him off the breast and standing him on the floor, where the earth soaked it up, as it did the droppings of chickens strolling casually in and out of the doorless entryway. These people were downright poor and funky, yet they had a pride and dignity that combined with their friendliness and made us enjoy every moment that we spent in their presence.

This young farmer's name was Vladimir and he'd been trying to get us to his house for several days, coming up to us along the tracks and offering to sell one useless item after another in the

Vladimir Leyva Guillen, with his father and his white mare, their thatch-roofed home in the back.

faint hope of getting some of our dollars. These people live very isolated, far from tourists, except for the fact that their farm is beside the narrow gauge mainline of Central Rafael Freyre, which means that during each sugar season at least one or two cars of photographers drive by in clouds of dust almost every day, chasing the trains. With so much Rafael Freyre trackage to cover, few of these tourists stop near this farmer's territory, but when they do he's all ready for action. He offered us first a necklace made from a bathroom plug chain, then a smaller necklace that he claimed was real silver, and finally a thin brass version with a homemade little cross, for which he wanted the sizeable sum of $10 U.S. When none of these things got our attention, he told us to wait and rode off in a hurry on his little white horse, returning soon with a small feed sack, from which he produced a live chicken. "Five dollars U.S," he said in signs. He was unable to comprehend anyone sleeping overnight without a cookstove at hand, though I tried to tell him that our hotel serves complete meals. He finally managed to get a dollar from me for an older

Cuban coin that he said contains silver, though I bought it as a souvenir, not for the mineral value.

The next day we followed trains along that narrow gauge line several times, passing our friend once or twice. He waved eagerly and looked somewhat dejected when we didn't stop. The day after that we drove out again hoping for some early morning photos, only to learn that instead of the usual two trains with steam engines, there was only a single train, and it was powered by a little Russian diesel. So I told Okan, "If only we knew where our farmer friend lived, we'd now have time to go and visit him."

To our surprise and good fortune, there he was by the side of the road, astride a skinny white mare who was accompanied by her suckling colt. He had on a straw hat and wore a big smile on his lanky, light-skinned face, especially when we pulled up and stopped. He looked proud as a prince when he heard that we'd visit, then led us up a narrow dirt path and through a rickety gate, past growing vegetables and palms to a little collection of thatch roofed bohios, which are Spanish campesino adaptations of Cuba's original native dwellings. The main one of these was his mom's house, where he brought us first, apologizing greatly that his father was cutting cane out in the fields and could not welcome us. The mom repeated this story, then offered us little cups of "cafe," that thick, potent stuff so different from the watery java that's popular back home. A few thumbnail sips of this stuff left me yearning for a cookie or cracker to help soak it up and to shore up my unprepared stomach. When I told them that I mainly drink water, they quickly fetched me an enamel cup full, direct from the well in their yard, warm tasting stuff from near the surface, perhaps also risky for my stomach, especially with all the homes and livestock so close around. There were two smaller houses for our friend and his brother, plus their wives, each of them having a small child. Stalls outside the houses held pigs and chickens, and I was surprised to note that each member of the family appeared to care for his or her own, rather than keeping all the livestock "communal." Still, the complete setup was certainly an old time traditional extended farm family of the kind that we see less and less of in the industrialized world.

"My house is your house," said our friend's mom, for which we thanked her. When I asked if we could take their picture they didn't say yes, but instead told me, "please!" They'd had no family picture taken since the sons were young boys, there being no camera in the neighborhood (nor could neighbors be seen from their compound, which is rare in Cuba).

That family must have thought they'd died and gone to heaven, when Okan asked our friend for the brass necklace and cross, paying him the requested ten dollars. We learned later that they'd never had such a sum of money in their household before, nor did our friend truly expect to get that much for his necklace. I'm not sure that they realized it wasn't worth even half that much, and that Okan was just buying it to help them out. At any rate, they expressed immense gratitude.

......Right now I'm sitting in a big easy chair out on the porch of our little Don Lino cabin, right beside the ocean. The continuous sounds of incoming waves crashing against the rocky coastline would probably lull me to sleep, if it weren't for a constant disco beat coming from somewhere in the distance. It's an annoying Cuban habit, playing such beats day and night, the volume usually turned up so far that everyone around is forced to listen. Such beautiful sounds of nature otherwise, including lots of crickets and a fair number of songbirds, their tunes combining pleasantly with the surf, but all of it tainted by this undecipherable, "boom, boom, thump-dee-thump, boom, boom, thump-dee-thump," over and over and over again.

This afternoon we spent some time parked along the fence of the Rafael Freyre sugar mill, looking in wistfully at the steam action around the railroad shops, where strict regulations have so far not allowed us to go. Would be some good photography, but even a telephoto lens couldn't capture it properly from outside the fence. As we watched, a young black fellow came over and started talking to us in decent English - first person we've really conversed with around here. He said this part of Cuba is considered especially conservative, and its people are far less interested in the outside world than most others. There's nearly a million people living in Holguin province, about 2,000 of them in the

Santa Lucia area, of whom most work in connection with the
sugar mill.

This young fellow had been a worker there himself for a
while, but found it too hard and dangerous. He said there are
dangers from noise, chemicals and difficult machines. The people of Santa Lucia have recently become aware of the possible
health hazards caused by living so close to this operation (the
smoking plant sits right at the foot of town) and that a lot of
them have eye and respiratory problems which they blame on
the materials coming out of the mill's two tall stacks. He says
others get sick from the poison fumes and sprays which are used
in and around the mill itself. It's no wonder, since the whole
thing operates by 1910 standards and there were no environmental concerns back when it was built. Unfortunately, today there's
no money for a much needed upgrade, while the alternative of
just closing it down has everyone worried.

During our visit to Guatemala in '64 the plantations were having a bad banana harvest, so you and I saw less train traffic than
we would have a year earlier. The same is true here in Cuba right
now - looks like this will be the smallest sugar crop since the
Revolution - or maybe since the early part of this century. Even
the government admits it will be below last year's 4.2 million,
down from seven million in 1993. A real setback for Fidel and
the country, considering all the other economic woes. The government blames a combination of things, including the extreme
shortages of fertilizer to boost depleted soils, along with a lack of
fuel and spare parts to run the machinery. The media back home
puts major blame on what they call "low worker's moral" and a
"massive worker absenteeism," but during our visits to various
sugar mills I don't get the feeling that either of those is anywhere near that big a problem. The main hope is tourism, which
averaged only 30,000 people a year in the 1970's, but is now up
around a million.

One small but conspicuous difference between right-wing and
left-wing dictatorships is that in Guatemala we could find a Coke
or other bottled soft drink in the most remote places. Do you remember the warm ones we enjoyed at an open-air, thatched

roofed hut way out in the middle of a jungle? Here, except at the tourist hotels, restaurants and some stores, a "bottle of pop" is not to be had while travelling the roads of Caribbean communism.

There's another very noticeable difference between my visits to Cuba and our 1964 trip to Guatemala. We were barely more than teenagers back then, and accordingly poor. Remember how I peddled one of my three cameras to a store owner for a fraction of its worth in order to pay for the last night's hotel room in Guatemala City? We had no insurance or credit cards, nor do I recall any emergency plans. Guess that's the difference between travelling as a carefree teenager then and now as a responsible father.

Our meager budget back then didn't allow us to think about paying to get special photographs, much less renting a whole train, but here in Cuba that has now become possible. For instance, our goal at the moment is to charter a train to be pulled by a little jewel of a locomotive, a tiny 30-inch gauge 0-6-0 that was built brand new for this railroad by Baldwin Locomotive Works back in 1882. Nicknamed "Chiquita," discussions are ongoing with mill bosses in the "uptown" Santa Lucia office about firing up and running this little thing. The whole idea came about after we learned of its existence from our friend Rodolfo Betancourt, chief of trains and transportation, who said the locomotive *could* be run, adding that he had proposed it be set aside for special tourist purposes. That's when I said to him, "How about asking the bosses if *we* can be the first tourists?" I said we'd pay cash for the opportunity. Cash is a big deal everywhere in Cuba these days, even at a sugar mill. So far the response has been, "maybe yes," so we're waiting from day to day for a firm decision.

Meanwhile, Rodolfo began to feel badly about the delays, so as a consolation he offered to arrange for two locomotives to pull a train, making a "double header," great for dramatic photos. The only catch, he warned me, was that the wooden cowcatchers in front and back of the engines (they run both ways at Rafael Freyre) would not allow them to be coupled directly and the bridges couldn't handle the combined weight, so there would have to be a caboose in between. Also, this doubleheader couldn't just be run anytime, it had to fit in with traffic schedules, which meant we had to check in at the mill several times each day, spending the balance out along the railroad line, or else resting at our resort beach ten minutes away.

Finally this morning at our first mill check Rodolfo anxiously told us to hurry some kilometers out to the village of Bariay, where the Peluda branchline train and its Baldwin 2-8-0 were waiting in the siding for the arrival of the mainline train, hauled by a similar locomotive. He said the two would then join their trains and bring the load in together. Needless to say, I drove that little Nissan like a race car, only slowing down now and then for some of the larger potholes and sharp rocky edges.

We spent the next couple of hours with that steam doubleheader, all our cameras getting a workout, as we recorded the dramatic event from many angles. My most frantic moment came right after we rounded a sharp bend to where the road and tracks suddenly run parallel for a ways. Okan was in the back seat shooting video while I tried some one-handed, slow shuttered panning shots with my automatic Nikon. But damned if the thing didn't choose right then to run out of film! So, dodging those same big potholes while also trying to keep Okan at the right spot so his camera would get both locomotives, I steered with one hand and used the other to, first rewind the film (automatically, lucky for me) then open the camera, pull out the exposed film, take a fresh roll from its sealed Kodak box, fit it into its camera slot, pull enough film leader forward so that the automatic mechanism could grab it and get it going, after which I still had to slam the camera shut, advance the film to start, then hurriedly fire off a few frames before we reached the spot at which the road and tracks cross each other, where I slid our Nissan to a dusty stop. Fortunately the train also stopped, since I had asked the crew if Okan could board here and ride a short ways in order to get some on-board footage. Every once in a while my photographing work comes up with some memorable touch of excitement, which more than once has been when my film ran out.

During a Northern Ontario winter I had to change film in a manual camera, using only one freezing hand and my mouth, while holding onto a steel ladder with the other, standing in an icy wind some 40 feet up on a spindly sand tower, looking down at one of our favorite wilderness passenger trains.

Back to Rafael Freyre, we later followed a single steam engine hauling two old tank cars and a caboose over a seldom used branchline that ends by a dockside oil tank at an appropriately named place called Puerto, where the tank cars are regularly refilled. This took place beyond a gate controlled by armed guards. We could see a Cuban navy boat tied up in the background, so we didn't even try taking any pictures, though it was sure a unique setting for a narrow gauge steam train. We did get some nice shots of it leaving the little port town later on, taken from next to a hillside vegetable stand where we had visited for a while with several friendly folks. It was a government stand, of course, with only three items: green tomatoes, red peppers, and green peppers, available only with the proper ration coupons.

A kilo of tomatoes (about a dozen medium sized ones) cost the ration holder a mere 65 centavos, while a bushel bag of peppers (maybe two kilos) was two pesos, which is still just a few pennies to us. One old woman was having a coughing fit, after which she came over and begged us for medicine, saying that none had been available for a long time. She could barely talk, her voice was so raw. Unfortunately, all we have with us are cough drops and even they were back at our hotel room, miles away. There's a dreadful lack of medicines in this country, mainly because of the U.S. blockade, so we did bring a variety of basic drug store stuff for most of our friends.

.....Another day has passed since my last notes, and what an unforgettable experience we've had this time! Something I've always wanted to do is rent my own train, in this case a caboose and a little steam locomotive. It had finally been decided that the day's rental would cost us $60, which seemed fair enough. By the time the last paper was signed at the office, we could hear the tooting of the little machine's whistle down in the millyard, where delighted crewmen were taking turns running her up and

The small size of Central Rafael Freyre's Chiquita, *on the right, is obvious when compared to the facing locomotive, which by itself would be considered a small narrow gauge engine.* Chiquita *has worked on this railroad line for over 110 years!*

down the yard, while I thought with frustration of the photos I was missing.

How was the price of $60 decided on? Keep in mind that no one at the sugar mill had ever experienced this kind of a business transaction before. Our friend Rodolfo handled negotiations on behalf of the mill and asked how much we'd be willing to pay. I hesitated to say, not having done this before either. Suddenly another friend piped up, "How much do you pay for your rented car?" I told him "sixty dollars per day." There was a brief whispered discussion, then Rodolfo said, "Alright, the rent for Chiquita is 60 dollars." Settled. That's one deal I'm sure Hertz or Rent-a-Wreck will never match.

But alas! The old girl hadn't been fired up in years, so she suffered from old age ailments, mostly minor in nature. A badly leaking water pump got worse from the running back and forth before we arrived, so the elderly engineer was forced to shut her down less than half an hour after we finally got there, and just before we were to take off with the engine and caboose. We were promised that by next year all the problems would be fixed so we could complete our ride. For me, just the experience of the rental itself, plus a few fine photos showing the 113-year old locomotive actually steaming down the tracks made the whole effort well worth while.

From Rafael Freyre we drove all day, leaving the province of Holguin and heading homewards, our next (and final) goal being one more visit with other narrow gauge friends near the coastal town of Caibarien. This meant driving into the night (which is exceptionally risky in Cuba) and also taking a chance that the only place with rooms near that area would have one available for us. In fact, the *first* challenge was to even find this place, a vintage resort called San Jose del Lago, because its various thatched huts and rickety motel buildings are scattered in a jungle-like setting around a small, hidden lake, barely visible when driving along the dark, narrow, winding highway.

We did find it, and were greeted at the gate by a friendly young fellow wearing fatigues and holding an army rifle. The office was to our left among a thick grove of trees, with no sign at all, but with a door standing open and clerks waiting behind a plain counter. We paid $17 for two beds and were not surprised that it was a pretty rustic room, including sagging mattresses, well-worn sheets, a broken Russian TV, an old rusty fridge, and a toilet with neither seat nor paper. This resort is operated for Cubans on holidays, not for tourists.

My first desire at the end of long travelling days is always for shower, so I rushed in there and made a couple of large cockroaches run off without pausing to give me a second look. Cold water only, as expected, but it felt fine. When I was finished and tried to turn off the flow all I got for my efforts was to have the whole faucet fall apart in my hands. I got a little more wet before sorting all the parts out.

The stately dining room down by the lake had seen better days, but the atmosphere was so totally Cuban and different from the tourist restaurants that we enjoyed the experience, even with the menu (a single one for both of us, in Cuban fashion) written solely in Spanish and listing almost nothing that I recognized. We took wild guesses and ended up with an interesting variety that included a ham steak, some kind of hamburger, a good rice and tomato mixture, plus a big plate of fresh tomatoes and cucumbers. Simple, but very tasty. With tall glasses of fresh-squeezed orange juice, the cost was $9.50 for the two of us. I only had a twenty dollar bill so the poor waitress had to walk a quarter mile up to the motel office for change.

Afterwards we took a lakeside stroll down to the office ourselves so that I could pay for a second night, not expecting to be back until late tomorrow from our photographing and visiting. There was a small crowd standing around in the lobby, watching the communal TV, but neither of the lady clerks nor anyone else seemed to understand my desire to pay in advance. About the time that I finally decided to just let it go, an old man sitting in a big chair on the porch tapped his wooden cane loudly and called for me in Spanish to come and sit by him. Soon after that a young lady appeared, talked briefly with the clerk behind the desk, then the two of them came over to us.

"You want to pay for your room?" she said fairly clearly. "Oh, you can talk English," I said happily," explaining why I would indeed like to pay for a second night. I don't know if that was some kind of code word or what, but suddenly one of these two pretty young ladies said, "Come with us to your room." When I looked hesitant, the other one said, "Give me your key, please," which baffled me so much that I shrugged my shoulders and complied.

The two young ladies then led us up along the semi-dark tree-lined trails, Okan and I saying nothing, but exchanging glances and wondering greatly. When we got to our room, one of the ladies unlocked the door, reached in and turned on the light, took a quick glance around, then motioned us inside, saying, "Here is your room," to which I said thanks. Then the other one added, "Is there anything else?" For a moment or two the four of us stood there in silence, suspense in the air as if we were waiting to announce a winner. Finally I said, "no thanks," wondering very much what the "else" might be, but hesitant to ask and find out. They just nodded their heads with looks of disappointment and left, and now I'll leave you as well, saying: Adios!

Varadero,
April 9, 1994

Hi Star

Almost time to come home, so here are my final lines from Cuba. Fantastically successful trip - all we have left to do is bundle up our film and get it safely back to the Canadian Rockies. Hope all these letters reach their proper destinations as well. Between them and the photos, there's over a month of hard effort, so I'm going to carry them with me on the three connecting flights, not taking chances by putting them in our luggage.

Yesterday we met the closest we've seen yet to a Cuban hippie, a fellow named Eusebio, with a ponytail, bright-colored clothes and an earring (left ear). He was with two well-dressed, long haired young beauties, the three easily standing out from the rest of the crowd at the downtown Matanzas train station, where we happened to pull into the taxi area so that I that could make a quick check for a potential travel photo.

Eusebio spotted us and came right over to ask where we were from. When I said Canada, he pulled out a letter from his backpack addressed to a fellow near Toronto and asked if we'd mail it for him. I said sure and threw it on the dashboard, then waved farewell, seeing nothing worth photographing and in a rush to be on our way. But he stopped me and asked if we could do him one more favor, which I figured was going to involve money. By this time we're down to our last dollars, having given most of it to our friends. But instead, he was trying to get a ride for the two girls, who were heading back home from vacation and had ended up at the wrong train station. "Could you drive them to the other one?" he pleaded. How could I refuse? Not only were they nice looking ladies, but the "other train station" happened to be our next destination, though for a much different reason. You see, it serves a famous electric railroad that was built and named for the Hershey chocolate empire back around 1920, and is still running with its original vintage American equipment between the cities of Matanzas and Havana. So, in moments we had the ladies and their suitcases in our car, all of us waving goodby to Eusebio as we pulled out into the heavy traffic. I never expected to meet this guy again.

The girls spoke no English, so I asked in Spanish where they were headed. "Ciego de Avila," was the answer. That can't be, I told them, the Hershey station has trains going only towards Havana; Ciego is in the opposite direction. "Yes, yes," they assured me, "the other station has trains going to Ciego de Avila." Impossible, I insisted, and they in turn were just as sure they were right. Finally I said, "look, it's much closer back to where we just came from, so let's return there and clear this up." They made no objection, but were obviously not pleased that their chauffered ride seemed to be coming to such a quick end.

Eusebio was still standing with his bright clothes among the station crowd, looking perplexed at the girls in the back seat, but when he heard our problem he said his own train was an hour late so he'd come and show us the right place. He laughed about the electric train, saying that indeed it would go nowhere near where the girls were headed. There's a *third* train station in Matanzas, it turns out, an ugly new one located in the midst of a train yard way out at the edge of town.

Eusebio is an artist and musician, the only one we've met so far, a fellow much dissatisfied with his society because he wants to practice his talents without government control and supervision. Like the musician-artists I knew in the sixties, his thoughts and attitudes are probably indicative of changes coming to Cuba whether he directly helps to make them or not. "The young will soon change Cuba from the ways of the old," he assured us. "Over 60 percent of us were born after the 1959 revolution. We are the children of the revolution and now we want some of *our* ideas to be heard." When I asked if he had any desire to leave the country he shrugged and said, "Sometimes, yes, when I'm frustrated and see no hope. But most of the time, I want to stay here and help make a new Cuba."

Okan and I got out to help unload the girls' luggage, for which we were rewarded with hugs and kisses, while a big crowd of bored waiting passengers stood nearby and watched. It's interesting how little unexpected encounters become meaningful events in life - Okan and I will probably never forget those girls, yet we were with them for no more than 20 minutes and never even got their names. But we did get Eusebio's, on the envelope of that letter, so I'll probably surprise him and write from home. The churches in Cuba are also benefitting from the new openness and are slowly coming back to life. This afternoon we had a visit with Father Rivera, a surprisingly old-fashioned Catholic priest who has been serving his parish all these years. "I was ordained to serve God before the revolution, so why should I have let it change my way?" he said, inviting us to sit down with him on one of the wooden benches in front of the old Spanish style church that he administers near downtown Santa Clara. Although he wore no long robes or other conspicuous church symbols, he still would have stood out anywhere in Cuba with his white collar and black suit. "This church has remained open through all that time and now things are finally getting better for us. I have lived to see the beginning of a miracle." Whether that's what this new tide of change will bring to Cuba, or to its churches, remains to be seen, but the good Father spoke as if he were already getting closer to heaven.

"Many of the young are starting to look for answers in the Bible, coming to attend church, especially now that our political and economic system is failing. They are looking for answers, answers that they cannot get from their parents, nor from the authorities. It is a time of renaissance for the church, a blossoming that began just in these last few years. It is like good perfume, you don't have to talk a lot about it but everyone knows it's there."

"When the government drove people away from the church, as they did until lately, it seemed we might have to close down altogether. It was difficult to get funds for anything, even from the people. Sometimes I would only baptize a few dozen children, perhaps a hundred in one year, but this year I've already baptized 635. A few years ago hardly anyone asked for church burial, while now I do several each week."

When I asked Father Rivera how other religions in Cuba are doing he got that old-world look of disdain, then coughed a bit before admitting that they must be doing alright. Having read about this subject before our trip, I asked if young Cubans seemed to have as much enthusiasm for the Catholic church as they do for other kinds. He looked away as if awaiting a confession, then whispered, "The young seem much more interested in groups such as Asamblea de Dios (the fundamentalist Assembly of God), and of course in Santeria. But perhaps this is because we Catholics tend to be so stiff and serious, while those others have lots of music and action." I was surprised by his candidness, which perhaps helps explain how he managed to keep his church going all this time.

End of another day in the small town of Guaimaro, in the province of Camaguey, with an old church bathed in sunlight while on the street are parked a white Willys convertible and a red '51 Plymouth.

Santeria is well suited to Cuba, having originated here through a combining of other faiths. During Cuba's long slave era many blacks kept alive their African heritage by dressing its spirits and rituals in Catholic names, masks and symbols. Thus the spirit of war that is known in Africa as Chango became known in Cuba as "Santa Barbara."

"Many Santeria followers come to my mass on Sunday morning," the father proudly claimed, though I doubt that my tocayo Adolfo would be one of them. He's more a young man of action, so he needs an active way of expressing his spirituality. The priest would be like a statue by comparison.

On leaving the church yard we were trailed by a bunch of little kids calling out "chicle." I guess to them we look like sugar daddies, a couple of fellows in a new car who *must* be carrying some kind of neat goodies that they just might be willing to give away. I can relate to this from my own days as a poor kid in southern Germany right after the war, when ordinary families like mine had barely enough to live on. The rare times that foreigners came to our neighborhood in cars (we had none, otherwise), a few of us kids would invariably stand around, keeping back a little distance, saying nothing, just hoping they might pull out some treats for us, though it seldom happened. Our best bet in those days was to stand at the curb when an American army convoy rolled by, hoping that the soldiers (or "Amis," as we called them), recognized our plight. Sometimes they tossed out sticks of gum, else candy, or even canned goods. Now I'm an "Ami" of sorts myself in Cuba (actually a "Canadiense") giving out gum, candy and the occasional piece of money in lieu of army rations. Once or twice I've seen myself in one or another of these Cuban kids, maybe a little Adolfo, standing back a bit from the rest, not knowing that life will soon bring him to other continents and other people.

It's especially enjoyable to give things away to kids we've gotten to know. For instance, at Mal Tiempo there's a little guy named Yusley who wears a white straw hat with a red bandana tied around it, a really "cool" dude, skinny and maybe about four foot ten, with a handsome brown face and a shy smile. He always stands out in the crowd that invariably surrounds us at this friendly mill. If we're taking pictures, they all know to move behind us, yet they stay so close as to become our shadows. Sometimes they seem like bothersome gnats or mosquitoes, and they don't mind danger if they have to follow us into someplace like the busy locomotive shops. Running away from flies would be easier than getting rid of these kids. Our only peace comes when we go for a ride on the trains, which they are not allowed to do. All but Yusley that is. He gets to climb up on the engines because the crews like him and give him extra liberties. Now and then somebody loans him a pair of gloves, so he can handle the chores of fireman, getting guidance as to how much each valve and lever needs turning. He's about 12 now, so he just might get to work on the line yet, but *if* so he will no doubt be among the very last and it will be a fleeting experience. Even in Cuba old machines have to eventually wear out, and none more so than those old steam engines on narrow gauge lines like Mal Tiempo. When Yusley is my age Cuban kids will marvel that he was alive "back" when there were still narrow gauge trains. I gave him an extra pair of gloves as a step in the right direction, but I have to wonder about his future. On another day I also gave him a couple of dollars, the very first American money he's ever had. With it he has entered an economic system most of his young companions do not yet know, since they live way out in the country where tourist money doesn't come around much. Where will these first real dollars eventually lead him?

"In Canada does your son have a bicycle?" Yusley asked me one afternoon when Okan was in another part of the railroad yard. When I said yes, he told me, "I don't have one yet, but someday I will." I said if he were in Canada my son might give him his, since he no longer uses it. Why not, he wondered, so I told him that he now has his own vehicle. What kind, he eagerly wanted to know. How do you explain a four wheel drive pickup truck with chrome rollbar, bright orange paint and huge bigfoot tires to a Cuban boy who has never seen such a thing, a boy who barely daydreams for his own bike. Hot rod magazines are not among the limited number of government approved outside readings, and we never saw any real hot rods like Okan's cruising the streets. I made an effort to explain this to Yusley, but I think he lost track of what I was saying. He seemed awed by the fact that the tall boy from Canada actually owns his own truck. Most Cuban *dads* don't enjoy such a luxury, let alone school age boys.

When I asked Yusley what he wanted to be someday he answered predictably, "an engineer." But when I asked him again later, he admitted, "I'd like to go to America, or Canada, maybe to have my own car like your son." I laughed, then he also laughed in his own shy way, so I hugged him and wished him well. He tucked the money I gave him down into the pitiful remnant of a sock.

By the way, back in Matanzas we went to a government store so Adolfo could show us Cuba's version of a supermarket. It seemed unreal to walk into what could have been a thriving store only to see row upon row of empty shelves and glass cases, with just a small part of this downtown establishment actually in use. Off to one side of the main entrance stood three counters behind which some white-coated employees tended to the customers, about a hundred of whom were standing in several long lines, coupon books and pesos in hand.

The first counter had a layer of crushed ice on which were displayed one pound slices of "fish steaks," which according to Adolfo are "sometimes available," rationed at one per person per month. They were probably shark or some less popular species, caught locally and considered not good enough to send overseas or to serve in tourist restaurants. "Our waters have many lobsters and shrimps, but you will never see them for sale in here," Adolfo said somewhat bitterly. "Our country is so bankrupt that we sell all our good food to tourists and foreigners the same as we do with the meat raised on Cuba's farms and ranches - the beef, sheep, pigs and others. They don't even give us the meat from old horses, and we have plenty of them."

On the next counter were stacked two kinds of sugar, brown and off-white, each kind being packed in small paper bags according to ration quantities. There was also a container of ground coffee, though Adolfo says it's pretty bad stuff compared with what he's tasted at tourist restaurants. Generally it's mixed with dried and ground peas (chicaro) to make the quantity seem greater. This makes it stronger and more bitter, but many Cubans don't seem to mind.

The last counter at the "supermarket" was the longest, with rice from China (rationed at 3 kilos per month), dried peas from Japan, cooking oil from Spain, plus boxes of crude wooden matches from Singapore. That was the extent of the day's offerings, and it was available by ration card only. Considering the near starvation food supply, it's no wonder UNICEF announced after a recent study that the average Cuban lost over two kilograms of body weight last year compared to the previous year. You only have to look at the population as a whole to see that there's a mass diet program in effect. You'll have to look very hard to find a fat or "weight challenged" person in Cuba today (other than the tourists, who often stand out as a result).

Adolfo took us for a coach ride through Matanzas, paying the driver three of his precious U.S. dollars for a couple of hours, insisting that we are his guests. The coach was a fancy red one with flowers painted on the back, pulled by a single black horse that responded easily to the commands of our straw-hatted driver, who was kind to his animal, for a pleasant change.

We stopped to say hello to several of Adolfo's friends, including the elderly babalao who is his teacher. We found him sitting on the wooden floor of his simple little house, leaning back against the wall and seemingly in a trance. His Santeria altar and sacred things lay nearby, and there was a book in his hand. It turned out he was having a divining session for a patient, an elderly Spanish lady who was seated before him on a little wooden stool. I felt guilty for intruding, but when he opened his eyes and saw us, he had an instant smile, acting as mellow and friendly as last year when Iniskim was with me. I'm hoping young Adolfo learns this part of life from the old guy, along with all the ritual knowledge, since right now he's about the most nervous and fidgety character I've ever been around, chewing his nails between bursts of high speed monologues (especially when he talks Spanish, as he did to his numerous friends, always at a fairly loud volume).

The carriage ride ended in front of Adolfo's apartment house, where we went up the familiar flights of broken steel and concrete stairs to his family flat, where his mom and dad were waiting with dinner. Adolfo joined us, but in typical Cuban fashion the parents - as hosts - sat and watched. Boiled potatoes, some pieces of meat, rice, fried banana slices, fresh bread and a strange tasting orange type drink made up the meal. As usual, it was put together especially for us, and was not indicative of the family's own daily menu.

Adolfo's dad said he regularly works six days a week, and also on some Sundays when he's a "voluntario, working free for the country." Adolfo's mom said "no, no," not her. She works as a dental nurse six days a week, but has no interest in performing voluntary work on her only day off. The dad said the volunteer work is mostly at his regular job, but during the sugar harvest it is also out in the fields, cutting cane. At those times even the bosses come along, getting sweaty and dirty with the rest.

When I asked if he likes the nearby tourist resort of Varadero, he said without hesitation that he wouldn't feel comfortable there because it is only for "tourists and the elite of Cuba." When I asked if in this system everyone isn't supposed to be equal, the whole family laughed and said, "yes, that was the revolution's ideal, but it has never become the reality. Some are elite, while most of us are not." Still, their plain, small apartment had more "things" than many other homes we've visited.

Adolfo showed us the new family pet, a red chicken named "Rookie," in honour of a character in "Star Wars." The black market also has new videos - mostly pirate copies - though like most families, Adolfo's has no VCR. His dad shook an index finger vigorously back and forth as he told us earnestly, "Rookie no for eat!" It's luxury enough for the family to get Rookie's three or four eggs a week.

"No lights today," said Adolfo apologetically, a common problem in their apartment block, or actually throughout the city. No running water either, his dad told me while showing us a large plastic garbage pail which they fill up when the water does run. He says it comes from a well in the neighborhood, but needs electricity to be pumped in. No wonder Cuba is showing interest in solar power, which pleases me a lot, since the lamp that I'm typing this by (back home at my desk) runs from a solar panel, It works well, and in the Canadian Rockies we don't have half the sunshine that they do in Cuba.

Well, I'm hot, sleepy and eager to get home, so I'll say good night and save the rest for when we finally sit down together.

Energy-efficient delivery service is common in Cuba, where a horse and wagon like this represents opportunity for its owner to earn a few pesos.

Dear Readers:
Since we've been back home, several of the friends mentioned in these stories have written me letters. Here are some of the more interesting ones (presented verbatim, with grammatical errors) the first one having arrived written in English with Canadian stamps and a Toronto postmark, delivered second-hand.

Pinar del Rio
August 15, 94

Hi Adolf!
I felt very surprise when I received your letter, since your name means nothing for me; just when I read your letter I remember who you are and our meeting at the train station in Matanzas province. I'm very glad to know that you haven't forgot me and your letter when reaching to me means that I'm not along in this foking country.
Since I met you it has been not so much changes on my life, just worse and worse and I felt very bad because of living in such a country where we don't have what is more appreciate by a human being "freedom." We must hide our own feeling to survive, cause everything is reduce in a slogan, "Socialism or death" and you can imagen to survive upon these hard and tough situation.
I can tell you that I spend most of the time looking for something to eat, every day is worst to find it and in the black market prices are very high; what is given by our government is not enough to live and unfortunately you find everywhere shops full of everything you need, but just for tourist. And for a few people having family in the U.S.A. and they receive money from them. That's the only way to survive here; all these is somewhat ironic 'cause we work during the month and the State pay us on Cuba money and finally they sell us things by dollars only.
Concerning eduction, I can tell you that some high and junior high schools are gonna be closed next course, since there are not enough matricula to begin the course. And lots of professors are going for courses cause they have not work; it is really hard, as you can see.
About my own life, I can tell you that now I'm unemployed and it's not permitted to work privit-

ly. I don't know if you know that I'm a painter
and it's very hard nowadays to live being as artist, 'cause no one needs art nowaday on this terrible situation. My life is very hard and for being unemployed I'm on the risking of going to
prison for four years. Theres a new law which is
for people who don't work, we are obeg to work
with state just for nothing, 'cause finally what
we are payed is not enough to survive.

Your money got to me and I appreciate it. But
I want you to know that I write you first 'cause I
enjoy it, second because I like very much to have
friends abroad. Anyway, if your wanna help me sincerely, I'll appreciate whatever you do for me
cause I do really need it. But you must be sure
about the post office, since I've got a friend in
England who sent me 300 dollars in a letter to
help me and the money don't arrived to me.

Please reite me everytime you are free and of
course remember me. It will make me really happy,
since I need it. Tell me about your son, your family, your work, your country, your own customs,
everything you think I'll be interesting on.
Greetings - Ever your friend

Eusebio

P.S. I'll try to send you this letter with a tourist because if people at the government read it is
not good for me and I'll be in a problem! Write
soon!

Santa Clara
April 14, 1994

Dear Adolf
    I'm Roger, the young fellow you met in Santa
Clara who served as translator to you and "Rubi."
We spent a very nice time together at Rubi's house
and had a cup of coffee. You showed us your family
album and for me was a new and nice experience.
Talking to you put my mind for a moment or two to
think about the first human being that trod our
land, and the whole continent. I'm very sorry myself for the loss of the Indian heritage here in
Cuba, who were desolated by the Spanish. But I'm
still happy because now I know there are people
like you and your family and friends that are
keeping your culture ahead.
    Here, as I told you we're going through a touch
and go situation, but we're doing our best to hit
back the odds. I guess all over the world people
face handicaps to achieve goals. Let's see what
comes on. In the long run we will find it out.
    I have to tell you that the next "29" of this
month I'm looking forward to getting married. My
fiancee and I will come to live in my house.
    If you have the opportunity to send me some
books that you have written, or also any magazine
about pop music, or any tape recorded about it, I
will appreciate it very much.
The best luck for all of you.
Till then, your friend

Roger

(also written in English)

Cienfuegos
April 15, 1994

Dear Friend
   Even though you left Pepito Tey just a few days
ago, I have missed you very much, because we had
very good times together with the trains and the
steam engines and our visits.
   It would be a pleasure for me to meet you again
and would be glad to be able to know all your family if they are all as you do.
   I don't want to boder you so soon, but I have a
little problem with my 6 years old child, she usually has asthma, and others problems, and I need
at the store with dollars, and i'ts imposible for
may to afford it because, I don't have any place
to find it out; so I apply to you in order to see
if you can send me a few dollars for its recurse,
and a pair of shoes because I can't find them anywhere.
   Really I our ashumed to write you for the first
time and ask you for help, but you know the cur-
cunstances we are living now, and I don't have any
other chance. My greetings to Okan, and you receive a hard hand shake, from your friend

Ramon
                    (also written in English)

Santa Inez
October 10, 1994

Dear Friend Adolf
  Hearty greetings to you and your family from myself, my wife Rosa, my mother Gisele, my brother,
and also my father, Roberto.
  We are just poor farmers, but we are very hon-
ored for your visit to our home. It is the first
time any foreign visitor has come to our home. We
will always remember this, so we thank you for
this privilege.
  Perhaps you have heard the news about Cuba, that
changes are coming more quickly than when you were
here. For us farmers it is especially important
that the government now gives us permission to
sell some produce. This way we can try to earn a
little extra money, and at the same time help out
some of our poor brothers and sisters in town who
cannot grow food. They have very little to obtain
at the government stores.
  Of course, the big problem for us now is the
transportation. You saw how we live, we are all
poor farmers out here in these mountains. We cannot sell produce to each other. The nearest town
is Santa Inez; it is not so far away, but there
are not many people there and, on foot it is still
too far for us and we cannot carry much produce on
the two horses we own. Our neighbour has a wagon
and horses, so maybe he can bring our produce to
Santa Inez and sell it for us along with his own,
but then he has to keep some of the money for doing this. We are not familiar with such a money
system. We have only heard about it from our parents, who were still young at the time when it
ended. Now we are nervous to learn about it and
try it out. But we don't know for sure how far we
can go with it, until the government tells us.
  For instance, we cannot sell the milk from our
cow to anyone except to the government agency in
exchange for coupons. Of course we cannot sell
the cow, nor the meat if she dies. We must use
her for work only and to make more milk and cows.
We also cannot sell the meat of our horses, although we can sell our pigs and chickens and
goats. The government newspaper said, "The people
can buy whatever they wish," so my brother and I
will experiment to see what we can grow that they

want. If you are coming to Cuba again, is it possible to bring us some seeds of vegetables, and
perhaps some fruits? These are difficult to obtain here in Cuba, and we want to try other kinds.
 Tomatoes and beans too, if you have them, so we
can try them from Canada.
 The dollar went up to 120 pesos on the black
market soon after you left, but just now it is
back down to about 70. We are all trying to find
ways of making money because the government wants
to have us pay taxes, and we need to get food, and
maybe soon also we must pay to school our children. Where should we poor farmers get such money
from? We have no relations in the U.S.A.
 My cousin from here has been in Havana for two
years working in a restaurant. His parents got
word some days ago that he was among the balseros,
and that he left Cuba with some friends. They used
a raft made of tires and barrels and wood. All of
us in the neighborhood worry for him. I think
many who leave Cuba end up far out in the ocean
with no way to reach land, no food or water, maybe
a storm, maybe the sharks eat them. We once knew
a man in Santa Inez who disappeared that way. He
was never heard from again.
 My cousin was the only one who ever gave me
American money. He got it from tourists at his
job, and he gave me one dollar. With it I bought
my mother a new washbasin for her house. I have
thought about a job in Havana or Varadero, so I
could get dollars and our family could have a few
things in our home. My cousin taught himself to
speak english from an old dictionary, but I cannot
speak it at all. Such dictionaries are very difficult to find, so I do not have one.
 You asked if I have travelled elsewhere from our
home and my answer is yes! During my active time
in the army I got to see much of our beautiful island of Cuba. I liked the province of Pinar del
Rio, a very fabled looking place. I also liked
seeing some cities like Havana and Santiago de
Cuba, which I never saw before. Otherwise I have
always been here in these mountains with my mother
and father and brother. If I could get work in a
restaurant in Havana, it would be very difficult
living without them. What would I do with my wife
and child? We would not want to have a home in Havana. Some of the people from there are quite

crazy, and we hear it is from being in the crowded
city.

You wrote to me about the tipi camp of religious
Indian people this summer and I read aloud your
words to my family, and we are very glad to hear
that some people are still living like this. Many
of us here in the mountains have Indian blood in
our ancestry, but unfortunately we don't know anything otherwise about it. That is the story
passed down from my father's grandfather, and long
before him, that some of our ancestors were of
Cuba's original people. Also my mother's home and
my brother's home and mine that you have visited,
those are Cuban homes handed down from our original ancestors. We call them bohio, and they are
made just from native materials, mostly the palm
tree, and they work good for us. But someday we
would like a good stone house, perhaps with water
coming in a pipe and some nice windows and doors.
Do your tipis have windows and doors? Sometime you
should bring one to Cuba. I think the Cuban people will be very interested to see it.

You asked me to give you some details from our
news here in Cuba, so these are some things I have
learned from the radio and from our newspaper
"Granma." They say that 130 markets were officially opened for the people to buy and sell what
they want across the country on October 1. We did
not yet go to one, but neighbors say that it is
worthwhile to try. One neighbor sold rabbit and
pig meat for 100 pesos per kilo. Another neighbor
sold a grown pig for $25 U.S. The government pays
us 190 pesos for one month of cutting cane nearby
here, but we get no pesos for our milk, or for the
vegetables that we must bring to the government
warehouse. In order for us to grow more produce
we must work more land, so we are clearing a flat
piece on the hill behind our farm. We use the cow
to pull our plow, which we now made with fresh
wood so that it no longer breaks all the time like
it did when you were here. But the cow is old and
not so strong for this new land, which has not
been farmed before and has many rocks and hard
places. We must bring manure there before the
soil will grow much. We have not received fertilizer for several years, since the problems in
Russia and other places. Fertilizer in Cuba goes
to the sugarcane fields, since we need them most

of all to keep our economy going. We use everything we can for manure here now, but I don't know
if it will be enough for the new land.

This is all I can say right now, but I will answer your next letter right away and you can ask
me any questions you wish. Sometimes it is hard to
write exactly what I think, maybe because I am not
so smart, or because it might not be good to put
such words down on paper at this time. We shall
see what tomorrow brings.
Your friend in Cuba

Gerardo

(Written in Spanish and mailed from Europe)

House of Commons
Ottawa, Canada
March 7, 1995

Dear Adolf Hungry Wolf;
   Thank you for your letter regarding my trip to Cuba. I am pleased to see you share my interest in the country and I appreciate your sharing your views with me on this issue.
   I have long felt that Cuba is a country of great vibrance and potential. I have found the people warm and helpful. This is something I noted on my first trip to the country years ago before I was an elected Member of Parliament. I also admire the system of medical care and education that Mr. Castro has put in place.
   I am pleased that Canada's approach to Cuba is constructive and compassionate. I believe that our efforts to introduce economic reforms in Cuba and our continued trade with the island nation will have beneficial short and long term effects. I am strongly opposed to the American's continued economic embargo and have written to President Clinton in this regard.
   You asked for some thoughts about my recent trip to Cuba, and in particular my visit with Fidel Castro. I remember thinking it incredible that I was only six years of age when the bearded man sitting across from me. casually answering questions from our delegation, rode into Havana as the heroic victor of the Cuban Revolution. How could I have guessed as a six year old boy from an immigrant family that one day as a Canadian Member of Parliament I would get the opportunity to meet with this historic figure. More incredibly, how could I have guessed that 34 years later, Fidel Castro would still be the reigning president of Cuba.
   It is a very unique experience to be able to engage a world leader in a frank discussion at any time, but it is even more unique to be able to engage a man like Fidel Castro at the sunset of his political leadership, reflecting on significance of the revolution and the way forward for the small country. That was the backdrop for a recent multi-party Parliamentary delegation of which I had the good fortune to be a part.
   It is often difficult to separate myth from reality when analyzing

some briefing material. Before I joined my seven other colleagues, I was baffled by the range of divergent opinions on Cuba's continuing economic viability. Depending on whom you read, Cuba is described as everything from a threatening challenge to American free market values, to an unsuccessful communist experiment teetering on the brink of economic disaster. And its leader is described as everything from a decaying despot to a charismatic demagogue.

On the particular day of our delegation's meeting with Fidel Castro, his mood was reflective and reminiscent, as if our nationality had sparked a stream of memories about Canada's role in Cuba's history. For two hours he spoke with characteristic eloquence. He reminded us of Canada's long time friendship with Cuba and of our refusal to sever economic and diplomatic ties with Cuba even at the height of the Cold War.

He regaled us with reflections on revolution, human rights and economic alternatives. But what surprised me the most about Fidel Castro was not the substance of our discussion but the subtext. He demonstrated a sincere caring for individuals which I had not expected, a compassion toward human suffering everywhere that it exists in the world. He emphasized that the fundamental motivation for Cuba's foreign policy has always been to reduce human suffering and to fight for social justice. As an example of this, Castro told us of how Cuba recently brought over 35,000 Russian children who were victims of the Chernobyl disaster to receive medical care in Cuban hospitals.

This example brought up an interesting question; what was the relationship between Cuba and the former Soviet Union? Traditional thinking has always been that Cuba was a Russian satellite, receiving on average a million dollars a day before the Russian well dried up. Yet, when I raised this question directly, Castro took great pride in a foreign policy very independent of the USSR. According to him, Cuba had, at times, been at odds with the Russian government of the day. He told us that Russia was at times worried about "what Cuba would do next."

Changing the tone quickly from worries to accomplishments, Castro expressed the greatest pride in the accomplishments that Cuba has made improving the health and education of the Cuban populous. By South American standards, Cuba has achieved some outstanding results. Life expectancy at birth is 77 years, the highest in Latin America, and the infant mortality rate in 1992 was 10.4 per 1,000, the lowest in Latin America. Cuba is the only Latin American country to have been included by Unicef in the category of countries with the lowest infant mortality rates in the world, on a par with the industrialized nations. As well, according to government figures, the illiteracy rate in 1990 was only 1.9%. This high level of education and training in the country is being used to attract foreign investment in science-based and high-technology industries.

At the same time though, Castro is realistic about the economic and social challenges which Cuba faces in the wake of the collapse of the USSR. Up until the collapse of the East Block, the USSR pumped more than $1,000,000 a day into the Cuban economy and served as Cuba's largest trading partner. Come 1990 though, continuing aid and preferential trading arrangements became impossible for the USSR to maintain. Almost overnight the well dried up for Cuba and the economy contracted by 50% in the following two years. The result for Cuba has been the deepening of an economic crisis which they have been suffering through ever since.

While in Cuba, I observed many of the results of that economic crisis. Apart from the tourist areas, food is scarce. Every commodity is being rationed at levels North Americans would find shocking. Black markets are beginning to develop for currency and goods. Threre are even those who say that Cuba's excellent educational and health facilities are beginning to suffer.

Castro himself is most worried about the effect that this crises will have on the psyche of the Cuban youth, those who have no connection to a pre-Revolutionary Cuba. To them, talk of the revolution becomes rhetoric overwhelmed by the lure of consumer goods and political freedom. It will be this emerging group, Castro believes, who will be the catalyst for the greatest change.

Still, change is coming. Measures are being introduced steadily which bring Cuba closer to a market economy. Cuban citizens are now allowed to hold hard currency. Small businesses are more encouraged. Foreign investment is being sought out and secured with many countries, mostly via joint ventures. For example, over

100 joint ventures were in place by the end of 1993, with another 100 "in the pipeline." In total there are 34 countries which have been attracted to joint ventures and production sharing agreements with Cuba, including Canada. The diversity of these projects includes tourism, fisheries, telecommunications, medical technology, mining, oil, construction and agricultural by-products. Thus, while it is true that Cuba is experiencing very difficult economic times, the seeds of change have been selectively planted. Things are changing in Cuba and Fidel Castro seems to approve of that change. Economists are already predicting that Cuba has hit the bottom of their economic cycle and are beginning their recovery.

One thing is for sure; the economic changes that are occurring in Cuba are not being forced as a result of the US embargo and policy of political isolation. This policy has been a failure for 33 years and has served only to increase Castro's legitimacy as a world leader and to justify his heavy hand on the Cuban people. As Cuba emerges from the woods of economic disaster with the support for the Castro regime still intact, the continuation of the US embargo seems neither strategically nor economically wise for the US. Strategically, this policy will not help Cuba in making their transition to a market driven economy. Nor will it help them to increase democratic freedoms. Economically, it will not help the US companies to cash in on the many emerging business opportunities within Cuba.

Nor will it help to open Cuba as a potential market for US goods and services. Within Cuba, this embargo is viewed as a serious but not crucial obstacle to the transition and growth of the Cuban economy. Internationally, the US position is seen as unreasonable and unjustifiable. In a vote by the United Nations, 102 countries voted against continuing the embargo on Cuba. Only two supported its continuation; the US and Israel, the latter of whom has already established informal trade relations with the Caribbean nation.

Yes, I agree that time is running out, but not for Cuba's economic system. Drawing from the experience of this visit, including not only meetings with Fidel Castro but almost every senior official within the Cuban government, I believe that time is running out for the position of the US vis-a-vis Cuba. The US has a unique opportunity, given the tremendous importance of their trading position, to help

Fidel Castro's hair and beard have turned grey during the time he has been President and Commander in Chief of Cuba. Highly admired by some, deeply hated by others, he is unique among world leaders, durable almost beyond belief, and still much loved by many of his people. His singular dedication to their welfare - whether you agree with his politics or not - is seldom matched in our age of personal power and self glorification. This colour portrait of Fidel was sent by Cuban Secretary of State, Dr. Jose M. Miyar Barrueco, along with a friendly letter "conveying Fidel's regret" that my request to take such a photograph myself would be "difficult to arrange," and offering this print in consolation.

Cuba find its place in the "New World Order." If they act quickly that place could very much resemble the kind of economy that the US a serious but not crucial obstacle to the transition and growth of the Cuban economy. Internationally, the US position is seen as unreasonable and unjustifiable. In a vote by the United Nations, 102 countries voted against continuing the embargo on Cuba. Only two supported its continuation; the US and Israel, the latter of whom has already established informal trade relations with the Caribbean nation.

Yes, I agree that time is running out, but not for Cuba's economic system. Drawing from the experience of this visit, including not only meetings with Fidel Castro but almost every senior official within the Cuban government, I believe that time is running out for the position of the US vis-a-vis Cuba. The US has a unique opportunity, given the tremendous importance of their trading position, to help Cuba find its place in the "New World Order." If they act quickly that place could very much resemble the kind of economy that the US has tried unsuccessfully to force Cuba toward for 34 years. My mother always told me that you get more bees with honey than you do with vinegar. If the US administration would make maternal wisdom the centre piece of their foreign policy with Cuba, let alone with other countries, they could not only help to relieve the poverty of thousands of Cubans but through an ironic twist, pacify one of the last remaining perceived challenges to US capitalism in the Northern Hemisphere.

Cuba will outlast the US embargo, of that I am certain. They will probably also go a long way over the next five years toward a more market driven society. As for the question of political leadership, who knows. Given his ability to beat the odds, Castro himself may be still at the helm of the Cuban ship as they enter into the 21st century, making him one of, if not the, longest serving political leaders of this century.

I hope you find this informative and helpful. Thank you for writing.

Sincerely
Herb Dhaliwal, M.P.
Vancouver South

December 8, 1994
San Pedro, Cuba

Dear Adolf,

You asked me to write you letters about my "Grand Adventure" here in Cuba, and so far it's been pretty interesting.

As you may know, Jack and I dreamed for years about being able to escape the responsibilities of family and business life; find a secluded beach on a tropical island somewhere, and just relax for an entire winter. It took a lot of planning and extra work; we had to wait till the last of the kids were grown, and get completely out of debt. By the time we managed that, there wasn't much money left over, which is one of the reasons we picked Cuba. Besides falling in love with it during our vacation there last year, we saw ways where we could live on very little. We knew we'd have to find inexpensive accommodations right away, and do all our own cooking, otherwise we'd run out of money and probably be home before Christmas. But in a country where simply renting a house from it's owner is illegal, and grocery stores as we know them are non-existent, we also knew we'd have to be flexible and resourceful. I realized this could result in experiences that might be interesting, challenging and downright unpleasant at times, and so far I've been right. Fortunately, the pleasurable experiences far outnumber the other kind, and our Grand Adventure is all I hoped it would be.

We have found just the little cottage-by-the-sea we were looking for. It's quiet, private and best of all, inexpensive. How we came to find it is another story, so I guess I should start at the beginning.

November 1994

That final week of preparation in Canada was unbelievably stressful as we wrapped up our business affairs, said goodby to our families, and tried to stuff three months of supplies into four suitcases.

On the morning of our departure we awoke to find a foot of fresh snow covering the ground, which helped alleviate any misgivings we may have had about going away. As we trudged across the tarmac to our plane, we stopped to take pictures of each other standing knee deep in the snow. I experienced an odd sense of displacement when I realized that the next time I would see this airport, winter would have come and gone and it would be spring. I wondered what might happen in between.

The trip was long and tiring with an overnight in Montreal. I was getting pretty bored and travel-weary by the time we passed over the southern tip of Florida, but as we started our slow descent over the glittering blue expanse of the Atlantic, a feeling of giddy excitement began to come over me. Strong sunlight filled the cabin and I craned my neck for a first glimpse of Cuba. Finally the emerald island came into view, while all around us, huge, billowy white thunderheads towered towards the sky.

The heat and humidity enveloped us like a warm, wet blanket as soon as the plane landed and the doors were opened. I was soaked in sweat by the time we reached customs, some of which might have been from nervous anticipation about how they would react to my little laptop computer. As it turned out, the male customs officers showed only polite curiosity about it, but their winking and smiling threw me totally off guard. However, they were all *very* interested in our food supplies, and quite a crowd of them gathered to watch as things were taken out, examined and discussed. They took away our two bags of meat jerky, which was a real blow because it was meant to supplement our winter's meat supply. Oddly enough, they didn't give a second glance at all the little plastic baggies filled with unidentified white powders, that we knew were things like baking soda and garlic powder, but could have been anything. They also ignored the box of medical syringes we were bringing to a diabetic friend.

Our plan was to spend a couple of nights in Varadero to rest and regroup before travelling on. We lugged our baggage of 300 pounds plus and two bicycles up to our second-floor hotel room, showered, put on shorts and stepped out into the busy Varadero street. It hadn't changed much; a continual stream of noisy motorbikes, horse-drawn carriages, vintage American cars, bicyclists and pedestrians. We went straight to the beach, took off our shoes and walked barefoot through the sand and the warm, clear water. We were just in time to watch the sunset, a huge orange ball that dropped quickly below the horizon. Then we went into a pleasant little beach-side bar for chicken and beer. Within minutes we were included in the swirl of conversation and revelry that was going on, and I remembered that no one is ever a stranger long in Cuba.

The next day Jack wanted to visit his buddy from Canada, who was staying in a house in Varadero with a young Cuban woman and her child. The two men spent a noisy evening drinking rum and reminiscing about their exploits the year before. They had gone to Cuba ahead of me and rented a house together. When I arrived on the scene a couple of weeks later I was appalled to find them both in a perpetual, rum-induced haze, living out fantasies of being pursued by beautiful women.

Varadero, it turned out, is filled with "chicas," lovely young women, mostly between the ages of 18 and 25, whose main objective is to snag a tourist. They don't care if the men are old, fat, bald, obnoxious or married, these girls will pursue them with zeal. Some ask outright for dollars in exchange for sex, but many are willing to trade their affections for whatever benefits might come their way, be it a chocolate bar or a pair of shoes. The ultimate prize is a wedding ring, financial security, and the freedom to leave Cuba if they want.

Jack and his buddy, like many middle aged men before them, had been totally swept away with all this adoration, an enthusiasm I obviously didn't share. I wanted to find a place more suited to couples, and Jack had reluctantly agreed. We ended up spending the rest of our holiday at a quiet resort area about 200 kilometers away.

Now here we were all together in Varadero again, the two men gleefully reminiscing about their wild adventures the year before. As I sat listening to them, unpleasant memories came flooding back and I was anxious to get away from there all over again.

We were supposed to leave the next morning, so I got up early to get everything ready. Jack was hungover and uncooperative, but I was determined to get going, so I dragged most of the baggage downstairs myself. Sweating profusely in the 30-degree heat, I finally managed to stuff everything (including a sulking Jack) into our rental car. I had never driven in Cuba before and had no real idea of how to get to where we were going. However, any anxiety I may have had about that was overcome by the sheer relief of seeing Varadero in my rear-view mirror.

Our destination was Rancho Luna, a resort area near the city of Cienfuegos, in the province of the same name. That's where we had ended up the year before and we met some nice people there. We even stayed with an old Cuban couple in their home....

It was less than a four hour drive, but it took us all day because I made a wrong turn and got lost. Asking for directions was hopeless because no one understood our limited Spanish. Jack's demeanor gradually returned to normal, especially after we left the monotonous sugar-cane country and started travelling past the scenic hills and rivers of Cienfuegos.

When we pulled up to the old couple's house, their son Carlos, a dark, thin man in his forties, was leading the family goats through the front gate. Before the car even came to a stop he had my door open and was giving me a bone crushing hug. We had written to let them know we were coming, but not the exact date, so I was surprised to notice that the old couple were dressed in their best clothes, no doubt for the occasion. After more hugs all around, we were shown to "our" rocking chairs on the front porch and were assured, Cuban style, that we were "in our home." We sat down, the view being even more breathtaking than I remembered; the sparkling blue-green Carribean in front of us, the white-sand beach disappearing into lush green jungle on the left, and in the distance, rising above it all, the misty blue Escambray mountains. The late afternoon sun began to bathe everything in a warm, golden hue, and as I basked in it's warmth, the glow of friendship swirling around me, I could feel my body start to relax for the first time in over a week. I felt like I had indeed, come home.

The Rancho Luna Hotel is situated about a mile from the actual village, so we checked in there that night, instead of taking the old couple up on their invitation to stay with them. We hadn't realized this was illegal when we stayed there for three weeks the previous year. We didn't find that out until the very last night when the police raided the place. This time we planned to ask Immigration for official permission to stay in a private house, and we didn't want to do anything that might jeopardize our chance of success.

The rental car was expensive, so we turned it in that night at the hotel. Carlos had agreed to meet us the next morning and take us into Cienfuegos by bus, and to translate for us at the Immigration office.

It was already hot by eight the next morning when we met at the bus stop. The bus was nearly an hour late, and when it did come it was jammed with people and went barrelling right by. "The bus is full," Carlos said, his voice filled with resignation and disgust. He suggested we "auto-stop," which meant hitchhike. Cubans often have to wait long hours in the heat to travel this way, he explained, but vehicles are more inclined to stop for women and tourists. Being both, I was sent to the roadside to wave vehicles down.

The temperature continued to climb, so fortunately a rusty green jeep appeared before long and screeched to a dusty stop. We jumped in the back, where we found nothing to sit on except the dirty, steel floor. We didn't dare complain about that or about the thick black smoke that belched steadily into the cab from a hole in the floor, during the twenty minute ride into town.

The Immigration office was located in an old, unmarked cement building. Carlos led us through a narrow waiting room filled with sombre looking Cubans sitting on blue plastic-webbed chairs. After a brief conversation with a woman in an olive-green uniform, we were ushered into a small room with a high ceiling and a tall window encased in bars. It was totally devoid of any decoration other than a large faded photograph of a huge crowd in a square. It was beastly hot and I could feel the perspiration streaming down my midriff as Carlos spoke rapidly and at great length in Spanish to a serious young man who ignored us other than an occasional brief glance. Carlos was assuring him that we were a responsible couple looking for a quiet place to spend the winter where I could write, and that there would be no problems with drunken parties, illegal activities or chicas in the house. Cubans are not permitted in tourist hotels without official permission, so it has become a practice for foreign men to illegally rent houses and use them as a place to meet with chicas. These places are delicately known as "bang-houses."

After a while the young man left the room and returned with another whom we understood to be the chief, a tall, attractive fellow with intense brown eyes and steel grey hair. He asked a few questions, watching us carefully as we answered. Finally we were told to continue staying at the hotel, and to return in three days for an answer.

Back out in the street we offered to buy Carlos lunch for his trouble. Instead of taking us to some pleasant sidewalk cafe like we envisioned, he led us a long way through the hot, narrow, streets of Cienfuegos, where the sights, smells and sounds of hordes of people going about their daily routines swirled around us. Most paused to stare as we passed.

Eventually we came to a long cement building where Carlos knocked at one of several tall wooden doors. It was answered by a young man, who stood aside to let us enter a small sitting room containing a couch and two easy chairs that were straight out of the

Typical Cuban street scene, with household furniture being moved by horse and carriage.

'50s. There was also a small coffee table and an old Russian TV, while on the other side of a partial divider a dining table was set with a white cloth. The cement walls were clean, painted white, and adorned with tacky plastic flowers. It was only then that we understood this was a private home used as a restaurant, probably illegally. The usual tourist fare was offered; chicken, fish and lobster at prices somewhat lower than the hotel, but still expensive for us, considering they were in U.S. dollars.

We ordered our food and asked for a cold beer while waiting. The young man was almost comical in his efforts to do everything just right. Stiff and formal, he served our beer with a white cloth draped over his forearm, as might be more fitting of service in a grand dining room. With a sombre demeanour and great delicacy he placed well-used, cardboard coasters on the table, then, using a red linen cloth to hold the bottle, poured the beer from a foot or so above the glass. We watched mesmerized as he repeated this until we had three foam filled glasses.

We sat drinking our beer in the stifling room for a very long time. At one point the young man went out the front door and came back a while later with a bag in his hand. We were again left alone with our long-empty beer glasses to stare at the walls and wonder what missing ingredient he'd gone for.

Finally he announced that lunch was about to be served and we had to suppress our smiles when we noticed he had donned a red bow tie, apparently to complement the moment. My fish was whole and fried, complete with skin, head and tail. Jack and Carlos' "chicken" was a large carcass with dark meat, most of which had been removed. To our shock the bill was over $21 US, expensive for us on our limited budget. We made a mental note from then on to always establish in advance where we were going with our friends.

Back at the hotel that afternoon, we sat pool-side and enjoyed a drink called Cuba Libra; a most pleasing combination of mellow Cuban rum, cola and lime juice. We discussed our options if Immigration turned down our request, which we both felt was very likely, and studied a map for alternative locations. We were looking for something not too far away, on a beach, remote enough that we might be able to rent a house illegally. A place called San Pedro

Playa looked interesting. It was in the countryside, near Trinidad, less than an hour's drive from Rancho Luna.

The next day after lunch, on the spur of the moment, we decided to hitchhike to San Pedro. We got a ride almost right away in a little Russian Lada. The man and two women in the front seat looked surprised when we said where we were going, telling us they could only bring us as far as the first junction. After they drove away, we were left alone, standing on the deserted road in the hot sun. It was very quiet out there in the countryside, with not a vehicle in sight. We figured one would stop for us, but what we hadn't bargained for was no vehicles at all.

We'd about had our fill of looking at the surrounding fields when a nice '54 Chevy came racing along, the driver stopping to offer us a ride. There were two men in the front, speaking mostly with each other, leaving us to admire the fine condition of the car's interior, trying to ignore the frightfully fast pace we seemed to be travelling along the narrow, winding road. They were turning off at the next junction, but in very limited English the driver offered to take us on to San Pedro for $30. Jack said it was too much, so the price was quickly lowered to $20. "Still too much," Jack said to me. "Besides, we're supposed to be on a grand adventure." So out of the car we went.

As the car roared away we looked around and found ourselves at the top of a hill with a most beautiful view. The valley below was filled with fields of green and gold, dotted with orchards and palm trees. Farther back were green rolling hills, and behind them the same mountains we could see from Rancho Luna, only now much closer. We stood on the hot road talking about destiny and other things that gave us the opportunity to witness such a "buena vista." Jack said to me, "If we'd taken the man up on his offer, we'd be $20 poorer and have missed this beautiful view!" No sooner was that said when the same car came roaring back. Screeching to a stop, the young man yelled out the window "10 dolar!" Grand adventure, buena vista or not, it was too good of a deal to refuse, so we jumped in.

It took another half hour to get to San Pedro, travelling first east towards the mountains, then south along a flat strip of land about a mile wide between the mountains and the sea. There were no real towns, just a couple of isolated villages and farms. Eventually we came to a faded sign pointing down a little hill to a compound of blue buildings set on a point of land, the Caribbean behind, sparkling in the afternoon sun. A chain blocked the entrance, but after a short conversation with our driver, a tall, young black man in a tattered uniform let us pass.

We parked the car and walked around the buildings to a big open area bordered on two sides by the sea. The place had a pleasant looking restaurant, an outdoor bar and a little outdoor dance floor. There were several two-story motel style units, but what really caught my eye was a neat row of individual little blue brick cabins that faced the open sea.

It all appeared deserted, except for a thin faced man behind the bar. To our surprise and delight he spoke fairly good English and told us that the little cabins were available to tourists for $12 a night and that we might get a cut rate for long-term. We asked to see inside one and found it to be simple but clean, containing two single beds, a bedside table, a wooden wardrobe, two blue rocking chairs, and a small but decent bathroom. Best of all, there was a fridge.

We were tremendously excited with this discovery, knowing that if our request to rent a house was turned down, this would be a legal and affordable option. As if icing on the cake, it turned out that cold beer at the little bar was only sixty cents, so to celebrate we bought one each for ourselves, our driver, and the friendly thin-faced bartender.

Our driver lived in Cienfuegos, so when he returned us to Rancho Luna that evening, we asked him to meet us the next day at the Immigration office. The following morning Carlos again took us to town, only this time the bus stopped. It was almost as packed as before, so we spent the trip crammed in with the rest of the standing passengers.

When we got to Immigration, the answer, as we suspected it would be, was "no." Our driver was waiting for us outside as promised and we asked him to drive us back to San Pedro to arrange for a cabin. Before leaving town we stopped to see my friend Rosa, a pleasant young woman I had become friends with the year before. It was her day off, so she decided to come along with us for the drive.

It was a lighthearted group of five that travelled to San Pedro that day, a trip that took just over an hour. When we arrived, Carlos and the driver disappeared into the little administration building while the rest of us waited in the car. When they returned, Carlos told us that the manager said the place was closed, and that they didn't want any tourists.

We were shocked, our high spirits suddenly dashed. Carlos said there was a similar place farther down the road where we could probably stay instead. We continued driving another half hour through the deserted countryside, then turned into another seaside compound. But this one appeared dirty and poorly maintained, not at all to our liking. We waited a long time for the manager to show up, but no one did so eventually we just left.

Discouraged and perplexed, my mind raced as we started on the way back. I stubbornly refused to accept that we couldn't stay at this lovely, empty place, so I asked Rosa if she would come with me to try changing the manager's mind. This time when the driver stopped at San Pedro, the two of us women went inside.

Rosa spoke at length with him. At one point I could see he was telling her about problems with power failures and water shortages, so I interrupted and asked her to assure him that we didn't mind and would really be no bother at all. Their discussion continued and, to my delight, he started to agree. Not only that, but after a bit of persuasion he gave us a reduced weekly rate. Rosa and I were ecstatic and slapped our hands together in a "high-five" as we walked back to the car and the waiting men.

In high spirits again, we returned to Cienfuegos where Rosa's mother served us a huge lunch. Carlos and our driver waited outside while we ate, a situation that seemed unusual only to Jack and I. We then went shopping for things we would need to set up housekeeping. Our first stop was one of the new "free markets," a street-side section where a very limited selection of household items were sold for pesos. We bought a kerosene stove, a bulky, crude looking thing that came with a bicycle pump. We also bought a small, homemade hot plate, some pots, cooking utensils, candles and two little kerosene lanterns.

Next we went to one of the new "dollar stores." Air-conditioned and fancy by Cuban standards, for us it was more like a poorly equipped general store. All kinds of merchandise, from televisions to food and clothing was on display, but selection was very limited. There were shelves of cooking oil, spaghetti and cola, but no fresh meat, eggs, milk or bread. We tried to get fresh vegetables at a nearby agri-market, but the counters were mostly empty, with only small cloves of garlic and onions for sale. We finally returned to Rancho Luna with our purchases, which had cost less than $50.

The next morning, after our last hotel breakfast, we walked to the village to meet our driver. Being Cuba, he couldn't pick us up at the hotel because it's illegal for private car owners to drive tourists around for a fee. It's probably illegal in Canada too, but in Cuba there are eyes and ears everywhere, watching and willing to inform. Our driver arrived on schedule and it took careful stuffing to get everything into the big car. The air was incredibly hot by the time we were ready, then we had to stand around and wait another half hour while he tried to get his engine started. Meanwhile, a passing fisherman sold us a half dozen lobster tails (one the size of a small cat) for $12.

The manager at San Pedro had said he would meet us at noon to check us in, but when we got there, he was nowhere to be found. We waited in the suffocating heat for about an hour, until finally a slim, nervous black woman appeared seeming to be in charge. However, she was uncertain and confused, carrying on an animated conversation with our driver before leading us to a small office. When she began filling out a form, I showed her my credit card and somehow wasn't surprised when she shook her head no. About that time I noticed a telephone with a crank on the side, sitting on the counter. I asked for the phone number, and was told "13," not a good sign. For the first time it occurred to me that besides being in the middle of nowhere without transportation, we were out of the range of electronic communication.

We were given a key and shown to the first cabin, closest to the restaurant. About 20 feet in front of it there was a big rock where a group of Cubans now lounged to watch as the car was unloaded. When everything was stowed inside, our driver tossed back a glass of rum, wished us luck, and left.

We now took a good look at our new home. It was clean with fresh sheets and bright orange spreads on the beds. Jack discovered an interesting looking electrical device attached to the shower head, which presumably heated water as it ran out. The bare wires caused him to speculate that this might give a whole new meaning to the term "hot shower." The fridge had been turned on and seemed to be working well, so the first thing we did was put the lobster in the freezer.

We began unpacking our baggage, finding a broken bag of flour in Jack's suitcase and a box of margarine that had melted into an oily mess. Everything else had travelled pretty well. There were two large bags of powdered milk, a second bag of flour, several dozen packages of spaghetti sauce mixes, dried soups, rice seasoning mixes, and pudding mixes. Also peanut butter, canned meats, tomato paste and all kinds of other stuff we didn't think we could get in Cuba.

The door of the cabin had been left open, helping the curiosity of the crowd outside to become unbearable. As the unpacking progressed, I noticed a regular stream of people strolling casually by the open door, slowing down for a good look inside as they passed. Without wanting to appear rude, but feeling that way anyway, I closed the door.

We spent the rest of the afternoon getting things unpacked, finishing just in time to catch the sunset. We went outside to the now mercifully deserted yard and sat on the cool tiles of the outdoor dance floor, from where we had a clear view of the Caribbean stretching out of sight to the south and west. After the blazing orange ball dropped below the western horizon, wispy sunstreams of pink, orange and blue radiated across the sky. As they too started to fade, a bright sliver of moon shone above it all, while to the north, lightning flashed inside enormous pink, glowing thunderheads, making them look like huge, heavenly, light-filled rooms.

We sipped a cold, 60 cent beer and felt smug about our success in finding this little tropical paradise. There's a sandy beach for swimming, rocky cliffs for catching fish and lobster, even a garden site for Jack. It's also quiet enough for me to write, and all that at a price we can afford. It all seems so perfect....

Over the next few days we settled in, first cleaning the cabin with strong disinfectants, figuring the creepy crawlers wouldn't like the smell and might stay away. I baked bread and peanut butter cookies in the toaster oven we had brought from home, while Jack got busy organizing the garden plot and more or less figured out how to work the kerosene stove.

We decided to hitchhike to Trinidad to call our families and let them know where we were. There were no cars around and we had no idea about the bus system, but confident in our abilities to get a ride, we stood beside the highway a couple hundred feet from the bus stop, which was crowded with Cubans. Eventually, a big truck with a flat steel deck rumbled up and came to a squeaky halt near the bus stop. All the people started running over to it and a young Cuban woman waved at us, indicating we should join them. We hurried over to where people were frantically getting up, while others were getting down. They all made a point of helping me climb aboard, making me realize that, as tourists, we were regarded as something just a little less than royalty.

The truck bed was pretty high off the ground and after we sat down I discovered, to my horror, that there was nothing at all to hang on to. Some people were standing up at the front, clinging to the back of the cab, others were sitting, grouped in the front, and they seemed to have some sort of stability. But where we were, all we had to grip was a small hole in the deck. Feeling uneasy as we started out, my concern soon turned to sheer terror as the truck began travelling down the road and I realized that with any bump or sudden turn, I could go flinging over the edge. Frantically I grasped on to Jack who sat calmly watching the scenery. An old man sitting behind me offered his packsack to sit on and a small black girl, sensing my fear, looked at me with sympathy in her eyes and offered me one of the straps on her knapsack to use as a handhold.

For the next thirty kilometers the truck careened around corners and hit many bumps, stopping regularly to let people on and off, while my fellow passengers in the back swayed to and fro, laughing as a group if a bump was particularly bad, staring often and curiously at us. Evidently in this part of the country tourists are an unusual sight, especially riding on the back of trucks.

After what seemed like an eternity, but was actually a half hour, we arrived in Trinidad, most of the crowd getting off at the outskirts. This allowed us one of the premium spots at the front of the deck, where, by standing up and hanging onto the back of the cab, we were treated to a good bird's eye view as we travelled through the historic city's narrow, winding cobblestone streets. We learned that only one of the two local hotels is right in town, and we had to hike up a very steep hill to get to it. There we were charged $7.50 US for a three minute phone call to Canada, and were told that there are no fax machines anywhere in Trinidad.

December 13. 1994

We have moved to a different cabin. The first one turned out to be far too public, with the nearby restaurant providing front row seats to whatever was happening at our place. Our new home is located at the far end of the complex, closest to the point of land where a small bay meets the open waters of the Carribean. The front of the cabin faces east, and is only a few steps away from the steep, rocky banks of the bay. A row of broad-leaved Uva trees provide shade, while their thick bent trunks are perfect for hammocks.

Looking left, we can see where the bay ends in a wide sandy beach. A slow, shallow river emerges from thick jungle-like growth and cuts a narrow channel through the sand. Above it, a huge cement bridge connects the two sides of the bay. On a hillside behind the bridge is perched the tiny village of San Pedro and beyond that are the steep slopes of the Escambray mountains.

To our right, all that separates us from open expanse of the Caribbean is a grassy strip of sand about 100 feet wide, ending in rocky banks that drop down 15 or more feet to the water. A few little shrubs are growing in the sand, but nothing that interferes with our view of the sea and sunset. A crooked little path that starts beside our cabin, winds its way through the grass to the point. It is out there that Jack has decided to put the garden.

It's a lot more quiet in this location. The restaurant seemed to be the focal point of the community and there was always a lot of noisy conversation, laughter and singing going on. Otherwise, there don't seem to be any radios or other sources of music here. Sometimes in the evenings, if there is electricity, the young people go out to the little dance floor and play around with an old TV that's encased in a wooden box. If they're lucky they get some music, then they'll hang out singing, dancing and relaxing. It reminds me of something our grandparents might have told us about, and I wonder if in 50 years these kids will be telling their grandchildren about how it was for them in the "old days" when they had to make their own entertainment.

We're doing our share of roughing it as well, and it's a lot of work for me. I get up before sunrise, tiptoe out to the front porch and try to do a couple hours of writing before Jack gets up and people start coming and going. Cooking and cleaning takes up a good part of every morning. Nothing is quick or easy here, as I have to make all our bread and baked goodies from scratch. Washing dishes is also complicated, since there's no sink except in the bathroom, and of course no hot running water.

The water is usually turned off from seven at night till seven in the morning and the electricity goes off most evenings. When there is

While young men in many countries take pride in keeping their vehicles clean, those in Cuba lucky enough to have horses perform more basic washing rituals.

no moonlight, it's black as coal outside and our little kerosene lamps and candles do a pathetic job of lighting the inside. I'm learning to cook dinner early if I want to do it with any kind of convenience; while there's still daylight and I can use the hot plate. It has only one temperature, and often gives me shocks, but it's still better than the kerosene stove, which gives out good heat but is complicated and time consuming to light. First you have to pump up the tank with the bicycle pump, then you have to pour alcohol into a little tray and light it. After a while you turn on the kerosene, and if you're lucky you get a hot, hissing blue flame. If you aren't, you get a smoky yellow flame and you have to start all over. When you turn the stove off, you brace yourself for a little mini-explosion that usually occurs within a few seconds.

Personal hygiene is a real challenge. There are two options: a cold shower, or a sponge bath using a bucket of warm water. I usually select the latter and have learned how to get quite an effective cleanup with a minimum of hassle. Hair washing is another matter.

Jack keeps busy with the garden, where he has planted lettuce, tomatoes, carrots, radishes and onions. He hauled in some soil and mixed it with the sand, then fed it with fertilizer brought from Canada. Finally, he built a tall stick fence to keep out the goats, even putting a chain and lock on the gate to discourage the kids.

For our big move to the new cabin, we had some unexpected but welcome help from our good friend Santiago. I should explain here that we met Santiago the year before in Rancho Luna. We were walking along the beach and spotted him coming out of the water carrying a nice string of fish. We had been trying to get some fresh fish for the hotel chef to cook for us, so we approached him and asked if his fish were for sale. He was very lean, but in a fit, sinewy sort of way, had kind brown eyes and a quick, warm smile. He spoke a bit of English, and stood ankle deep and dripping in the water as we negotiated a price. When we agreed to pay $4, an unmistakable look of delighted relief flashed across his face. Jack and I both got the feeling that even though we may have been paying more than necessary, the extra money would probably help someone who was having a hard life.

After the business of the fish was completed, we stood and chatted for a while. Jack asked him if he knew where there was a pretty shell he could buy. The fisherman led us down the beach and along a rocky path to a house where he said there was one for sale. This turned out to be the old couple's house, which is how we met them. While we were in the house looking at the shell, the old lady had motioned us farther into the house and showed us a large, clean, bright room with an ocean view, saying that they rented it out for $5 a night. We had ended up checking out of the hotel and moving into this house for the remainder of our holiday, not just to save money, but to give us a better chance to experience Cuban life and meet the people. In those following weeks, Santiago came to the house to clean his fish every day, and we got to know him well. A straightforward, sincere man, he was always cheerful and ready to help in any way he could. We understood he was very poor, yet he never complained or asked for anything.

We were surprised to learn that he fished by swimming for hours along the reef, dropping down a baited hook when he spotted a fish. An intelligent man with a college education, he had worked many years as an electrician. But when the "special period" hit (the Cuban term for the hard economic times brought about by the end of Soviet support) Santiago could no longer survive and support his family on his electrician's wages. He had turned to fishing; the four dollars we paid was double what he could earn in an entire month at his trade. During our stay at the old couple's house in Rancho Luna we grew very fond of Santiago, and liked him best of anyone we met in Cuba. When we returned to Canada we kept in touch, writing back and forth.

Now, during our second stay in Cuba, on the morning of our move to the new cabin, we were treated to a surprise visit by him and his friend Jose, a small dark man with flashing black eyes. They had started out from Cienfuegos at four that morning and it had taken them five hours to reach San Pedro. Santiago's English was much improved and he told us he had been studying the Spanish-English dictionary we gave him the previous year. I brewed up some fresh Canadian-style coffee and handed them each a cup, along with a couple of chocolate chip cookies. They were both delighted by the cookies, but I think somewhat appalled by the coffee. In

Cuba they drink it strong and syrupy, tossing back a tiny cupful like a shooter.

Pleasantries and refreshments over, we moved everything to the new cabin. When that was done I left the men drinking cold beer on the porch and tried to prepare a good lunch in my unorganized new kitchen. There weren't enough chairs to go around so Santiago insisted on sitting on the hard tile floor. He assured us he didn't mind and said he often sleeps on the floor. Not for the first time, we wondered about his home life and situation and that night, after they left, Jack and I talked about it. We both felt that with his resourcefulness and willingness to work, Santiago would do well in Canada if he ever had the chance to go there. We decided to do what we could to sponsor him.

As we talked, a young black man appeared carrying a bucket and a small, brown bottle. His name was Pedro and he lived in the village nearby. Earlier that day he had passed by our cabin and stopped to chat with our visitors. They told him about our problems of cooking when the electricity was out, so he had brought us a backup stove of sorts, kind of a Cuban version of a barbeque. It was a metal bucket with a hole cut in the side and a recessed wire grate across the top. In the bucket was some "carbon," homemade charcoal. The little brown bottle was filled with gasoline with which to start the carbon burning.

We offered him a glass of rum and sat chatting while the sun set. Although he spoke no English at all, he was one of those people who seemed able to communicate quite well anyway. He told us he is 26 and single, and that his father is a policeman, although Pedro himself doesn't agree with many of the laws, or even abide by them. He said there are deer in the surrounding mountains and that he likes to hunt, but it's difficult to get a permit, so he's only ever shot one.

I asked him if there were any cats I could adopt to help keep the bug population down around the cabin. He laughed, pointing his fingers towards his mouth, indicating that people had eaten them. I heard in the news back home that Cubans were getting so hungry they were starting to eat cats, but this was the first confirmation I had in person that this was actually happening.

Pedro was dressed in typical poor Cuban style, denim cutoffs in the final stages of disintegration and a thin muscle shirt that wouldn't be considered thrift-shop merchandise back home. After two drinks of rum he left, and I wondered if I should have invited him for dinner, which had been cooked and set aside during the course of the visit.

The whole question of when to offer people food and drink and when not to, has been a problem for us. For one thing, we aren't familiar with the customs and don't know what's appropriate and what isn't. Some people, no matter how poor or starved looking, will accept nothing, regardless of what they have done for us. But others will hang around for hours, apparently looking for a handout for no reason other than being there. Some, if offered a drink of rum, will stay until the entire bottle is gone. We feel bad that we can't help all the people of the village, but even if we could, we know that if we did, our place would become a hangout for everyone wanting something. We value our privacy and just don't want people around all the time.

One day, as I was sitting on the front porch writing, a boy of about 12, wearing khaki shorts and a hat, sat with his back against a tree right in front of our cabin and stared at me for the best part of an hour. Other than a polite "hola" I didn't encourage conversation. "Don't you suppose anyone ever taught him that it's impolite to sit in front of someone's house and stare at them?" Jack said when he came in from the garden. I thought to myself that it's more likely his parents and the other adults around him do the same thing. In fact, earlier that morning the elderly gardener who pokes his rake sporadically at the sand and picks up leaves, sat in the same place and stared, just like the boy.

Jack had been totally unsuccessful at fishing during the day, so one night after supper he decided to go out to the point and try his luck in the moonlight. I sat quietly alone on the porch, and in the pale, ghostly light a horribly thin dog silently appeared and stood staring at me. Her backbone and ribs stood out sharply and I couldn't believe an animal could be so thin and stay alive. I went into the cabin to see if there were any scraps, finding some bananas I had tried to fry, but had only made inedible. When I set them on the ground, she lowered her head and stared at me with great caution.

When I stepped back to give her some space she leaned forward and practically inhaled them. I went back into the cabin, searching for something more, and found a piece of fruit a passerby had given me earlier that day. It looked revolting, like pieces of slimy fish (I discovered later that it's actually quite sweet and tasty). I put some of this down on the sidewalk and again, she gobbled it up.

After that I saved our few scraps for her and she started coming around regularly. One day, when I had nothing else, I gave her a small piece of cheddar cheese. I don't think she could believe her luck, as she sat down and stared at me for a long time. On another occasion I set down two halves of an old, stale bun. She took one in her mouth and quickly disappeared, so I picked the other one up and waited. She soon returned and began looking frantically around for the other piece. I called to her, and at first she ignored me, but finally she looked up and saw me holding it out to her. She slowly came closer, stretched out her neck and took it from my hand, very, very gently.

Living together day and night in a tiny cabin has resulted in some new interpersonal challenges for Jack and me. Away from our busy lifestyle in Canada we have lots of time to notice what's going on with each other, which isn't necessarily good. Everything, from which bowl to use for the chocolate pudding, to the location of the clothesline, has become an issue of debate.

Jack doesn't have as much to keep him busy here as I do; this in contrast to Canada, where he's always on the go and I have a lot less household work. One day I watched him working in the garden, silhouetted against the sky and sparkling sea. I was reminded of a scene from the movie "Papillon," where Steve McQueen and Dustin Hoffman are prisoners on an island (which in fact, was probably not far from here). Steve McQueen is the rebel who will die before he quits trying to escape, but Dustin Hoffman accepts his life there and even has a little garden, kind of like this one.

Jack would be more like Steve McQueen, with too much energy and rebellion to passively accept a restrictive situation. And although he has been as enthusiastic as me about this place, I have to wonder how he will be able to handle the quiet isolation in the long run.

The days are slipping by and starting to blend into one another now. Life in Cuba is so different than home, but already it feels like we've been living this lifestyle forever. The slow, laid-back pace, the heat and the effort required to do even the smallest chore. Also the endless search for food. Only time will tell if this place will be suitable for the entire winter. It could prove to be a bit too quiet. Either that, or the entire three months will just slip away and it will be time to return home before we know it.

Having nothing better to do than tend a little garden patch beside the Caribbean was the fulfillment of a long-time dream.

March 1, 1995
San Pedro, Cuba

Dear Adolf

Three months have come and gone since I arrived in Cuba and strange as it may seem, it's hard for me to remember the life I left behind in Canada. I've just been given a special extension on my three month tourist visa so I can get married! But I guess I should backtrack a bit first....

When I last wrote in December, I was wondering how Jack and I would get along in the isolated setting of San Pedro. Well, as Christmas approached the weather turned stormy, which was an apt reflection of what was going on inside the cabin as well. Being in such close contact, all kinds of unresolved issues began coming into sharp focus.

It started the week before Christmas. I was missing my children and family, feeling sad that I wouldn't be able to share Christmas with them. Jack was cranky and unsympathetic, saying he wanted to ignore the occasion completely. In the end we compromised, agreeing to spend Christmas with our friends at Rancho Luna.

We stayed with the old couple, and I spent a quiet Christmas eve visiting with them and the various people that stopped by the house. Jack went with Carlos to a big dinner and party at the Cuban restaurant nearby. I think he was craving the dancing and socializing because he cheerfully rose early with me Christmas morning for a walk along the beach to watch the sun rise. Later that day we called our families back home, and before returning to San Pedro, made arrangements to meet Carlos five days later. In Cuba, New Years is the big celebration of the year, and Carlos had invited us to spend it with him and his family in their Santa Clara home. The plan was for Jack and I to catch the early bus into Cienfuegos the day before New Years eve. Santiago would meet the bus and take us around town for a bit of shopping. At noon we would meet up with Carlos, and go with him to Santa Clara on the train. As it turned out, a lot would happen before that.

In the days leading up to the new year, there were various celebrations around San Pedro. One night a party was held for the workers which Jack and I were invited to attend. Everyone was singing and dancing to salsa music that blasted from a tape player, but for reasons I still don't understand, except an excessive consumption of rum, Jack became angry and stormed off in a huff. Back at our cabin he threw his things into a suitcase, saying he was going to Varadero the next day instead of Santa Clara. In the heat of the moment, after the tension of the previous couple of weeks, I was all for the idea.

The sun was just rising over the mountains to the east and the air was already warm at 7:00 a.m. as we climbed the hill to the San Pedro bus stop that second to last morning of 1994. We both remained stubbornly aloof, holding on to our own self-righteous attitudes, although the high emotions from the night before were giving way to more rational thoughts. I was planning to continue with the trip to Santa Clara, but Jack said that he would be trying to find transportation to Varadero.

The real bus never came. Instead, an old, canvas covered army transport truck stopped. At first I misunderstood it to be a vehicle simply offering to give us a ride, so I went to get into the cab, but a crowd pointed me towards the back. I walked around the side to find people being hoisted up a steel ladder, and we were told it would cost three pesos to join them. Only then did I realize that this *was* the bus.

The back was crammed tightly with people standing and clinging to the rusty steel ribs that supported the canvas. As my eyes adjusted to the darkness, I peered farther up into the bowels of the box and could see dozens of eyes staring curiously back at me. People were sitting on benches along each side and down the middle, with still more people lying or crouching in an overhang at the very front.

We stood in the tightly packed crowd as the truck lurched along. I fought nausea from riding backwards in the dark, as exhaust fumes filled the truck. Thankfully, before long, a disembarking woman specifically designated her seat on one of the wooden benches for me. Jack wasn't as lucky and had to stand, hungover, for the whole trip, providing me with a certain amount of smug, sadistic pleasure.

Even though the "bus" was very late, Santiago was waiting for us, looking like a tourist in his fresh white T-shirt, belted walking shorts, white socks and sneakers. He looked surprised and concerned, but said nothing, when Jack told him about his new plans. The train and bus stations are located side by side in Cienfuegos, so it was a simple matter for Santiago to check both for departures to Varadero. There were none. Jack decided to come along to Santa Clara after all, surmising that he might be able to find transportation from there. I wouldn't have admitted it for the world, but when he said that, I felt a wave of relief.

As we walked around Cienfuegos, the clear morning air replaced the exhaust fumes in my lungs, making me feel better. Carlos met us as planned, but said he found someone going to Santa Clara in a car that we could ride for $6. This would save us standing for hours on the hot train, so we quickly agreed.

Sitting in the huge back seat of the vintage Chevy, Jack and I noticed the strong smell of gasoline almost right away. The driver was carrying on an animated conversation with Carlos in the front, and whenever we expressed our concerns he kept assuring us that there was "no problem, no problem."

But when we arrived in Santa Clara, again nauseous from fumes, we discovered there was indeed a problem. A spare container of gasoline had tipped over in the trunk and saturated Jack's suitcase. The driver appeared utterly unconcerned about the dripping mess and cheerfully accepted our money before bidding us a happy new year. The thought was not returned.

Carlos' house was a grand affair built before the Revolution by his grandfather, who had been very wealthy. It had stained glass windows, beautiful ornate tiles, and antique furniture that would fetch a fortune back home. We received a warm welcome from his wife and daughter, then were shown to a large, main floor bedroom which was also filled with beautiful antiques. Our first job was to take everything out of the gas soaked suitcase and set it in the back yard to dry in the sun. Then, while Carlos showered and his wife prepared dinner, Jack and I sat alone on the front porch and talked. A level of sensibility had settled over both of us by then, and we agreed to try working things out. We would start by having a good time over the weekend, with the trip to Varadero forgotten.

The next day we explored Santa Clara, which was alive with a festive air. In the evening several close friends of the family came to the house where a modest dinner was served. The group was very musically inclined, with guitar, violin, flute, piano, various little rhythm instruments and song, everyone participating into the early hours of the morning.

Festivities were interrupted just before midnight when we were all handed a glass of tepid water, which we were told not to drink. Jack and I stood holding our glasses with uneasy anticipation, wondering if somehow we'd end up getting wet. Then, just before midnight, we were all ushered outside where, on the stroke of twelve everyone threw their water onto the street. It was explained to us that this is a Cuban tradition symbolic of washing away the old and starting fresh with the new. We stood in the street, laughing, hugging and wishing each other a happy new year, and through the dark night we could hear the sounds of many other people doing the same thing.

The next night the five of us squeezed into Carlos' tiny car and drove towards the centre of town. We were going to see the "Carnival," although Jack and I really had no idea what that was. As we neared the square, the streets became clogged with throngs of people, so we parked the car and joined the merrymakers on foot. At the square there was an almost solid mob of people. Folding chairs, reserved for ticket holders, were set up along the sidewalk and Carlos led us to ones he had purchased earlier that day.

We sat and watched for a very long time as endless streams of people of all ages, colors and various degrees of sobriety milled around us. Finally, in the distance we could hear drums and trumpets from a procession coming up the street. It was a sight like I'd never seen before. In the lead were two or three dozen costumed black people, performing precision dance steps to a frenetic, pounding beat. A cluster of men were beating wildly on various kinds of African drums, following behind, while others whacked on the bottom of frying pans which were mounted upside down on boards. Still others played trumpets that blared out a simple, repetitive melody which reminded me a lot of the Campbell's soup jingle, "Mmm mmm good, mmm mmm good, That's what Campbell's soup is, mmm mmm good." A thousand voices sang along in words we couldn't understand. The musicians were sweating and intense and were surrounded by a group of men who moved along with them, presumably to provide moral support.

The intense pounding of the drums and the disjointed dance-walking of the performers was one of the most vital, yet primal sights I've ever seen. As the group passed by, the crowd joined in behind making a solid mob of dancing, singing, laughing people filling the street for a half block or more. After a while another group came down the street and, except for different costumes, the whole thing was repeated. This happened again and again, continuing long into the hot, humid night. I felt like I was watching some ancient ritual brought over from Africa and preserved through all the years of slavery. It was an exciting beginning to a new year, but only a prelude of what was to come.

Back home in San Pedro things quickly settled back into a routine. We developed friendships with local people, especially one family that lived down the road. The brother and sister in their thirties became our close friends and we would see them pretty well every day. Their mother insisted on taking over the job of our laundry, and every few days would stop by to collect our dirty clothes, delivering them back clean, ironed and folded, refusing payment of any kind.

We were given a key for the cabin next to ours to use for storage, which gave us a lot more room in our cramped little place. It also gave us a "guest cottage" of sorts for overnight visitors. This was mostly Santiago, who became our right hand man and frequent companion, bringing us food and supplies from the city. He was also our guide and translator on various excursions. He never seemed to mind searching for the items on our shopping lists, nor in making the long trip out to San Pedro laden with heavy bags and pack-sacks.

Our lack of transportation was inconvenient and frustrating, so we asked Santiago to find a private car we could rent on a monthly basis. He located a red, 1978 Lada for a reasonable price, so finally we had the freedom to travel at will. Although we were now well established, dark thunderheads of dissent loomed on the horizon. Problems that had surfaced before Christmas soon flared up again, and by the full moon in January the situation had come to a head.

As these things often do, it started with a silly misunderstanding and blew up from there. Furious, Jack disappeared into the night with the car and a bottle of rum. I stewed and worried for hours, but when he finally returned in the early morning, babbling drunkenly about an encounter with a chica in Trinidad, it was my turn to be furious. His suitcase got packed, and the trip to Varadero was on again. But this time was different: now there was transportation!

We had previously planned a trip to Cienfuegos for the next day, and had already arranged for Santiago to meet us there. Now a new twist was added; a stop at Rancho Luna to see if Carlos would drive with Jack to Varadero, drop him off and return the car to me at Rancho Luna. I would stay the night at the hotel and wait.

This time, unlike the earlier crisis, everything went exactly as planned. The car started, and Carlos was not only home but thrilled with the prospect of an overnight trip to Varadero. I suspect he didn't understand the full impact of the situation, while he happily packed a bag and joined us in the car. However, Santiago understood completely and looked deeply troubled when we met him and explained the new plan. Still, he agreed to take me shopping and make sure I got back to Rancho Luna safely that night.

Jack and I said a cool goodbye in the street and after the two men drove away, an odd sense of unreality set in. As Santiago and I walked along the streets of Cienfuegos, I felt a numbness, with an underlying feeling of dread. I kept expecting to hear Jack call out my name, turn around and see him there, we would patch things up, everything would be okay, and we'd continue on. But, that didn't happen.

Santiago found a car to take me to Rancho Luna, then came along for the drive, waiting outside while I made sure my friend Paul was in the hotel. We had met Paul the year before and become good friends. A kind hearted, retired Canadian, he spends winters at the hotel, and that night he sat and listened patiently while I told him all about my problems.

It was an emotional, restless night for me, and by the next day my anxiety levels were running on overload. I wondered if Jack would return with Carlos, which he'd hinted he might, if not to patch things up, at least to find another place in the area to stay for the rest of the winter. I had told him that if he stayed in Varadero, there would be no getting back together for us. Ever.

In the heat of the moment I had truly wanted to see the last of him, but we'd had upheavals like this before and when things settled down we managed to work it out. This time was different. I was perfectly aware of what he would be doing in Varadero and I couldn't spend the rest of my life with a man who could leave his partner of eight years alone in an isolated place in a strange country while he went to chase around with chicas.

As the day dragged on, I paced restlessly around the old couple's house, waiting for Carlos to return. When the little red car finally pulled up in front of the house, my stomach took a sickening lurch, as I saw that he was alone. A suffocating cloud of panic descended over me and suddenly I was desperate to get back to San Pedro, where I could deal with the situation in private. But nothing in Cuba is ever that simple.

First I had to get gas, which meant a detour into Cienfuegos. Besides that, the clutch was giving off a strong burning smell. Santiago, who had returned to Rancho Luna that morning, offered to go into the city with me to help find gas. Two fishermen friends of his, needing a lift to town, also came along.

Dark storm clouds hung low in the sky and I was choking back tears, as we started out for Cienfuegos that late afternoon in January. The two fishermen chatted quietly in the back seat while Santiago sat beside me in front, eyeing me silently. It was all I could do to keep control of myself, and of the car, which I now discovered had loose steering and almost a total lack of brakes, in addition to the overheating clutch. It was hard enough to navigate on the highway around the endless stream of bicycles, horses, buses, and potholes, but things got worse when we reached the city and it's pedestrian version of rush hour.

Shortly after I dropped off the two fishermen, the heat and strain finally became too much for the clutch and it gave out completely. With a foul burning smell filling the air and an ungodly howling coming from the floor, the car refused to go farther. It was all to much for me as well, and turning off the engine, I burst into tears. At that point, Santiago took over.

We left the car and walked to his friend Jose's house, which was not far. After explaining the situation to Jose, Santiago told me to relax and left me there while he went to deal with the car. Jose's house was a clean, pleasant, upper level of a duplex, and the first thing I did was change from my hot jeans into a pair of shorts, wash my face and brush my damp sweaty hair. Santiago returned to say a mechanic had been found, the car towed, and that it would be fixed by the next day. In the meantime, we would have dinner at Jose's house and I could stay there that night.

After handing me a tiny glass of red wine, the two men disappeared into the kitchen to make dinner. As I sat alone, the setting sun filled the room with warm, golden light, and I began to feel better. At one point they came to see how I was doing. I must have still looked pretty miserable because Santiago told me, "It is the custom in Cuba to be happy and cheerful, even when there are problems." I decided to try to adopt this attitude in future. We ate a meagre dinner of rice, beans and salad, after which Santiago went home. Jose gave me his room, saying he would sleep on the living room couch.

The next day I waited impatiently for the car to be fixed. When it finally was, the bill only amounted to $16. I was anxious to get home but it was getting late in the day and I dreaded the thought of driving the unpredictable little vehicle alone through the isolated countryside. I also worried about how I would manage with some of the practical things that Jack had always taken care of, such as operating the kerosene stove. So I was relieved when Santiago offered to drive back with me to help me get set up.

I felt good when we left the crowded city streets and began travelling through scenic countryside. However, that feeling evaporated instantly when we reached the cabin, as desolation hit me with an almost physical force. While Santiago busied himself with unloading the car and lighting the stove, I wandered down the crooked little path to the garden. As twilight gave way to darkness, I sat for a long time on the point, looking out to the sea. I thought about all the things Jack and I had done together, all the things we had planned. Everything we had worked so hard to build up, our past, present and future, was all gone. I sat alone in the darkness and tried to come to terms with it all, searching for the strength to go on.

Santiago stayed a couple of days and was as kind and supportive as a friend could be. He worked quietly around the two cabins, getting everything organized, offering a sympathetic ear when I wanted to talk, but leaving me alone when I didn't. He worried about how I would manage there alone, but I assured him I would be fine. After I was settled, he instructed the night watchman to keep a close eye on my cabin then caught a bus back to Cienfuegos, promising to return in a few days with food and supplies. So, as it worked out, I was alone when I got sick.

A pain that started in my midsection kept getting worse, and by the time Santiago returned I was in bed with a fever. I had started taking antibiotics brought from Canada, but they didn't seem to have any effect. He was alarmed and asked the village "medico" to come see me.

I was more than a bit apprehensive when a young woman who looked barely out of puberty arrived at the cabin. With Santiago translating, I described my symptoms. She took my blood pressure, poked around my stomach, and looked curiously at my bottle of pills. To my dismay, she then produced a large, antiquated looking syringe and gave me a painful shot in the hip, supposedly for pain. I silently cursed my bad judgment in not keeping a few of the small, disposable syringes from the box we had given to Carlos.

I had another bad night and word that I was sick had travelled around the village. The next morning my friend's mother appeared at the door to offer her medical services, which I understood were more of a spiritual nature. I would just as soon have passed on that, but didn't want to be impolite, so with Santiago and her husband looking on in approval, she got a towel from the bathroom, stood in front of me, and began a series of towel foldings, mumbled prayers and signs of crosses. She then told me to hold one end of the towel up to my stomach while she held the other end and measured out lengths. I had absolutely no idea what was going on. Finally, she gave me a concoction of baking soda, water and lime juice to drink down fast. It tasted ghastly.

When her duties were seemingly dispensed, I offered them some Canadian style coffee and, while I reclined on the bed, the three of them sat around and talked about how tasteless it was.

Since I wasn't getting any better, Santiago insisted I go for proper medical attention. He asked Lorenzo, my friend's father and a bus driver by trade, to take us into the city in my car the next day. I was relieved to have someone else in charge, and slept all way.

Our first stop was at Jose's house. I was beginning to understand that he has a lot of connections. Although I didn't realize it at the time, they decided to take me to a Cuban hospital where a doctor would see me for free. Tourists are supposed to go to an International Clinic where dollars are charged for services.

We drove to a hospital for children, where Jose disappeared inside. He returned and told us to follow him to a kind of open air emergency waiting area. There we sat and watched as an endless stream of people went in and out, most carrying children who looked anywhere from very sick to very healthy. I was amazed at the lack of noise with so many kids around. No wailing, crying or whining, no parents speaking sharply or smacking anyone. All the children appeared well dressed, even when the parents wore clothes that were old and tattered.

I expressed concern about being treated by a children's doctor, but was assured the physician would be qualified. Eventually we were called inside by an attractive woman of about 35. She led us down a crowded hall into a tiny examining room, motioning for me to sit at a small desk. Seated on the other side, she began asking questions in Spanish, and with Santiago translating, filled out a form. I could see her write Jose's name at the top, so I'm guessing that whatever went on that page is now part of his permanent medical record. Some of my symptoms were of a rather personal nature, not something I would normally discuss in a group, especially with men. This didn't seem to bother these two in the slightest. As Santiago translated, Jose freely added his own opinions. I was quickly learning that in Cuba, modesty and privacy are luxuries, and like all luxuries there, not even considered an option.

Other unidentified people squeezed into the tiny room until eventually there were seven of us participating in the conversation. I contemplated the unhappy prospect of a physical examination with this crowd around, but to my relief, Santiago finally motioned towards the door and said the welcome words, "go now."

When we got to the car where Lorenzo was waiting, the entire story was related to him. As we drove away, I was told that the doctor needed a urine sample and we were returning to Jose's house to get it. At that house everyone stood around watching as Jose briskly scrubbed out a little brown bottle. While I was sent off to produce the sample, a spartan lunch of rice, beans and salad was prepared. After lunch Jose got on his bicycle and headed back to the hospital, the little brown bottle now in a plastic bag swinging from the handlebars. He was to return with the results in a few hours.

By then I was feeling a lot better so we went to the Boulevard, a pleasant pedestrian-only shopping district, to get a few items I needed in the cabin. While we were there we ran into Rosa, who was brought up to date on the events of the previous week. She looked at me with concern and said she would return to Jose's house with us to await the results.

Jose returned with the happy news that I had a kidney infection and that I should continue with the pills I was already taking. I say happy because this meant no more tests and because I had a good supply of the medicine. Cuban coffee was then served and all the details of my "problem" were again discussed among the group. That subject finally exhausted, we all got in the car and headed downtown.

Earlier on the Boulevard, we had run into several people who said they "heard" there was a fax for me at the Jagua Hotel. I told everyone back home to fax me at the Rancho Luna, but for reasons still unknown to me, a fax had gone to the Jagua, which is right in Cienfuegos. Not only did people on the streets of this sizeable city (pop. 120,000) seem to know who I was, but they also knew where my faxes were. This was my first indication that although electronic communication is terrible in Cuba, the grapevine is healthy and thriving.

It was just getting dark as we drove down a wide, main street. Suddenly we saw a man standing in our lane, facing us, feet planted wide apart, arms outstretched. Lorenzo honked the horn and raced the motor, trying to get him to move, but the man stood firm, a grim look on his face. We lurched to a stop and immediately another man appeared from a house, carrying an old woman with blood all over her face. She was crying and wailing, with the many people around all extremely agitated and upset.

Rosa, Jose and I jumped out of the back seat and the man put the old lady inside, then climbed in himself. Other people tried to get in too, but Santiago, in the front seat, more loud and commanding than I'd ever seen him, firmly told them that only *two* people could go. They drove off to the hospital, leaving the three of us standing on the street in the dwindling light. We were told that there had been a power failure and as the old woman was being helped to her bed, in the darkness, she had fallen, hitting her head on something sharp. It is law in Cuba for all vehicles to provide emergency transportation if needed.

The car soon returned, and we continued on to the Jagua, dropping Rosa off on the way. After we picked up the fax, we decided to eat dinner at a peso restaurant nearby, which was not really legal for me. There are two monetary systems in Cuba, pesos and dollars. Things available for pesos are barely affordable for Cubans, but ridiculously cheap by our standards. Tourists are supposed to purchase everything in dollars or else with pesos purchased legally at an enormously inflated rate. But black market pesos are readily available, so peso restaurants are more or less off limits to tourists.

I was warned not to speak English, or better yet, not to speak at all. Surrounded by the three men, yet still feeling conspicuous, I was brought to a pleasant room with nautical scenes painted on two walls. A third wall consisted of windows that offered a clear view of the darkened western sea. We sat at a small table, and wine was ordered. It was sweet and yellowish with just about the worst possible taste I could imagine. The men, however, thought it was wonderful.

After a while we were shown into a nice dining room, with windows overlooking the sea on two sides. A four piece band played soothing contemporary music. A single menu was brought to the table as is customary in Cuba, one person reading from it and everyone discussing as a group what should be ordered. I wondered if I would be asked to leave or if the police would come and arrest me, but nothing happened. The food was bland but passable and there was plenty of it. The total bill was 50 pesos, equivalent to an American dollar.

Our next stop was Santiago's house which turned out to be not quite as grim as it looked from the outside. I then met various members of his family. As we sat and visited, his little niece bounced around, playing and flirting with everyone, unmistakably the centre of attention. After a while, Santiago motioned for me to enter one of the rooms farther back in the house. There, his mother, who has Parkinson's disease, had been roused and propped up in a chair, a sheet tied around her middle to hold her upright. She was painfully thin, wizened and stooped, dressed in a ragged but clean nightgown. Talking was obviously difficult, and her hand shook as she gripped my hand, uttering various things in Spanish which Santiago interpreted as he tenderly stroked her hair. I was beginning to see how, in these homes crowded with several generations, there might not be enough food or basic necessities, but there is always an abundance of love and attention, especially for the very young and old. The economy might be in serious trouble, but the family unit is strong and healthy, and I suspect this explains the warm caring nature of Cuban people in general.

There was a carnival downtown, and remembering the one at Santa Clara, I said I would like to go for a while. One of the people in the house was Santiago's cousin Angela, a beautiful young deaf woman of about 20. Thrilled to be invited, she changed rapidly into a sweater, brushed her long, thick, black hair and we were off.

It turned out that this Carnival was geared for tourists and totally unlike the one in Santa Clara. Tourist were seated in chairs on one side of a street while across from them a couple with microphones talked in English and introduced various acts. Farther back and to the sides, crowds of Cubans stood and watched. When we arrived a man was doing tricks with a dog. That is to say, the dog was doing the tricks, not the man. The clever little poodle jumped and skipped and did somersaults.

Next came a fashion show with glamorous but haughty looking women, dressed in all kinds of outlandish outfits, stalking back and forth. Suddenly the power went out and the fashion show came to an undignified end. The power returned a few minutes later then a band began to play. There was sort of a dance contest wherein three tourist couples were persuaded to compete in front of the crowd. Judging was done by a show of applause from the audience, the winner being an aged gentleman wearing a polo shirt, bermuda shorts, long, white socks and white loafers, having a ball with a very young, attractive Cuban woman on his arm.

With the organized events over, the audience was invited to stay, drink, dance (and spend money). Music began blasting over the loudspeakers as the Cubans began dancing and having a good time. Our little group was no exception, and thus we spent a most enjoyable evening. The music was loud enough for Angela to feel the vibrations and she was eager to dance with anyone who would dance with her. At one point she took my hand and, pointing to her eyes, indicated she wanted me to come with her to look around. We had been standing with the Cubans, but now, as we walked towards the tourists, I realized I was eager to communicate in English. But most had already boarded the special buses that were waiting to take them back to their hotels, and for the first time I felt a sense of being isolated from people of my own culture. From then on I looked forward to opportunities to mingle with other English speaking people.

That night Lorenzo and I both stayed at Jose's house, where I was again given the bedroom, leaving Lorenzo and Jose to argue over who got the floor and who got the couch. They both insisted on the floor.

Santiago blamed himself for my being alone when I got sick, so he returned to San Pedro with us the next day, determined to stay until he was sure I was okay. I didn't realize it at the time, but all the brake fluid had leaked out of the car during the night and Lorenzo drove the entire distance back with no brakes at all.

The next day his son came to fix them for me. I made lunch for the three of us, which we ate outside, while two of the little black children from the village watched sorrowfully. Feeling like a monster, I finished the last of my sandwich, knowing that if I gave them any they and most of the people in the village would be here all the time.

I knew Santiago had seen his share of hardship and hunger, so I asked for his advice on how to handle the situation. He told me that he thinks it's better to give most to one really needy person, rather than a little to many.

Everyone around here feels especially sorry for one little boy that hangs around the cabins, a cute little six year old named Lazarito, who is the oldest of three children living in squalor with their single mom. Filthy, skinny, and probably hungry all the time, he never asks for anything. In fact, the shy, sad little boy seldom speaks at all.

One day as we sat on the front porch Lazarito became excited, talking and pointing to a gaggle of brightly dressed children who were crossing the beach. I understood these were all the children of the village going to a special party, but he couldn't go because he didn't have any clothes. I decided then that if I could only help one person, he would be the one. I discussed this with Santiago, who was very pleased with my decision. He didn't talk much about it, but I knew he felt especially sorry for Lazarito because his own childhood had been as bad or even worse. He had grown up before the Revo-

The end of another day on the shores of the Caribbean finds Santiago the fisherman reflecting on changes he has seen and greater ones that still lie ahead.

lution and it's social reforms, sharing a one room hovel with seven other people, with hunger a way of life. The Revolution changed that, first by giving his family a better, if still very modest house. Then, like many children from very poor families, Santiago was taken from home and sent to boarding school in Havana where he received a good education. He went on to college and spent several years studying to be a teacher, but was conscripted into the military shortly before he received his degree. During his military service he was trained as an electrician. He enjoyed that trade, so continued working at it after his discharge several years later.

But Santiago's compassion for Lazarito went further than that. His own son and only child had died at the age of three, and Santiago's marriage had failed after that. He devoted the next fifteen years to the care and support of his sick mother and disabled brother, so never remarried. Still, he loved kids and would have like to have more. Now, he enjoyed being able to spend time with Lazarito, helping him out and teaching him different things.

I gave Santiago the blue 10-speed bike that Jack had been using. It was my son's old bike in Canada, where most people would just junk it. But Santiago was thrilled. Not only was it the first bike he ever owned, but it had gears, almost unknown in Cuba.

As time slipped by peacefully, my mental and physical health improved. I heard nothing more from Jack, and gradually put things into perspective. I realized our relationship hadn't been working for a long time, but we had always been too busy with life to notice or to have dealt with it. The split had probably been long overdue, so after the initial shock and adjustment, I knew it was for the best.

One night after supper Santiago and I went for a walk and noticed the restaurant was filled with people. We were told they were government workers who had been brought to San Pedro for a special weekend of relaxation. After a while, in the little outdoor bar, a young man started singing soft, slow South American songs accompanied by a guitar and bongo drums. The dance floor was filled with couples, and all around people sat, talking, laughing and drinking rum. A soft warm breeze was blowing in from the sea, and as I sat beside Santiago on the edge of the dance floor, I felt peaceful and content. I looked up at the sky and saw it was filled with brilliant stars.

I thought about those same stars shining on my home back in Canada, and I tried to imagine what it was like there at that moment. It seemed as far away as the moon, and with my emotional distress now only a distant memory, I felt like I could stay in Cuba forever.

But there was more to it than that. The spark of friendship between Santiago and I was igniting into something much more; stronger feelings were catching fire. Later that night, when we walked back towards the cabins, we stopped to look at the stars. As we sat on the seawall, the only sounds in the warm dark night were the waves lapping softly against the rocks. Then, in that most romantic of settings, we shared a gentle kiss. It was neither the kiss of a comforting friend, nor one of urgent passion. After a thoughtful moment I said, "So *that's* how it feels to kiss a Cuban!" That made Santiago laugh, because he had never kissed anyone who *wasn't* Cuban. It was a light-hearted moment, but the course of our relationship suddenly changed, and would never be the same again.

We were together all the time after that, spending hours talking about our lives, our dreams, and our hopes for the future. We took long walks, as he taught me about the flora and fauna, the fish, the birds, the trees and the flowers. He told me about the people of Cuba, his country, and how much he loved it there. Most important, by example he taught me about human kindness, family values, being happy with what little you have, and sharing. Although poor, I could see that in many way he was far richer than most people. The more I got to know him, the more I realized what a truly special person he was.

One day we drove to Sancti Spiritus to visit his brother Rudolfo. He and his wife weren't expecting us and had no idea who I was, so were surprised to see Santiago with a tourist woman. We spent an enjoyable day with them; before parting we all went to a nearby Cuban resort for a pool-side drink. It was there Santiago confided to his brother that we had become romantically involved. This was met with a great deal of approval and enthusiasm. Santiago had put his own life aside to take care of his family long enough, Rudolfo said. There were seven other kids in the family and it was time to let some of them take over and for Santiago to get married again. With this comment ringing in our ears, we started back to San Pedro.

Between Trinidad and Sancti Spiritus there is a beautiful little valley where green and gold fields are studded with royal palms and surrounded on two sides by soft, green mountains. Now, as we drove through it, the setting sun filled this valley with shades of gold and pink, the mountains a dusty blue. I felt good about the day and thought about what Rudolfo said. I realized that, despite our cultural differences, Santiago and I had developed a deep emotional bond. I didn't know where it all would lead, but I did know one thing: with him I felt happier and more peaceful than ever before in my life. And I knew something else. I had fallen in love - and I didn't want to leave him behind.

Outrageously impulsive as it was, when the idea to get married surfaced, we both embraced it wholeheartedly.

To say my family was surprised when I phoned home with the news is an understatement. Their reactions ranged the full spectrum between dismay (my father) and guarded delight (my mother). Despite the shock, everyone soon rallied and did everything possible to make it a reality. Documents were sent, my mother made travel plans and my girlfriends back home put together a bridal outfit for me to wear. Our Cuban friends, although no less surprised, were equally supportive and enthusiastic.

As the weeks went by, my kidney infection came and went and came again. I tried to touch up my roots and my hair turned orange. The owner of the car asked to borrow it back for a day and never returned, leaving us once again at the mercy of the Cuban bus system. My documents disappeared into the black pit of the Cuban courier system so that the wedding had to be postponed. Money was getting low and food supplies brought from Canada started running out. To make matters worse, the San Pedro cantina rum barrel ran dry.

But in spite of setbacks and difficulties, these were wonderful, happy days for Santiago and I. When we had to make the stress filled trip to the city, we would look forward to our return to San Pedro, where tranquility awaited us. We worked, swam every day, entertained friends and enjoyed each other's company. Santiago's English was rapidly improving, while my Spanish was getting good enough so that I could hold my own in a group of Cubans. Tourists were seldom seen, except for the occasional bus or rental car that zipped by on the highway. I was beginning to forget what life was like back home and rarely thought about it anyway.

When I had been in Cuba nearly three months we realized I was supposed to have my visa renewed every 30 days. Fearful that I may be in trouble, Santiago first went alone to the Immigration office to talk to them about it. He was told to bring me to the Jagua Hotel the following day and they would meet us there. As we sat and waited, I saw two men in olive green uniforms coming towards us and I recognized them right away as the same two that Jack and I had met with. The grey-haired one's eyes riveted on me in recognition. After we were seated by the pool, they asked Santiago what happened to Jack. He gave them a quick rundown of the events, his announcement that we were getting married bringing warm smiles and comments of approval. The atmosphere was friendly and informal after that, my visa updated, then extended for an extra month.

March 10
Farewell to San Pedro

After two stressful days in Cienfuegos, where we literally chased a mail truck down the street and finally located my missing documents, a wedding date was set for three days later. Santiago had more business to attend to in the city, but bribed a seat for me on the sit-down-only special bus so I could return to San Pedro ahead of him. I arrived home, hot and tired, mixed myself a Cuba Libra (a rare treat these days) and sat on the front porch in my rocking chair.

With my time in San Pedro drawing to an end, I reflected on the events of the past months, and about this place that I have come to love. The view from my vantage point on the porch changes constantly, yet remains unchanged, and this could be my first day here or one of a thousand. On the beach to my left a never ending game of baseball continues, with barefoot players of all ages, clad only in shorts. An enormous pig and several piglets wander around while a Cuban cowboy sits astride a horse that canters across the sand. People carrying sacks walk to and from the house that distributes basic rations. The occasional vehicle crosses the bridge, usually a truck filled with people in the back, or a tractor pulling something.

Half a dozen people are frolicking in the water, while off by themselves a couple kiss and do God-knows-what under the water. This is Cuba where often the most privacy a couple gets for God-knows-what is under the water, in a fairly well populated, public beach.

To the right I can see the point, the stick fence around our garden standing sharply against the watery landscape behind. Now abandoned, the tomatoes grew armpit high before it became a race over who would get to the fruit first. We ran a poor fourth behind the goats, kids and green worms the size of cigarettes. The little winding path through the sand and grass reminds me of my first days here with Jack, back when I wondered how the isolation would affect our relationship.

There have been good times and bad times during my Grand adventure in Cuba. It's been challenging and exciting, more so than I've ever experienced before. But without doubt, the last two months have been the happiest times of my life.

Relaxing on the porch of a seashore cabin between Cienfuegos and Trinidad.

March 21

My departure from San Pedro could have been worse. It could have been a nice day with all my friends gathered around to make me feel miserable about leaving. As it was, none of those things happened except for the part about being miserable.

We were leaving San Pedro for good the day before the wedding. I would be returning to Canada in less than a week, and until then we would stay at Jose's house.

The day started with a lurch at six in the morning when Santiago informed me we were supposed to have everything packed and ready to catch the nine o'clock bus, and that his brother-in-law Manolo would be arriving soon to help haul everything up to the highway It was the first I'd heard of this plan, which caused me immediate panic because I had nothing at all ready. Worse yet, I could feel the discomfort of my kidney infection recurring yet again. Feverish, uncomfortable and cranky, I was barely able to hide my irritation at a local friend and her two kids who loitered around the tiny cabin. I wished someone would just knock me over the head and put me out of my misery and it became clear there was no way I would be able to pack things up quickly enough to catch the bus, let alone assist in carting all the suitcases, boxes, sacks and miscellaneous other items up to the highway. In fact, as it turned out, the only thing I had the strength to do was take a third extra-strength Tylenol and lie down. When Manolo arrived we asked him to go back to Cienfuegos and hire a car to take us into town. It would cost $10 which we couldn't afford, but as I laid back down to rest, I realized that it was probably one of the best $10 investments I'd ever make.

After a while I felt better and was ready to resume packing. I made a luxury breakfast for us of boiled eggs, toast and peanut butter, then brewed some of the wonderful hand-roasted Cuban coffee given to us by friends. We were finally ready and by the time the big vintage car arrived, more people had also shown up and were standing around. It reminded me of our arrival in San Pedro under the watchful eyes of the crowd on the rock. Only now I knew each one personally, their kids and families. They had all been good to me, generous with whatever they had, especially their kindness and friendship.

As things were loaded into the car, I looked sorrowfully around for the last time, close to tears and wishing everyone would go away so I could have these last moments to blubber in private. But this was Cuba, where privacy is as scarce as good hamburgers, so I left them all at the cabin and walked alone down the crooked little path to the garden. It began to rain, and as tears streamed down my face, I poked around the garden, straightening the stakes for the now wilted tomato plants and picking up dead leaves. I took one final look at the sea, rough and dark with waves breaking over the reef, inhaled deeply, then walked slowly back to the cabin and our waiting car. Tears flowed freely as I hugged my friends and joined Santiago in the back seat. When we drove through the grounds, I looked for the last time at the restaurant, the little outdoor bar, and the dance floor. We passed the guard station and everyone waved. My heart ached as I watched from the back window until San Pedro was blocked from my sight.

Our wedding day began early, with Jose in the kitchen rustling up breakfast and also preparing the food for later. My body was now filled with Sulfa and penicillin and I was feeling reasonably well. People started filtering into the house before noon, and as a group they decided which of the borrowed clothes Santiago should wear. When ready, he looked handsome in a blue shirt, red and blue tie, white pants, and black jacket.

After as good a shower as one can have in a bucket of water, I slipped on the white crocheted outfit my friends in Canada had sent for me to wear. Rosa, my bridesmaid, looked lovely in a silky print pantsuit, her long black hair done up on top of her head.

The driver of the car that had brought us in from San Pedro the day before had donated his services for the wedding, so a group of us piled into the car for the drive to the lawyer's office. In Cuba, marriages between tourists and citizens must be performed by a government agent, kind of like a justice of the peace, though most people just refer to them as lawyers.

Our group, along with some total strangers, crowded into the small, utilitarian office. My interpreter was a striking black woman wearing a blue floral dress. She stood behind me, softly translating the long list of commitments and promises. After Santiago and I both uttered "si," at the appropriate times, my new husband leaned over and gave me a gentle kiss, not unlike that very first one in San Pedro. As before, it was a happy, light-hearted moment and there wasn't a shred of doubt in my mind that I had done the right thing.

Out on the street the mood of the group turned festive, so for the next couple of hours we drove around the city, taking photos at different scenic and historical spots, stopping at a vine and flower covered garden cantina to toast the occasion with a bottle of champagne . We made a quick stop at Santiago's house to see his mother, but she was too ill to be roused, so we headed back to Jose's place where people had already begun to arrive.

Cuban and South American music played on the tape machine while Jose, with Santiago's brother Papito, took over the duties of serving pasta salad and croquettes in little brown cardboard containers. Drinks from a donated bottle of rum were mixed sparingly with Coke. When that ran out, more bottles of rum appeared, each one at a less stage of refinement. Even so, no one seemed to mind drinking it straight, after the cola ran out. Even the die-hard party animals were gone by 10:00 p.m. and Jose also left, discreetly saying he'd be gone "for a couple of hours". This would be the only time for us to be alone before I had to return to Canada.

Santiago's paperwork to leave the country was all complete and we were hopeful that, as my husband, the Canadian Embassy would issue him a visa to allow him to return to Canada with me.

The day after the wedding, we made the long trip to Havana. I had never been to Cuba's capitol before and was fascinated with the grand old-world architecture and the narrow streets of the old section, where we spent the night at the home of family friends. We were treated to a motorcycle tour of the city, so I received a ground-level view of Havana at night sitting in a little sidecar.

At first I felt pride when we arrived at the stately grounds of the Canadian Embassy, the red and white maple leaf flag flying overhead. That feeling vanished when I was permitted entry through the big iron gates, but Santiago was told he would have to wait outside the grounds and on the opposite side of the street. Inside the building a receptionist behind a glass window offered me no information other than to wait. For the next two hours I sat in a hot stuffy room where I had a clear view of the street and of my husband standing like a cast-off on the other side.

Finally, he was also allowed to enter but ushered directly to an inner office, where I was not permitted to follow. After a very few minutes he returned, a stricken look on his face and a piece of paper in his hand. It was a form letter saying his application had been denied. With a sick feeling welling up inside of me, I tried to remain calm, asking for more information. I was told to go to a window on the outside of the building and there, from behind bullet-proof glass, a woman told me through a microphone that I would have to return to Canada and apply from there. She spoke at length about how busy she was and that she didn't have time to talk to me anymore about it. Thus brushed off after two days of travelling and hours of waiting, I left feeling both outraged and embarrassed for the shabby, insensitive treatment we had received from my own government. Worst of all, I realized that I would have to leave Cuba without Santiago.

March 23,
Canada

In the end, it wasn't as hard as I thought it would be, getting up at 3 a.m., driving for hours, saying goodbye to my new husband. The numbness I felt when the alarm clock rang continued right on through the trip and the two hour wait in the airport.

The night before, Santiago and I had climbed the steep stairs to the flat roof of Jose's house, and in the warm night air we looked at the full moon and the stars. He reminded me about the Cuban way of being cheerful even when things are bad, so I was determined not to make things worse than they already were.

We kept the conversation light during the long wait in the airport, and my feeling of numbness continued through our farewell when it was finally time for me to go. Passing through security I waved one last time and walked to the waiting plane. When the doors were closed, I shivered as the air conditioning replaced the humid warmth I had finally become accustomed to.

It wasn't until the airplane took off and banked sharply to the right, giving me a bird's eye view of the rapidly diminishing airport, that the magnitude of the time and space now separating Santiago and I began to sink in. Once in the air we quickly climbed to 37,000 feet, and as I looked back, the last thing I saw was the same as when I had arrived a lifetime ago....thunderheads towering over the emerald jewel that is Cuba.

So Adolf, that's the story of my "Grand Adventure." And although I'm back in Canada now, I'm sure life for me will never be the same.
Your friend,
Elaine

Postscript
October, 1996
Over a year and a half has passed since that day Santiago and I said goodbye at the airport, but he's still not in Canada with me.

As a sixth generation Canadian, I had no experience with our country's immigration practices, so the appalling treatment we have received both surprised and infuriated me. A minor glitch in Santiago's application derailed the process, and since then we have been at the mercy of bureaucrats in Ottawa who seem to have an attitude of casual contempt for people like us whose future they control. For the past year all anyone will tell us about his application is that "it's sitting on a desk somewhere and *maybe* will be approved by 1997." Actually, they don't tell *us* anything - inquiries must be channelled through a Member of Parliament's office which is passed along to us third or fourth hand. Ordinary citizens like myself cannot contact anyone in Immigration directly; even their names and office address is withheld. Faxes to the Minister of Immigration's office are ignored.

After Santiago and I had been separated for six miserable months, I returned to Cuba. We spent a wonderful winter together, but the following spring I had to return to Canada without him once again. Like a recurring nightmare, we have now spent another six long months apart. Meanwhile, our lives are on hold and the long wait has been both emotionally and financially draining. Yet, throughout it all, our committment to each other remains absolute, and there's still never been a doubt in my mind that we did the right thing.

There are many fascinating old church buildings throughout Cuba, though many of them have sat unused for years. This one is part of the old company town at the sugar mill of Simon Bolivar, in the province of Sancti Spiritus. Its roof has fallen in and nature is reclaiming where pews and alter once stood.

Third Visit to Cuba

Rancho Luna Hotel,
Cienfuegos, Cuba
March 28, 1995

My dear wife:

Since it still hasn't worked out for you and I to visit Cuba together, I'll write to you as Okan and I travel so that you can at least experience the journey with us in this way. We just arrived an hour ago and are wondering how long it will take us to get used to the heat. Okan is washing a few of his travelling clothes in the bathroom sink, having brought special soap for that purpose so as not to repeat the skin condition he got on his hands last year from using the harsh, lye-saturated Cuban hotel soap. When he's done, we're going for a night time dip down at the beach, into the Caribbean.

It's always such a contrast to sleep one night in a fancy Canadian airport hotel, enjoying all the modern luxuries, then to fly down here to Cuba into such a totally different social and economic world. Our flight went smoothly this time, using Canadian Airlines to avoid last year's bad experiences on that old Russian plane and its comparable service. The only tense moments of our journey came while we were still at the hotel, waiting in the lobby to board the complimentary airport limousine. It was a hectic morning and they were running late, so we stood in line and watched the limo fill up before our very eyes, leaving us stranded in front of the hotel with a big pile of baggage and little more than an hour till flying time.

Lucky for us, a turbaned taxi driver just happened to pull up at that moment and willingly rushed us to the airport, where we learned that the plane was an hour late anyway. It reminded me of the time you and I took the kids to Germany while they were little, when less than two hours before flying time I was still correcting proofs for my next railroad book at the printer's office, so that we ended up speeding several miles to the airport in a frantic sweat, dragging kids and baggage through the doors in a rush, only to end up in a nearby hotel when the flight got postponed. Guess it's a modern version of what you sometimes see in those early flight films, where a man with wings strapped to his arms gets momentarily airborne, but ends up mostly just hopping on the ground.

Two of our three bags were marked with white chalk for inspection at the Varadero airport - the two with locks on them. After we got them open the young customs man got suspicious about my books and the large quantity of film, asking several times what they were for. While trying to explain, we were suddenly greeted warmly by my old friend Alex Chavez, whose work for years has been to meet arriving visitors from Canada and guide them to their hotels, and through the days of their vacations. He knew there wasn't much to do for us two "independents," but he still seemed real glad to see us. The customs man said right away in Spanish, "Hey Alex, you know these people?" When Alex said "sure," he was asked why I had such a pile of books and film. "Oh, he's an author; he writes about trains; he has friends on railroads all over the country, so he brings them books, and he takes pictures of them." We were immediately thanked for our time, given a big smile, told to close up our bags and go on our way. Like I keep saying, it's a friendly country.....

Stepping from the air-conditioned lobby into the tropical heat, I heard someone call my name and there stood our train station friend Eusebio from last year, looking somewhat tense and pale, another fellow at his side. You may recall that I wrote to Eusebio last winter when I thought I'd be coming down here alone, asking him to join me for part of the trip. I wanted his company, thinking it would be fun for a change to have an interpreter along. But when he didn't write back, my plans got altered, so I forgot all about him. Unfortunately, *he* didn't, and there he was, ready to spend the next two weeks with me. He was quite let down that I no longer needed him, all the more so because while hitchhiking from his home in Pinar del Rio, tired from previous long hours of working in the fields, he fell asleep and some other hitchhikers got off with his bag, which contained all his clothes, papers and money. He'd arrived at the airport broke the day before, then spent all night trying to sleep on a bench in the lounge, where he incidentally met the other fellow, a Canadian who'd also lost his gear and was broke, though fortunately he was flying back home the next day.

By renting a car right at the airport we were able to skip the resort area of Varadero altogether this time and head right out into the country to visit our friends. We dropped off poor Euse-bio at the same downtown train station in Matanzas, where he fig-ured that some of the U.S. dollars we gave him might buy a fast

Here's my friend Walfrido of Central Fructuoso Rodriguez, near Matanzas, just back from work in the field with his father, on the right. Walfrido spent some time in East Germany as a sol-dier and student, learning to speak an interesting version of Cuban accented German, by which he and I converse. It's not too bad in person, since we can include some Spanish and many hand signs, but our letters must be nightmares for the postal censors. The garden supplements his family's meager rations with crops of beans, rice and several kinds of vegetables, some of which are in the sacks around Walfrido and his dad. We met Walfrido on our first visit to Cuba, while photographing a rare old 1896 Rogers tank locomotive switching cars into the near-by mill, where he was at work unloading cane.

ride back home. He'd really been anxious for this opportunity and put a lot of effort into getting time off from farm work, while his mother lay sick at home, and there was also a younger brother to take care of. Their food and other needs are barely met by whatever few dollars Eusebio is able to come up with from friends like us. I felt quite badly and made a note to be more careful in the future about telling anything to my Cuban friends by mail in advance of my coming. He'd taken what was only a suggestion of mine and turned it into a fully planned agenda.

So, in less than two hours after getting off the plane we were visiting with the family of our friend Walfrido, he of the proud good looks and muscular body, living with his two skinny little-black parents, along with his equally handsome and muscular brother and their pretty sister. They were all there - except him; he was down at his uncle's garden doing some work. The Fructu-oso Rodriguez village was exceptionally quiet because the sugar mill wasn't operating this year. Its cane was being taken by train to a neighboring mill where Walfrido and his fellow workers go and take turns putting in their hours, though from the sounds of it that mill is already overstaffed and his need there was minimal. Walfrido finally showed up, soaked with sweat and out of breath, having received word of our arrival and then run all the way home.

After a short visit we left, and by late afternoon reached the town of Cruces, its narrow crowded streets lined by the facades of many old buildings, tall stacks of the sugar mill Mal Tiempo smoking nearby. At the mill we first went to our special friend Efren, who was home alone. His youngest sister was having prob-lems with a pregnancy in Havana and his wife had gone there by train to help. "No woman!" he said dejectedly about himself in English, having learned some words from the dictionary I gave him last time. He gave us juice, then brought us through the mill-yard to greet our other friends at the locomotive shop. After a short visit with all of them we drove here to our beach front ho-tel, half an hour and a world away.

Efren said the number of tourists who come to photograph

trains at the sugar mill keeps growing every year. But he still insists, as he did last year, that we're the only ones who've stayed long enough to eat with them and become friends. "Most just ask a few questions, take pictures of trains, then drive off in a cloud of dust." The largest contingent apparently comes from England, and he said they are the least friendly, generally travelling in tour buses, else crowded several into one or two rented cars, sometimes travelling in convoys. He was annoyed by the action of one recent character, who threw handfuls of candy into the crowd of kids that usually gathers around foreigners, then video taped their mad scramble for the handouts, which insults the pride and honor of most older Cubans. He said another fellow took his shirt off to give away - in itself a well meaning gesture - but instead of handing it to someone he threw it into the gathered crowd then let them fight over it while he recorded the scene. I can hear him telling friends back home, "Look at the poor buggers, they'll kill each other for a capitalist's shirt."

Efren claims Americans are sometimes even worse than Brits because, according to him "they won't give anything at all to anybody." As an old soldier under the revolutionary hero Camilo Cienfuegos he'd naturally find it hard to welcome Americans after all these years of bitterness, and there are still many others in Cuba like him.

Things in general appear to be looking up this year, according to Efren, who said that Mal Tiempo has already filled its sugar quota. Last year's harvest fell way short, but this year they've met the quota and still got enough unharvested cane to keep them busy at least another two more weeks. Vegetable gardens are growing everywhere this year, and the weather has given them good results. Lots of tomatoes and cucumbers, even potatoes, of which there were hardly any last year. The U.S. dollar is down from 125 pesos to 40, as of today. Efren was proud that the peso is getting more even with the dollar, though he didn't mention that in the process everything else has become much more expensive, especially on the very important black market.

There was an accident on the narrow gauge railroad last year, right after we'd been here and had our thrilling trips at the throttle. Locomotive No. 1345 got away on its own from the shop, after one crew member moved it around and forgot to put blocks under the wheels. It headed out of town (luckily the switches were set right and no one was crossing the tracks out on the main road) then it ran alone down to the big curve about two kilometers away - where last year's crew set up a smoking double header for us - and there it derailed at a good speed, turning over in the process. It took only one full day for the crew to get it back on the rails, using nothing but jacks and manpower. This year it's back at work and looking fine. Also last year, a mill worker heading home after dark took a shortcut through the narrow gauge railroad yard, walking between two cars that suddenly got moved and coupled up, killing him in between. Dangerous railroading, Efren says earnestly.

Old and dangerous the sugar mills may be, but Efren insists that there is now big German money in partnership with Cuba for their continued operation. If anyone can modernize Cuba's mechanical sugar operations you'd think it would be the Germans, in which case old narrow gauge lines like Mal Tiempo - and the half dozen others that we visit - will not last much longer. A fleet of Mercedes trucks and trailers will probably take over, though with world sugar prices so low, one wonders if *any* improvements would help. Maybe it would be better just to build theme parks for tourists out of the old mills and their trains, with the hope that local populations will be better sustained.

When I made this suggestion to Efren I thought he might laugh, or even get upset, having enjoyed his life on the sugar railroads. Instead, he not only agreed that this might be a hope for the future, but surprised us by saying that one such plan is already in the works for Mal Tiempo. About an hour out of town the narrow gauge tracks cross a crystal clear stream and a smooth-rocked gorge over a dramatic bridge built in 1910. Last year the crew stopped there for us and waited until we climbed down to water level before rumbling back across with the train, smoking it up for our cameras. It turns out that beside the stream is a pool of warm mineral water, so the government plans to build a health spa there and bring its guests out aboard special trains for which the cars are already being built in the FCC shops at Camaguey. They will be drawn by Mal Tiempo's last original engine, No. 1221, built for the mill back in 1920. Efren was quite proud that visitors would be hauled by this old engine because as locomotive shop foreman he had supervised the efforts needed to keep this machine alive all these years. Rather than turning into a rusting hulk headed for scrap, it's now destined to become a tourist star.

Travelling through a transportation timewarp! That's the subtitle of a colour photo book my sons and I have been assembling from our visits to Cuba, and this photo illustrates that theme very well. We're at the edge of Central Mal Tiempo, where the narrow gauge railroad crosses the community's gravel boulevard, which winds its way to the nearby Santa Clara - Cienfuegos highway. Some of our friends at the shop are aboard locomotive No. 1320 on the left (built in 1909 by Baldwin of Philadelphia). We've also got a few cowboys, a horse-drawn coach, plus the classic black '57 Oldsmobile four door sedan. Pictures like this take a lot of effort to set up, but the rewards are precious snapshots of a bygone time.

Hotel Inglaterra
Havana, April 4

Our introduction to Havana might have been better at some
time other than the afternoon rush hour. Guess I'm spoiled from
driving in the Cuban countryside, where there is seldom any
heavy traffic, nor even much rush. Lots of both upon entering
Havana, with the usual honking, speeding and stalling so common to most cities.

Those are among our first impressions of the biggest and most
famous Caribbean city. It seems crowded, noisy, intriguing, old,
dangerous, and sometimes uninviting. This last was a problem,
since we didn't know anyone and needed to find a good, safe
place to stay. Over a million people in a region of the world
where anything more than a village is big. The wide beach front
highway from Varadero to Havana via Santa Cruz del Norte reminded me of coastal San Pedro in California, or maybe the
south end of the San Francisco Bay, else some place in New Jersey on a hot summer afternoon. Nondescript houses scattered
among huge fuel storage tanks and industrial sites, surrounded
by barren dusty soil, crisscrossed by a tangle of roads and railway tracks, the scattered immenseness of it all making a strong
contrast to the luscious green countryside around Cienfuegos
where we've been this past week. The dense, foul city air soon
filled our nostrils, which were used to scents far more fresh and
clean. I didn't expect to like Havana, and those first glimpses did
nothing to change my mind.

We entered downtown on a famous wide road called the Malecon, which circles the waterfront of the city like part of a wheel,
with every street a spoke leading towards the hub. Ocean waves
splash against an immense wall on one side of the wheel - the
Malecon - while old buildings line the other, with stormy waves
often spraying over their facades, when police have to close the
road to traffic. No storm on this day, just a high tide of crowds,
many strolling the sidewalk, others sitting on the wall next to the
water. Guys and girls hugging, individuals of both kinds waving
to us, calling out what they had to offer, whether it was cheap

fuel, cigars, love or money. But all I wanted was a decent hotel room.

The task of finding one seemed daunting for several reasons, among them the knowledge that some hotels here are really expensive, yet I couldn't locate my list that said which ones, nor did I trust my Spanish enough to ask anybody on the street. Wherever I looked, the people appeared untrustworthy, though I don't necessarily blame that on Havana, since I get similar feelings in New York and L.A. (though not so much in Vancouver, and even less in Zurich). Coming there directly from our country friends, not to mention our own country living, made me feel somewhat like a coyote just turned loose at a cattle auction.

One Canadian friend had told us about a fabulous old hotel somewhere downtown, whose atmosphere alone sounded quite interesting. But when we located it on a dark and narrow side street, there were numerous unsavory looking characters hanging out in front, along with several policemen, two of whom were checking out the only car parked nearby. It looked like a hotel for Cubans only, which would mean cheap and uncomfortable. Adding to my concern was the Havanautos clerk who had warned us not to leave the rental car unattended anywhere in the city, or it might be missing wheels and other parts, for which I was liable. So we cruised around for a while looking up and down other narrow streets, all of them crowded with people who seemed to stare at us, while we were still wondering where we should go to stay. There were endless ornate old Spanish buildings, decorated by scrollwork, stonework, big columns and wrought iron grills. Many of them were cracking, crumbling and faded, with some already collapsed or in the state of collapsing, others having their embellished front walls held up by old telephone poles propped in at angles, like old dowagers whose jewelry only adds weight to the wrinkles, for whom a face lift is probably already too late. Old Havana is a Unesco world heritage site, but I suppose Unesco funds are getting nearly as scarce as Cuba's own....

We suddenly came out onto a wide boulevard passing the city's Central Park, where our eyes were first drawn towards the architectural grandeur of the nation's Grand Theatre, then right next door we noticed the smaller but also very antique looking Hotel Inglaterra. It had a clean front, facing a wide sidewalk, plus a parking area conspicuously located in between the boulevard's opposing lanes. I quickly pulled in and stopped by a dozen other tourist cars parked in the angled spaces. Directing my parking enthusiastically was a pot-bellied, middle aged fellow in tight sweater and baggy pants, a big smile on his face and a plastic hotel I.D. card pinned at one shoulder. In poor English he said, "I'm here all night, I'll watch your car."

Drag race of old timers in downtown Havana, as our '52 Chevy station wagon is passed by what looks like about a 1949 Packard. Across the way is Cuba's National Theatre, one of Old Havana's architectural gems. The Hotel Inglaterra is just beyond, with Havana's Central Park to the right.

We had passed the National Hotel a couple of times during our search, but its big oval driveway and uniformed doormen told me a room there would cost too much for our budget and I was right. The Inglaterra is less pretentious; for a dollar an elderly "bellboy" gladly hauled our five bags from the street up to our room, where a double glass door opens out onto a balcony. From there we can look right down on our car, or out at the heart of Havana, which is surrounding it. What a sight! A couple of new plush beds, a big clean shower, the fanciest room we've yet seen in Cuba, at a price of $60 U.S. Reasonable for us seasoned travellers, though a vast fortune for any one of the hundreds of thousands of people that live in this city day and night. They know how much we tourists have to pay to sleep here; it's no wonder they stare at us wherever we pass them.

Maybe this kind of guilt is what helped keep me awake my first night, but the main cause was no doubt the unending, nerve wracking downtown noise. For what rest I got, I could just as well have stayed awake and gone around blowing on one of those silly party noisemakers, and I would have saved myself 60 bucks! So now I'm sitting on an antique Spanish rocking chair near the massive wooden front door of our room thinking about the fact that this is Havana's oldest hotel and its first guests might well have been in here talking about the "wild American Indians" killing General George Custer, which had just happened a few seasons before this establishment's grand opening.

The rental car was like having someone else's child to look after, a big worry when we got to Havana. One American friend came to this city a couple of years ago after a long day of filming trains, driving the same kind of four-door Nissan like we had. He and his brother parked on a busy downtown street and went into a big hotel for a meal. My friend's professional-sized video camera and big tripod were left in the back seat, covered by crumpled clothing and other stuff. When they got back from their meal the police were already there, taking notes from a witness who said a man walked by, smashed one of the Nissan's side windows, opened the door, grabbed the camera and tripod, then made his escape in a car that stopped briefly. That valuable camera gear will be mighty conspicuous to sell in Cuba, especially with police taking down serial numbers and all. Besides, the robber missed the tripod's fluid head and the camera's rechargable battery, two things impossible to get in Cuba, without which the gear is almost useless. Smooth move, outsmarted by technology. For my friend, his reason for being in Cuba suddenly ended, since he goes mainly to shoot videos of trains.

Speaking of shooting videos, Okan was sure sorry he didn't have his available when he suddenly persuaded me to rent an old American car and its driver, a big, tough, Spanish looking fellow. For three bucks we got to cruise through the narrow, dark streets of downtown Old Havana in his unique baby blue '52 Cadillac stretch limousine, trying to keep from sliding around on the smooth, naugahyde-covered bench seats while our chauffeur spoke to us willingly, played loud, scratchy rock and roll music on his original dashboard radio, and shifted the gears of the rumbling Russian tractor motor with a hefty four-on-the-floor. The designers in Detroit would look aghast at their one time pride, feeling faint from its belching diesel fumes, as would the Batista general who was its original owner. I had to chuckle at the incongruity of it all, cruising through the heart of socialist Havana in the ultimate symbol of American capitalism. Okan meanwhile was trying to think of ways to bring that weird blue rig back home for his personal pleasure and for his friends; he says it is now his favourite car in all of Cuba.

Downtown railroad stations are often interesting places for photography, just like downtown people and downtown traffic. All three go together, so it's just a matter of finding good angles and the right lighting. Besides, our self appointed goal to document Cuban railroading would not be complete without a visit to the country's biggest and busiest train station, Havana's Estacion Central.

The recent growth in tourism inspired the FCC to open a branch called Ferrotur, with the idea of attracting tourists wanting to travel by train. I first saw a display of theirs at a table in the lobby of a fancy Varadero beach hotel, including a fuzzy brochure that extolled Cuba's scenery and the ability of trains to bring visitors where they could see some of it. Several daytime round trips were offered, with very reasonable prices quoted in U.S. dollars. Ferrotur was supposed to block sections of seats on designated trains so that tourists could step up to a ticket window a short time before departure and get aboard, even while Cubans stood in line for hours and days to get their tickets.

Central Station's Spanish architecture and tall, imposing twin towers make it a national landmark, but the office for Ferrotur was in a nondescript little fenced patio down the tracks away from it, presumably as another attempt to separate tourists from the Cuban masses. Although there were several staff members in this office, we were told we'd have to wait for "the boss," even just to get information. There were some bare plastic seats, but no smiles or offers of friendship. I've heard that all Cuban tourist services used to be run in this fashion, but for us this was a first experience.

Central Station in Havana, with passengers boarding an express train whose brown and yellow coaches can be seen going around the curve way ahead. The locomotive at far left is one of 50 built in Montreal and sent to Cuba in 1975, causing much political uproar with some Americans. They are considered Cuba's best locomotives by crews and shopmen alike.

For the next half hour we sat and watched as little happened, except that several mangy dogs got booted out while trying to "cruise" through the open office in their search for eats. A switch engine backed into the terminal with a string of passenger cars, after which a particularly ugly and skinny dog was allowed to come in and lay down in the middle of the floor, where he proceeded to scratch himself mercilessly, while a clerk at the nearest desk chatted away on the telephone, leaning back in a comfortable office chair, idly riffling through the kind of train timetable book I had come there to see. This was not good service.

Eventually a chubby little man near retirement age came in and sat down at the best of several desks, though like the others he didn't acknowledge our presence. He lit a cigarette and looked out the window at the train until one of the others told him that we were wanting to ride the daylight train from Havana to Santa Clara.

"Well, sell them a ticket for No. 17," he said without turning from the window. "It departs at 14:20 and will cost them $10.80 each." One of the clerks performed the necessary formalities (including passport check).

We hurried back to the hotel, packed our bags, then took a taxi to the station early, though the train ended up leaving nearly an hour late. We passed the time in silence, sitting with our mound of baggage on those same uncomfortable plastic seats in the Ferrotur office, watching the boss and his unfriendly crew shuffling papers on their desks and sometimes answering phones, while a mixed crowd of mostly young Cubans in semi-uniforms, (train attendants, it turned out) were laughing and frolicking nearby, waiting for the car cleaners to finish their work in the train so that they could go aboard. Through all this wandered that ugly, mangy grey mutt, scars all over his face attesting to hard fought meals in his train yard territory, where others like him also scavenge for the few edible tidbits that a poor, hungry nation accidentally drops.

Eventually the heavy wrought-iron gates at the other end of the terminal were opened, releasing a crush of human traffic out of the big station building, swarming towards the parked train across the tracks from where we sat. That surprised me, since I'd let myself assume that as dollar-paying tourists we'd receive priority seating. Not until the main rush was over did one of the office clerks signal with her hand that we should proceed. Struggling with our baggage, I asked for further directions, to which she gave me a pained expression as though the answer should have been obvious, then showed with her hand a route clear up to the main station, around the tail end of the train, then back up towards the front on the other side. She then returned to her desk work and ignored us, leaving me to wonder how much of a rush there was to our upcoming walk, since it was almost time for the scheduled departure and no one had explained that the train was delayed.

Maybe this was planned by some cynic within Ferrotur, who thought it would be good for train riding tourists to be seen and inspected by the whole trainload of passengers, as we now had to walk up the train's entire length right underneath their windows, with our big load sure to attract attention. With hunched shoulders we lugged the heavy baggage through the thick, hot air of the Havana harborfront, thinking unkind things about those unfriendly people back in that little tourist ticket office.

Our car turned out to be sixth from the front, which meant we had 17 cars to walk down then back up again, though luck was with us as a baggage handling friend from our earlier station visit showed up half way through our struggle, his cart recently emptied and ready for the next load. He looked at our tickets, threw on the bags, then added so many more boxes and suitcases from other passengers that he could hardly get the rickety cart started and had a hard time steering it once it got moving. In fact, he managed losing parts of the load once or twice, at other times coming within half an inch or so of the numerous passengers and various steel posts that stood along the way. I gave him a dollar as a tip when we finally got to the door of our car, though I noticed no one else giving him anything, not even a thanks. I guess among Cubans you do your job and don't expect compliments.

The FCC mainline snakes its way out of the dead end downtown station area for the first couple of kilometers on an elevated steel trestle, something like a big ride at an amusement park. Rusty ships were tied up to the docks on our left, factories and warehouses carpeted the right, while up ahead an ancient stone fortress dominated the hilly landscape. Unfortunately, these initial trackside scenes were about the most exciting ones of the afternoon trip to Santa Clara, the rest being mainly of sugar cane fields interspersed by small farms and expanses of fallow land.

When we first boarded the train, everybody naturally checked us out, but when we smiled they smiled back and after that they all pretty well minded their own business. Few people seemed to be travelling alone; there were several families with little kids and babies who wandered up and down the aisles, wearing minimal clothing, sometimes holding a bottle or dragging some pitiful looking toy. Moving trains present obvious dangers for kids wandering loose, with sharp curves and sudden brake applications liable to cause falls, but no one seemed particularly concerned. The naugahyde covered seats were clean and comfortable, while the linoleum floor looked well maintained. Only the windows were stained from the daily passing of burning sugar cane fields, plus the lack of soap for washing. The stubble in all the fields is burned after harvesting, the results being that in Cuba you're seldom without the sight of smoke during the sugar season. Flames would suddenly leap up beside the open train windows and smoke would come rushing in, the hot smell rudely and quickly invading all our senses, the loud crackling sounding as if it were a campfire of dry mountain pine instead of green and yellow cane stalks. Each time this happened there was a frenzy as everyone rushed to close the windows by their seats, always a bit too late to keep out the powdered ash that came swirling in with the smoke, covering all of us and everything we had. Meanwhile, with the windows suddenly closed for a few moments, the inside of our car would immediately heat up in the tropical weather. At times there were just short breaks between the burning fields, so that the lowering and raising of 30-some windows by a carload of passengers took on the air of a Broadway play,

or at least some kind of schoolyard puppet show. All of them up
- slam, slam, slam. All of them down - slam, slam, slam. Over and
over. Imagine the wear and tear on the old equipment, not to
mention everyone's ears and nerves.

What is train travel without food and something to drink? No
diner, no snack bar, just a couple of old men pushing a tall tin
box perched on the rickety bottom of what seemed to have once
been a grocery shopping cart. Little dry looking sandwiches
were available for a peso, while a big thermos had coffee, the
strong, Cuban kind, which was poured out into tiny cups with a
little dipper. One of the men wiped the cups between customers,
but we preferred just plain water and, like most of the passengers,
had brought our own big plastic bottle full. We also carried dried
food, so took no chance at sampling the caterer's wares.

A big change in Cuban train travel had gone into effect just
that previous season when Fidel said it was alright for people to
sell things to each other for money. Now, at each station stop a

Railroad stations in Cuba are still busy places, fairly safe and
tidy, recalling North American train travel from a bygone era.
This handsome grey stone building with dark blue and yellow
trim serves the small town of Aguacate.

handful of mostly women and girls walk up and down next to the tracks, just below the train's open windows, carrying cardboard trays with homemade edibles, generally tamales of sorts, beans and rice wrapped in thin white dough sheets, costing a peso or two. Hardly any of the track walkers had the look of food vendors, and their wares looked to us almost uniformly unappetizing. They just walked along until someone called out and asked what they had, the answer usually being given in low tones and without any sales pitch. Knowing that soap would be scarce in their environment kept us from being tempted to taste these trackside treats, even more so after we saw several potential customers handle the cooked goods, then put them back when they decided not to buy. Nothing of the mechanized junk food assortments available in train stations most everywhere else in the world nowadays was to be seen anywhere near these Cuban trains.

There were no other tourists aboard, except one chunky blonde fellow in shorts and T-shirt, every bit of his light skin sunburnt, apparently a German from the look of his worn rucksack and the writing on the map that he kept open on his lap continuously. He never looked directly at us during the five hour trip, though he sat just across the aisle and back one row. He didn't make contact with any of the other folks around him either, though these were otherwise cheerful and carried on a lively social interchange with each other, frequently smiling at us and exchanging some words.

The German fellow seemed typical of today's "rich world's kid," out for a glance at some exotic places, trained to watch them like TV programs, sitting silent and removed, one frame following the next, each one precisely noted and checked on the map, then left behind, probably forever. I wonder what kind of place the world would be if international travel changed its focus from luxury tourism to simple and meaningful exchanges of friendships; living with people of other lands, talking and travelling with them, working for a spell right alongside them, without maps, guidebooks and segregated hotels.

The majority of women at the station in Havana and on the

train were lightly dressed, seemingly more so than the men. One pretty mulatto mother just ahead of us nursed her little kid rather carelessly, when he wasn't running around with a dirty bottle in his hand. Others wore low-cut blouses, or else had loose open sleeves, with nothing else underneath (state rations allow for one bra *or* pair of panties per year!) In Cuba, women don't yell "sexual harassment" the moment a man casts longing glances; if anything, some appear insulted if they're not noticed. In Mexico, local men tend to resent foreigners looking at their women, who often dress just as temptingly, but Cuban men don't seem to be bothered. More than once we've visited with fellows who suggested to nearby girls that they should "go" with us. Telling them that I'm married and accompanied by my son only brings smiles and shrugging shoulders, or as one pair of definitely available ladies said to us, "So, pretend that we're mother and daughter!"

Arrival in Santa Clara turned out to be sudden and hectic, as we were busy leaning from windows, trying to to capture photo scenes with our cameras, when one of our neighbors suddenly said in excited Spanish, "Aren't you getting off at Santa Clara?" My eye still on the viewfinder, I casually answered, "Si!" to which several voices chimed urgently, "hurry up, get your bags out," while someone else went to tell the conductor. Presumably he already knew, since he'd punched our tickets, but he never said there would be any rush about it. The sudden urgency was compounded when the train stopped, then started rolling again. I had made it partway down the steps of our car with one of the big bags and was just climbing back up for another when a stern faced lady attendant blocked the exit and said we couldn't get off the moving train. There was a moment of panic, as I struggled for words in Spanish telling her that this was our stop and that I already had part of our baggage on the station platform. She relayed that information in a loud voice to somebody in the station crowd, who then kept their eye on the bag for us. It turned out we were only making a switching move, and there was plenty of time to get off safely. That wasn't the only occasion in Cuba when people have gotten us rushed and excited for nothing.

A couple of ugly Ladas were parked out in front of the station, their drivers watching to see if anyone needed them, but I spotted a nifty red and white '57 Chevy nearby, whose elderly Spanish driver got out proudly when I nodded to his inquiring stare. He filled the trunk with most of our baggage, then placed the rest on an old chrome luggage rack up on the roof. His wife rode shotgun, a plump elderly lady who said nothing, letting him and me do all the talking. Five to ten fares a day is his usual traffic quota, with most everyone paying in Cuban pesos, which have only limited value in his eyes. He lives and works for the occasional tourist customer like us, though he only gets two or three of them in a week. He willingly accepted my three dollar counter-offer to his five dollar request for what I knew was only a ten minute ride. Still, we got a bargain by downtown Vancouver standards, while he got over half a month's average wage,which would buy at least a few more litres of fuel for his gas loving car.

A note here about the "baling wire" that is often reported to "hold together" Cuba's aging fleet of American vintage autos, according to reports on radio programs, in newspaper articles,

Typical small-town Cuban traffic includes a dark green 1929 Model A Ford, a father and his son on a Chinese bicycle, and several homemade, horse drawn carriages waiting at the curb for local taxi service. This was just off the main Highway 1 where it passes through the town of Florida, near Camaguey.

and even in National Geographic magazine. Yet in all our travelling around Cuba I don't recall seeing one single old car that literally had any important parts held on with wire. We've seen many with missing lights, mirrors, bumpers and fenders; but parts wired on? I guess it sounds dramatic in literature, but welding is still the most common practice for repairing loose car pieces in Cuba.

Having told the driver of this old Chevy that we wanted Motel Los Canneyes, we then sat back and watched with silent pleasure as he fired it up, put it in gear, and drove away from the station *very* carefully, obviously having high regard for the machine. He told us that he bought it new before the Revolution, when he worked as the manager of his father's leather tannery. Later it sat by his house unused for years, but just lately he got it going again with some cash from a relative in the States, and now the taxi work supplements his family's meager rations of rice and beans and his pension of under 100 pesos. Our three dollars alone were worth one and a half times that amount.

During the ride I imagined being back with my teenage friend Randy, riding to the beach in his parents' '57 Chevy like this one, though theirs was brand new. The classic dashboard looked the same, and the old couple in front might just as well have been Randy's parents, although his dad was then still a young man, proud of having a fast, souped up two-door, whereas this old Cuban rig was a slow, rumbling four door. Interestingly, a sticker on its rear window advertised the decidedly capitalistic product Castrol, popular all over the country (for some reason...).

Motel Los Canneyes is somewhat unusual in style and location, a Cuban Flagstaff, Arizona, with just one single motel, way out of town and away from everything, hidden in a grove of thick brush. It's called a motel only because you can motor up near it, though a more accurate description would be "tourist village," complete with pool, bar, store, dining room, and several dozen little one-room cabins surrounded by well-tended lawns, palms and other tropical plants, *plus* a big, high fence. Something like the ancient Cuban native huts called bohios, complete with palm-thatched roofs, these rooms offer a touch of nature and privacy not seen much of anywhere else in Cuba.

It so happened that a train photographer named Nigel had the hut next to us, a young Cuban girl keeping him (illicit) company. "My little number got all up in tears," he told us in his Cockney accent, "when I told her she couldn't come back to Britain with me, and that I wasn't sending for her later." That's because he already has a wife and kids who think he is only in Cuba chasing trains, knowing nothing about the dark haired, pimple faced chica who was standing in the dark nearby waiting for him, while he sat talking to us, not thinking of her, as is often the way with those who lubricate themselves all day long with cheap liquor and then insist that it's "no problem." He met the girl four weeks ago, at the start of his trip, when he and a bunch of other Brits found the bookstore where she works in Santa Clara (where treasured copies of an *Atlas de Cuba* are for sale). "While my friends were still here we did *nothing* but chase steam from sunup to sundown," he said, "but now they've gone and I'm doing my own thing to wind down." That meant staying drunk at this tourist resort and hanging all over an exceptionally young Cuban girl.

"To get her into here," he explained willingly, "all I had to do was pay a one dollar fee and registered her name at the desk as a visitor." Officially, this allowed him to bring her to the disco. There are always a bunch of Cuban girls (and some guys) waiting outside the motel gates on weekend nights, all dressed up in the latest fashions, hoping some tourist will sponsor their way into the disco. But Nigel says he brings *his* chica to his cabin instead, for "play," claiming he chased off the security guard when that fellow came around to hassle them about it. If that's so, the liquor must make him feel pretty tough, since the guard carries a short barrelled, 12-gauge Defender shotgun slung over his back as he makes his regular rounds through the compound. Instead of giving him lip, it's just as likely that he gave the guy a couple of bucks to keep quiet about the girl. Nigel speaks fluent Spanish, being a language instructor by trade. Says he's been working in Spain for the past 15 years, but is now looking for a Canadian company willing to pay in U.S. dollars for his language services in Cuba. "Then I'll just stay and enjoy the steam and women, not to mention the rum. I'll have the best of both worlds." Guess he forgot all about his family back home.

We rented another car, but the next day it broke down near sunset, a long distance away from the motel, with both of us yearning for the shower and scrumptious buffet meal that beckoned after our day of chasing and riding narrow gauge trains. We had just come through a 40 km stretch of empty road lined only by thick greenery, an area with few homes and no telephones. While passing through the very old colonial town of Remedios, I decided to make a detour of a few blocks in order to snap an orange sunlit photo of an old Spanish style church. Suddenly the motor died, and I sensed by the way it did that it was good and dead.

We pushed the car against a stone curb that was so high that the door on my side couldn't be opened, then we tried the starter a few more times, but managed only to attract everyone's attention in the area with noisy electronic sounds that signalled "tourists in distress!" Several people came right over to help, but all they could do was join us in staring at the darned thing, its modern computerized motor being as baffling to them as to us. I decided to go look for a phone. Not far at hand, it turned out; we'd broken down right in front of the fine, old Hotel Mariotta, a historic inn recently rebuilt with rooms for tourists. A bronze plaque out front said that in 1899, during the war of independence with Spain, this same hotel was used for an important meeting between Cuban revolutionary hero Maximo Gomez and representatives of U.S. President McKinley, whose administration offered support to Cuba.

The next vehicle to come by on that narrow street in Remedios happened to be a flatbed truck and it nearly took off part of our car's roof in passing. Luckily, the driver was going slow and watching, so that he managed to stop just about the same time that several of us shouted. Had he roared on through, he might have felt nothing, but I would have had a big repair bill on my hands, in addition to the broken down car, since the insurance has $250 deductible.

So I went on into the Hotel Mariotta and asked in Spanish if we could phone the Havanauto man at Motel Los Canneyes in Santa Clara. Three brown-uniformed young ladies behind the sparse hotel counter exchanged glances before one of them said they weren't sure if that could be done. It wasn't the best start, I thought to myself. I also noticed that the sun was setting; the nearby aroma of food being cooked was reminding me of the promised supper at the motel. There was a restaurant to one side of the lobby here, where four more brown-dressed ladies stood, watching our plight, perhaps hoping we'd be stuck there so that at least one of the restaurant's empty tables would have patrons. However, the buffet at Motel Los Canneyes is notable for its quality and selection, so we both had our hearts set on that. We knew it would be our last chance before the next few days of unknown travelling and eating.

One of the clerks finally decided to call the local operator, who was told the whole story of our misfortune, then was asked if she could connect us with the car rental agency in Santa Clara. All of this was done exclusively in Spanish, with not one of them admitting to knowing a single word of English.

After a fair length of time we were told the phone was ringing, but there was no answer. This called for Plan B, which I'd been thinking about since the start of our ordeal.

"Can you call a taxi for us here in town?" I asked the desk ladies. The one doing the phoning laughed and they all shook their heads; apparently there were none. "Alright, how about a private car to rent," I asked, "for a trip to Santa Clara?" More head shaking. Again they said there were none. I tried to tell them in my frugal Spanish that I've seen cars on the streets each time I've driven through this town, and that I can't believe some of their owners wouldn't gladly make an evening run for some quick cash.

Nope, not available, they insisted. Then, one of the waitresses suggested phoning the police station to ask them what to do. That's when I realized these young ladies were not long out of their hotel training courses and in no way wanted to take responsibility for anything that hadn't been listed in their course books, which in this case apparently included tourists needing something other than room and board.

Finally a middle aged lady came out from a back office, dressed in the same brown uniform but apparently with enough seniority to take charge. Yes, of course, the police must be phoned if a tourist has problems. "Hello Police, here is the Hotel Mariotta and we have a tourist whose car is broken. He wants to know if there is a car in Remedios that he can hire to drive him to Santa Clara. Yes? Yes? No? There is no such thing available in Remedios? I will tell him. What should he do? You don't know? I will tell him. Good." She hung up and gave me a look of sorrow. "He says there are no autos to hire in this town." Then she suddenly glanced up at the ceiling and thought for a moment before she said, "You want to hire a private car? Wait, just one moment." The girls all stood around with an air of expectancy, eager to see how this old pro would solve the challenging situation. I wanted to walk away and flag down one of the old American rigs that periodically rumbled by on the streets outside (we were at a main corner). I wanted to wave some American cash at the driver and say, "Santa Clara - quick, for the buffet." But another part of me was of a mind like the girls, curious to let this scene play itself out.

"Hello Rosita, it's Maria. Yes, I'm fine, how are you? Yes, he's fine, and he's working. Oh is he? You don't say." She looked at the girls and made a face, then raised her eyebrows and nodded towards the earpiece. We could her the loud voice at the other end, but there was so much static that I couldn't make out a word and I sensed the girls couldn't either. Maria gave us clues by the way she kept making faces, shrugging her shoulders, nodding her head. Now and then she looked at me and made quick, jerking movements as if to say, "I wish she'd hurry up." Rosita apparently had a lot to tell Maria and it mainly had to do with her husband, though I doubt that he would have liked having it broadcast to the hotel lobby, including the local girls and foreign tourists. Maria managed to get a few words in edgewise, mainly to ask if Rosita's Jorge wanted to make some money taking a couple of tourists for a drive in his car. To Santa Clara. Oh, he won't go that far? How far will he go? Not far? Oh, because the car won't start? And because he's at the sugar mill, working? Oh well."

Having cleared that up, Rosita apparently continued with her gossip, while the hotel lady tried to say goodbye and hang up. I finally went outside to see if I could get hold of a car on my own. Okan had stood by ours to make sure no other passing vehicles threatened to damage it. Hearing the situation, he said we should try to start the motor once more, so I suggested he go ahead, thinking perhaps his touch might be different than mine, but he got the same lack of results.

"Pech!" said a voice in clear German behind me, meaning "tough luck." Normally I don't respond to that language in public; perhaps I have a subconscious desire to keep my distance from a place that is otherwise so remote to my daily life. But in this case I appreciated the tone of sympathy, all the more so when I turned and saw that it came from a plain-dressed young black Cuban with a big friendly smile. "Jawohl, Pech!" I replied, nodding my head and smiling back with resignation.

"Mensch, sprechen Sie Deutsch?" he eagerly wanted to know, so I told him, "I can, but only if we drop the 'Sie' and call each other 'Du.'" I find German sort of a stuffy language, and consider one of its stuffiest parts to be the different way people are addressed, depending on how familiar you are with them. I always figure Du is you, and that's good enough for me. He agreed immediately and said, "Of course, are we not friends?" To that we shook hands, while I learned his name is Pedro. He didn't mention that Spanish actually has a similar custom with the words "tu" and "usted."

"You have no idea how much this means to me," he explained a few moments later. "It's been six years since I've spoken German with anyone other than my wife." Your wife? "Yes, she is from Poland." And she lives here in Cuba? "Yes, about a kilometer from here, do you want to come and meet her?" Well no, I started to say, but he already understood, taking me by the elbow and whispering, "Of course, you have a problem, what can I do to help?" I asked if there were any private cars for hire in town, to which he said, "Certainly." But when I told him we wanted to get to Santa Clara right away, he whistled low and looked at me as if I'd said Miami or Paris.

"That is a *long* drive. I will have to ask around to see who has enough gas and a good enough motor for such a distance." He told us to wait by our car, leaving a large plastic bag full of red beans plus a small jug of kerosene. I told Okan that I had a good notion just to rent a room in this nice old hotel, eat at their restaurant, then continue in the morning. But it would mean wasting the money I'd already paid for our room at the Los Canneyes and I didn't feel we could afford that. Also, our baggage and personal gear was there, and besides, as I get older I find myself less willing to make such sudden changes in my plans, even in constantly changing Cuba.

About that time one of the uniformed girls looked out the hotel door and said I had a telephone call. For a moment I was baffled. Who knew I was here, except maybe the cop? But it was the Havanautos man in Santa Clara, who listened to our problem, then asked a few obvious questions about such things as an empty gas tank or broken wires. I said we'd already checked all that, were tired of waiting around, and were about to head for the motel with a hired car. Suddenly he got quite excited, insisting that we must stay by the rental vehicle and wait for him, that otherwise it might be stripped, or at least have its wheels stolen. It took me a while to convince him that it was fairly safe, sitting right out in front of the town's only hotel. Still, he insisted he'd be there "in an hour" to fix either the car or to pick us up. I told him not to expect us waiting.

Pedro was back when I stepped out of the hotel, trying without much luck to communicate with Okan in German and Spanish. The moment he saw me he called, "I have found a car and driver." Nobody with a big old Buick or a '47 DeSoto like I'd hoped, but instead with an ugly white Russian Lada, the skinny and elderly Spanish driver looking around nervously before getting out and coming over when Pedro waved to him.

"He wants $45 for the trip and needs some of it now to buy extra gas," Pedro announced, at which point I swallowed hard and came near to being more flexible with my plans. But when I told him the Havanautos man had called to say he'd be here to get us in an hour he just laughed and said, "I know my Cuban people. You'll be lucky if he shows up by tomorrow morning!" I had three options at that moment and none of them looked particularly good, but I had to make a choice right away. Finally I pulled out a twenty and said, "Here, tell him to hurry up, but I'll only pay forty altogether." The driver agreed, then said he'd have to get not only gas, but also some extra tires. In a moment he was gone, though the Lada didn't sound exactly like a Porsche when it took off.

"Thank you for agreeing to go with this car," Pedro said, "because this is becoming the best day of the whole year for me. Not only do you speak with me in German, but I have also gotten to meet Winnetou!" At that he looked proudly at Okan, conspicuous at 6'3", his long braids probably making him the closest thing to an old time Indian warrior Pedro could have hoped to see. During his three years in East Germany some time back, he'd read several books by the famous author Karl May in which the hero is a big Indian named Winnetou. "Oh, how I wish my wife and children could meet you two," he said several times, smiling with obvious delight.

Before our driver got back, we pushed the Nissan to the hotel side of the narrow street and parked it more safely behind a government car whose driver was the only occupant on the hotel's guest register. Pedro said the Llada would probably use 30 liters for the round trip, with a black market price of about a dollar each in their town. When it pulled up I let Pedro sit in front while Okan and I performed yoga to get into the cramped back seat. I thought it might be safer back there, since I correctly guessed that the driver would go fast. Quite worrisome to trust our lives that way to an elderly little stranger on Cuba's crowded and narrow highways at night, but what could we do? Among the nearest of several close calls was a fellow on a bicycle, no lights or reflectors, who suddenly loomed up out of the darkness as we were careening down a steep hillside, him wobbling all over the road either from too much speed, too much drink, or both.

After we got going, I asked Pedro to tell us something about Cuba. He laughed and said, "You want to know about the Cuban women?" I told him that would do for a start, so he began. "Well, you are a couple of handsome gentlemen, so you would have no problem getting any kind of Cuban women you want - black, white, mulatto - they would all go with you because they are all very friendly. You are tourists, so they know that you have things that you might give them. But even without that, Cuban women are naturally friendly to men. But you have to be very careful if the woman has a husband, because Cubans also get very jealous. I think it is the main cause of trouble in Cuba, fighting and killing over women. We don't have robberies, kidnappings, or such things, but we often fight over women!"

While I translated this to Okan, Pedro told the driver what he'd said to me in German about Cuban women, which caused the driver to get a glint in his eyes as he kissed the tips of his right hand fingers.

"German men and women are much different from Cubans," Pedro went on. "I think many of them lose interest in each other after they get married and have children. On the other hand, German women sure do like black men, at least the women I met. Sometimes I got invited home for a meal by one of the Germans I worked with, or by a fellow student at the technical school. The wives of these guys would often make eyes at me, but the men didn't get mad, one or two even left so that their wives would be alone with me. I was nervous about this at first, but the women always said it was alright, and there was never any trouble. I'd be killed for doing that here in Cuba."

Pedro said the best part was that all his life his tastes have been for white women, that he thinks they are much easier to please than black women, though he admitted that he didn't know this first hand. "To be very frank with you," he said in educated German, "although my whole family is pure black, I've never made love to a black woman. My friends tell me that the good ones make love to you all night so that you're tired and can't go to work the next morning." He laughed again good naturedly and then told the driver, who also laughed.

Pedro said he studied textile technology in East Germany, back in the years when Cuba was that country's little Latin brother and lots of Cubans went there to study and work. He met his Polish wife at the school and brought her to Cuba expecting to help set up textile plants for the government. But funds never became available, so instead of being boss over a quality manufacturing process he works as a mechanic on rough Russian-made harvesting machinery at a nearby sugar mill. He's highly dissatisfied with the situation but says that for now there's nothing else he can do.

"The Revolution was finished by the time I was born, so I never experienced life in Cuba before then. But my parents said to me I would never have been sent to another country and trained as a textile technician under Batista, even though he was part African himself. He was just a mulatto, and they always had more chances, while us pure blacks were just one or two steps up from slavery, still working for other people on their land. My grandfather actually was a slave as a boy, until about 1880. Nowadays, there is no difference among us Cubans as to the colour of our skin, except maybe in sexual tastes, like mine. This discrimination that they talk about in South Africa, or in the U.S., we have nothing like that here. I am just the same as my white neighbors, or my white wife, we all treat each other the same. Sure, sometimes we hate each other, but there are some blacks I hate more than any whites. Anyway, not much hate, mostly we get along with each other, just to survive."

At this point the driver interrupted and wanted to hear what Pedro said, so he was given another short summary. He then told Pedro several questions that he wanted answered by us, the usual things like country of origin, occupation, where from and where to. I was grateful that Pedro didn't translate most of this request, but instead continued answering my questions. I felt sorry for the driver, who obviously had never carried tourists in his car before and was eager to learn something about them. Pedro himself said he hadn't ridden in an auto for over a year. He shook his head and chuckled when he told us this, so I asked if he and the driver were good friends. He surprised me by saying, "Until this evening, I've never met this man before. He is as new to me as you are. I met him through a friend of a friend, when I went out to help you. If it had not been for my friends he would not have done this. No one else wanted to make this long journey, especially at night." I asked if it is true that people can now earn dollars on their own, as long as they don't use anyone else's labour.

"No, for instance, for the driver to do this officially he needs to buy a taxi license, and they are not easy to get. For that reason, if we were stopped by the police I would ask you to tell them that he is doing this for you just as a favour. Of course, it is no problem if you give him a gift of $40 at the end." When the driver heard what was said he shook his head and insisted there would still be a problem if we were stopped by the police.

"They would know that it requires at least 30 liters of petrol to drive to Santa Clara and back, yet by looking at my identification papers and ration book, they would see that I've only received 20 liters since the start of this year (five litres per month), so they would ask where the rest of the fuel came from. For that I could be fined or even put in jail." A sobering thought as we barrelled along through the night.

The opportunity to study in Germany came to Pedro through the military officer's training school in Havana, after he finished grade nine. They wanted him to attend a more advanced school in Santiago de Cuba, but he told them that he needed to care for his elderly parents and didn't want to be so far away, so they kept him in Havana three more years instead. "It was like they were punishing me, keeping me from going home." Cubans have much respect for their elders and show great care for their parents, so this part was tough in Pedro's life.

"As soon as my schooling was finished they sent me to Angola for two years. I was specially trained for my mission, but I can't tell you anything about it. They are still very strict about us talking. I was involved in a lot of fighting, and I wonder now why we even did it. We went there thinking the Angolans were our brothers, but they are very much different from us. Sure, we all looked somewhat the same, but their way of thinking and living is way different from what we know in Cuba, much more cold-blooded and primitive. In Cuba we are well educated, while most of them had never been to school. They knew little else but their tribal rules and superstitions, so it was really hard to fight a war alongside of them; our country lost a lot by trying it. I don't see anything that we gained. Several of my friends were killed over there, and not just by bullets, even by snakes and diseases. Another problem was that for two years all I saw were black women, and I never went to bed with one of them, so you can imagine how I liked it!"

Since Pedro was being so open with his thoughts, I asked him how he felt about the future of Cuba's current system and its boss. I spoke this last part very carefully since the words sound about the same in German, English and Spanish and the poor driver still thought we were working on *his* questions, not talking about Cuban politics. Pedro would now and then tell him a few things in Spanish but they barely covered what we were really talking about.

He said - like so many others - that "the boss" had been good for his country up to a certain point in history, but that now he is not able to bend enough with the needs of today's world. "Hardly anyone I know still believes in the system or in the communist party," he said with resignation.

"Those of us who are younger want more of the modern world, but I think it will take a new leader to satisfy that. We don't want violence or revolution, we just want some big changes, with freedom, dignity and respect for everyone. We want to elect our own leaders. We also want to make a decent living from our work. Those are the things that Americans and others in the world take for granted. But we don't want Americans, or even Cuban Americans, to come here and try directing our changes. We want to do it ourselves, with the pride that Fidel has given to us."

Ironically, Pedro has a younger brother whose life *is* the communist party - he's an official in the party's youth movement, and apparently he lives better than the average Cuban. The state gives him a car to drive, a newer apartment, clothes and some special foods. Not a lot, but the difference shows, Pedro says, although the brother is generous and helps his family. He makes 460 pesos a month, about double the average wage, but he has no more access to U.S. dollars than a sugar mill mechanic. This brother thinks the communist party will survive and lead Cuba into a better future. He agrees with Fidel, saying that political movements come and go, and that the time of communism will come again, at which point Cuba will be ready to lead. Pedro says such beliefs are very much in the minority, yet from my own travels and visits around the country I feel there is some possibility in these words. A form of socialism or communalism may yet be in the future for all of humankind. Worldwide shortages of crucial things could force everyone to live more simply, using whatever is at hand, as the Cubans have already been doing. They could, one day soon, be giving the rest of us seminars on simple living!

What a relief it was to enter our neon-lit motel oasis, the driver begging to park some distance away where it was darker, so as to be less observed by the entryway crowd, which no doubt included some "special" observers.

A short, intense relationship came suddenly to a quick end, as we paid, said goodbye, and rushed to the restaurant with just minutes to spare. "No problema," said the head waiter cheefully, saving us a table while we rushed to our rooms for a quick clean up. Everything we ate and drank for that next hour tasted twice as good because of all the hassle we went through to get to it.

April 9, 1995
Hotel Las Americas
Santiago de Cuba

It's Sunday night and we're in downtown Santiago, surrounded by the sounds of music and traffic again, but otherwise in a noticeably different atmosphere than anywhere else we've been in Cuba. For one thing, we're at the opposite end of the island from where we usually go. The Sierra Maestra range stands impressively between here and the rest of the country, sort of like the Rocky Mountains stand between the east and west back home. Havana and the nation's government have always seemed far away to those who live here, as is Ottawa for those of us in the west of Canada, or like western Americans feel separated by the Rockies from Washington D.C.

The distant rough highways that lead towards Santiago de Cuba from various parts of the island come together into a single, wide freeway that actually goes over a mountain pass. It might not make someone from Switzerland nervous, but nevertheless it comes as a great surprise to those who imagine Cuba as consisting of only flat lands and palm lined beaches. Gran Piedra, highest peak of the impressive Sierra Maestra, reaches 5,600 feet into the Caribbean sky, and at that height you're mountain climbing even in the Rockies. No wonder people at this end of the island consider themselves slightly aloof from the rest.

Driving through that mountain pass towards Santiago reminded me of Cajon Pass in Southern California, with similar dry hillsides looking like immense loaves of bread, sloping down into luscious green canyons, both places having mainline railroad tracks going through their midst. In Cuba the freeway takes the high route, while tracks of the FCC could be seen now and then where they snaked along further below. During my brief stint as locomotive fireman on the Union Pacific Railroad, I made a few trips in the cabs of diesel locomotives over Cajon Pass in the early sixties. Going through this part of Cuba made me wish there was a long-distance dome liner like our old "City of St. Louis," instead of just the FCC's plain overnight coach train.

I should mention the yellow frog that was sitting quietly in our shower stall the other night. A genuine bright yellow frog, about average size, looking like an amphibious Andy Warhol. It was back at that funky place called San Jose del Lago, where last year the two pretty desk clerks offered us "more" than room service. This year we got yellow frogs instead, two of them. Pretty creatures, though their yellow skin took a while to get used to, especially since it was only a few inches from my eyes when I first discovered it. I was well into an enjoyable cold water shower at the end of a long day, and I'll admit that it took me aback for an instant, say about a foot a back! But when I looked at it more carefully and realized it definitely was a living yellow frog and not somebody's prank, I enjoyed the unusual experience. To my surprise it didn't move away, even when I raised my arms during washing. What's more, when I got out of the shower and went to call Okan, there was a second one attached to the back side of the bathroom door. Said Okan, who had just observed a lizard go under his bed, "This place is a real zoo!" In the morning there were horses grazing on the lawn outside, with weird lake birds squawking up in the trees.

The room we have here now at the Las Americas is substantially better, with no bugs or frogs at all, except for a few mosquitoes. But we're paying about four times the rate, though that includes a TV on which we can watch American movies, even CNN, through a satellite dish. It feels strange to sit in Cuba and watch uncensored news, knowing the throngs of people outside cannot. I'm tempted to turn the set so that it faces the open window, then crank CNN up real loud. But I suppose that would mean getting a quick visit from some of the police we can see from our window, directing traffic and walking on patrol.

Not so long ago the Las Americas was Santiago's best hotel, but these days its rather open accessibility has been superseded right across the street by the post-modern fortress-like Hotel Santiago, whose five star high-rise rooms are virtually hidden behind one-way glass, with the hotel's lower levels consisting of solid brown walls that barely indicate what's inside. Between it and us there's a busy main road with a wide, green strip of grass and trees down the middle. At night this road is dimly lit, but at the top of the hill just past here a spotlight beams on the huge statue of revolutionary hero Che Guevara.

Speaking of hills, the whole city is built on them, with steep narrow streets like San Francisco's, from the summits of which you can look down over the city's rooftops and into Santiago Bay far below. There are railroad tracks on some of these streets, though no fabled little cable cars, nor anything else except the usual Cuban traffic, of which the bikes must frequently crash on those shiny strips of steel and their adjacent ruts. Considering the rustic mechanical condition of many cars and trucks, it makes me nervous to go down these steep hills with somebody else behind. I try to be extra careful at intersections, having had one really close call already when a small Lada zipped past our hood on a non-stop downhill run. Thank heavens these rental Nissans are light and have good brakes. It was startling to notice how quick an accident could happen. I don't think there were five seconds from the time I saw this car until it was again out of my sight.

"Where the Revolution Began" reads a large poster as you enter Santiago. Another one says, "Yesterday Revolution, Today Tourism, Always Heroic." Santiago de Cuba is the old home town of Bacardi Rum; you can still see the distinctive fortress-like factory, its antique walls painted a faded pastel yellow, where workers now produce a potent drink called Havana Club, with the capitalistic Bacardi name long gone. The Bacardi mansion, in another part of the city, has become the Palace of Pioneers, where Cuban students receive military education along with exposure to art and culture.

It was here in Santiago that young Fidel announced to the world in 1953 that he had his own ideas for Cuba's future, as he led a troop of idealistic students and friends in a bungled attack on Batista's Moncada Garrison. Although easily repulsed and nearly wiped out in the process, the actions of Fidel and his followers have been the cause of national celebrations on July 26 ever since. Fidel landed in prison at the time and would have been executed if Batista had been more ruthless. I wonder how

Santiago de Cuba is the island's second-largest city, with steep streets lined by old buildings similar to those in San Francisco. Santiago Bay lies between the city and the wild and rugged Sierra Maestra ranges seen in the background, from which Fidel and his Revolutionaries launched many raids.

many times the General later regretted that missed opportunity? We drove down to the dockside passenger station for photos but learned that no trains were due to come or go from Santiago until late afternoon, so we decided to get out of the city and continue on our way through the Cuban countryside. We headed east to Guantanamo, partly just to say we'd been there, but also to have a quick look at one of the least known sugar mills, although we'd heard its people were not so friendly. From there we had planned to take an alternate route north to Central Rafael Freyre, our favorite place of all.

Part of the drive to Guantanamo is over a wide freeway, nearly empty of traffic, but seemingly ideal in case of sudden need (as in military). The town itself was sizeable for Cuba, but not at all impressive. If American sailors got to come here on shore leave back in the days before Fidel, you wouldn't know it now. We were the only tourists in sight, and people stared at us on every corner. My one desire was to get a picture of the railroad station, preferably with a train, but even there I was disappointed. The building was ugly and modern, looking more like an abandoned third world prison compound than the railway base of a famous town. It was surrounded by bits of barbed wire fencing, with a total lack of trains, train cars or even personnel. Then I spotted a pair of legs on the second floor balcony of a squat concrete yard tower, making me think that perhaps here was someone who could tell me if there were any trains due.

Climbing up the partly broken concrete staircase I found a door at the top locked, with the reclining legs belonging to a figure that turned out to be a big, pathetic looking grownup, staring at me with a blank, dark face that said something wasn't all there, a huge, weird belly button extending noticeably out from under his dirty and ragged T-shirt. His reply to my question about anyone else being at work was so eerie and unintelligible that I said thanks and hurried back down to the car, looking back once or twice with a feeling as though he might have gobbled all the real railroaders up. I had actually hoped to track down a rumor that some antique American-made Brill rail buses were running out of Guantanamo, but this encounter, combined with approaching dark clouds and possible rain made us decide to get out of town and head north.

Rain fell harder the further we went, while our two lane highway got ever more narrow and winding. On hindsight, this was the first route we've travelled in our visits to Cuba that hadn't been driven before by someone we knew.

We did stop by a couple of cops, parked with their little grey Lada in the shelter of some roadside trees, to ask if we were on the right road to Sagua de Tanamo. But in the growing rain all they said was, "Si," and motioned us on. Surely they must have known what the conditions were like up ahead. We soon entered an area that was practically unpopulated, with the rain probably keeping at home what little traffic there might have been. Continuous sharp curves and steep hills forced me to drive slowly but I still found at times that the car would slide sideways or start to spin on the steeper grades.

I got tense and sweaty - somewhat like driving our own mountain roads during midwinter glare ice, but in this case definitely more unsettling for me.

Parts of this narrow jungle highway consisted of concrete slabs which seemed even more slippery than the asphalt. As we were headed up a particularly steep slope into a misty forest, we suddenly lost our momentum on a sharp curve, at the same time facing a grade more severe than any other, one side of which dropped off into a steep overgrown ravine dotted with palm trees. We'd nearly reached the top of this incredible grade when the car stalled completely and the wheels started spinning. I quickly put on the brakes, but they failed to hold us, as we began slipping down backwards. This all happened very fast; and when I noticed that we were going sideways I let off the brakes for a moment in order to straighten up. We did, but with the result of faster speed, so that when I again stepped down on the brakes the whole car just spun around in the snap of a finger, leaving us - to our amazement - facing directly downhill. We thus continued to roll and slide at a rapidly accelerating pace until we reached the bottom, from where I just kept right on driving as though it had been my intention to turn back all along, except that now I was shaking like a leaf in the wind. We barely allowed ourselves to speculate on what might have happened if the car had spun only partway around, with us going into the hidden ravine and its many tree trunks.

So that's how come I'm writing this tonight at the Hotel Las Americas, back in Santiago de Cuba, which we visited earlier, but thought that by now we'd have left far behind. Nice room at a reasonable price, letting us finally relax. While checking in, we were given the "once over" by half a dozen cops in blue uniforms who were sitting comfortably in the downstairs lobby watching a recent Hollywood movie about an airline hijacking on satellite T.V. (normally off limits to Cubans).

To make up for the photo work I had intended to do around Guantanamo, we went back out a while ago for a sunset drive around Santiago, our eyes set in the "camera viewfinder" mode, me with two Nikons and slide film, Okan with our new Hitachi Hi-8. First we went up and down the San Franciso Bay-like streets to reach the railroad station, where the crowd was thick but train action still non-existant. From there we drove through a neighborhood that went out to the edge of Santiago Bay, where a cool looking young dude sauntered over to us from a local sunset-watching crowd to beg for "un dollar." When I made no reply he upped it to two dollars, then went for five - putting on a whole show of strutting and talking in bad English to impress his audience. He reminded me of some chicanos I've seen in East L.A., or Latins in uptown New York City, the kind who look as if they'd just as soon carve you up with their push button knives than smile at you.

So, I told him, "Alright, you want a dollar, I'll take your photo," and when he agreed I jumped out of the car with my camera in hand. This took him aback for a moment or two, but when I pointed to a spot next to the water and aimed my camera, he moved there dutifully and tried to pose, but became immediately the object of whistles and catcalls from his dozen or so nearby buddies. This appeared to humiliate his pride, so he turned sideways to my camera, refusing to look anymore into the lens, getting more of that "cut you up" look than he already had. I snapped the photo hurriedly and gave him the dollar, which brought more whistles and catcalls, leading him to demand very firmly that he wanted five. When I said 'no' just as firmly he went to pleading about his poverty and his need for a pair of shoes, showing me loose soles on the ones he had on. But I'd decided early in the trip that a dollar per stranger would have to do, else there wouldn't be enough to go around. It's still a week's wages for the average Cuban.

Leaving the crowd by the water I had to slow down for a bunch of young boys who were playing baseball, but stopped to stare wishfully at us, then to shout in through the open window, "gimme a dollar!" So I stopped, backed up, hopped out with my camera and told them, "Alright, one picture, one dollar," to which they gleefully agreed. Without any coaching, they immediately formed two lines as if they posed for pictures every day. Sunset on the bay was visible in the background, while a fill-in flash brought out the details of the kids, up front. Several people watched this brief encounter from their doors and windows, but when I finally pulled out the promised dollar bill I noticed a sinister looking older man walking around the edge of the boys. Neighborhood watch committee, was my guess, but I just ignored him. Instead, I asked the boys in Spanish, "Which one of you will be Jeffe?" or boss, to which a quiet fellow immediately raised his hand, though several others then followed him. I told him, "Alright, you'll be in charge of this dollar, but it's for all of you here, not just for him alone." I told them to go buy a pack of chicle or a bag of candy, whatever the local black market has to offer for that precious dollar. They had applauded each of the two times I snapped the shutter, and now they applauded again. It seemed they had been trained in expressing their enthusiasm, though probably in school and for a much different purpose. At any rate, as one they all said thank you, in English, while I got back into the idling car and drove on, remarking to Okan what an easy and fun way this was for adding a little zing to an evening, especially for those kids.

Do you remember me talking last year about "Chiquita," the little beauty at Rafael Freyre that Okan and I fell so much in love with? The one we tried to rent? Well, this time we did it, went all the way through with it, riding her clear to Puerto Blanca and back. You do, of course, recall that "Chiquita" is a sweet little locomotive - Rafael Freyre's tiny 1882 Baldwin 0-6-0 switcher. She's a rare machine, seen by very few, and until now never ridden by tourists. Last year we did pay to rent her, but only got a few photos in the yard before the water pump gave out and they had to shut her down. All we got was a "sorry," but no refund. Well, this time there was no need for the sorry, thank heavens.

We're staying in rather plush surroundings, at the Hotel Rio de Luna, not far from the seaside village of Guardelavaca, since last year's Don Lino resort is at the moment only history. All its beach side cabins are getting a complete rebuild, after somebody decided the place was too choice for such Russian-era economical accommodations, though lots of people are going to miss it. Here, we've got a big room with satellite TV (which we don't watch), two queen sized beds (the first we've seen in Cuba) and a sliding glass door to a balcony looking out over flowers towards the beach and ocean below. All this for 40 something dollars, a special rate because they're just starting up.

We unloaded our baggage at the room, took time out for showers and some cold juice, then drove to the mill office at Rafael Freyre for a visit with our friend, Rodolfo. Again there were the strange feelings of leaving the luxurious beach side hotel and in just minutes entering a much different world of poor people and a turn of the century narrow gauge railway. That's why I'm trying so hard to encourage the idea of a theme park based on tourist railroading to all those who'll listen, especially Rodolfo.

The price to rent "Chiquita " is still $60, but this time Rodolfo said they would guarantee the engine to run, and what's more, we could ride behind it! He proudly said, "We built a car for it, just like you suggested." Last year I gave him a copy of my *Narrow Gauge Railway Scenes* book, which includes photos of special cars used by various lines to carry tourists. The Rafael Freyre crews had taken an old spare caboose of steel and fixed it up to allow better viewing, bolting down half a dozen seats inside its roofed shelter, with another dozen out on the open deck, thus making a practical carriage for special occasions. He said it had also been officially decided that the little engine and its car would be operated on the least travelled route, the scenic branch line to Puerto Vita, at whose dockside little "Chiquita" performed her switching work for many decades.

We nearly had to cash in our guarantee, for within an hour after getting the locomotive fired up it again had water problems, this time with the injector. Rodolfo apologized profusely and offered to let us use one of the bigger road engines instead, but we insisted that it had to be little "Chiquita," so we agreed to try again the next morning.

Sure enough, we got out of Santa Lucia at 7:30 a.m. same time as the day's first Uvila train, both our engines puffing and smoking side by side for a couple of thrilling moments until our line branched off to the left towards the coast, while the other went further inland. It was a pleasant trip, being pulled by a 113-year old locomotive that occasionally tooted its little peanut whistle and tried to sound very important. It was a quiet ride, as far as steam engines go, at little more than foot running speed, and with no real purpose other than to haul us two around. About halfway to the port we stopped on a little bridge over a pretty river, where everyone on board joined into a bucket brigade in order to fill up the engine's water tank. Our crew was an interesting mix of an elderly engineer named Dima, quite a young fireman, the elderly chief of the locomotive shop, a middle aged fellow from the mill office who was chief of public affairs, our friend the traffic chief Rodolfo, plus a pretty young lady in tight blouse and shorts who said she was a receptionist, though no one explained exactly what her role aboard the train was supposed to be. Perhaps she was intended as a flower of sorts in an interesting vase?

As happened last year, renting "Chiquita" gave us more or less free run with our cameras inside the normally off-limits shop and mill yard. We rode completely up and down in the yard during an initial test run of the train, thus getting to record the whole antique layout on video. The port area at the other end of the branch is even more off-limits to tourists and cameras than the sugar mill, mainly because of its use by the military. But the armed guard just unlocked the gate and waved us through, as our cameras rolled with the train to the very end of the line. It just so happened that a group of naval officers picked that moment to show up, immediately heading our way. We put the cameras down and thought there would be trouble, but instead their technical instincts had told them that "Chiquita" was quite old and unusual, so they wanted to know what it was all about. When

One of Cuba's rarest steam locomotives, little "Chiquita" at Rafael Freyre, a narrow gauge 0-6-0 built by Baldwin of Philadelphia in 1882. When my son and I rented her in 1995 she was 113, but had no problem rolling along with a home-made "tourist car." Here we were stopped for photos, halfway to sea on the Puerto Branch.

told that a Canadian father and son had rented the train for a round trip, the officers saluted respectfully and didn't even look at our cameras, even when I snapped a picture with them in it. The boss agreed that our photo privileges around the off-limit shop area could be extended after we arrived back with "Chiquita" so that we could take a couple of night time photos as well. In my limited Spanish I tried to explain my style of taking such photos, which is a follows: I need a parked, steaming engine, preferably two; also one or two crewmen, standing still by the engine cab as if ready for work. I also need someone aboard at least one of the engines to flash the headlight momentarily. If it stays on too long it burns out the picture. With my camera on a tripod I then open the shutter for a time exposure. Unfortunately, most Cubans aren't familiar with such a technique and these guys just couldn't comprehend it from my description. It takes a while for me to go around and fire a flashgun two or three times at the most important parts of the scene, such as the people, the wheels, the smoke and the steam. These people had experienced standard flash pictures, so as soon as they saw mine go off, they turned, moved, or walked away, thinking the picture was taken. My open shutter thus also recorded their movements, though only as ghostly shadows.

Another experience in the Rafael Freyre area was far more rewarding than even the pleasant travelling with "Chiquita." It took place at the very centre of our most favorite train photographing scene, a location we call the "Grand Curve." You've seen a big enlargement of it hanging on the wall over my desk since last year. (Note: it is now also on this book's cover). We spent four afternoons hiking to and from a hot, dry hillside to get that great view of the Grand Curve. One of my main goals while visiting Cuba this time was to go back again to that hillside and try once more, still yearning for the ideal combination of late afternoon sunlight and a passing steam train, along with blue sky and a few nice clouds, plus a bit of smoke from the locomotive. Last year we came close several times, but never did get all those factors at once. Never in my lifetime of photographing have I come near putting this much effort into one single picture, though fortunately this place offers something far beyond what my film and lens can capture - a warming of the spiritual senses, the soothing sight of forests and mountains that for me is Cuba's equivalent of our own family land in the Canadian Rockies.

We drove to this hillside right after our visit with Rodolfo on the first afternoon here, since it was sunny and the potential was right. Early each morning two trains pass outbound through our Grand Curve, though the lighting is wrong at that time and both steam locomotives are running backwards. Near noon they return with fresh sugar cane, this time heading up their trains properly, but the bright overhead sun makes for stark and unpleasant photos. In the early afternoon they both run out backwards again, returning "properly" - and into the lowering sun - sometime before supper, often just before sunset. The biggest challenge to getting this ideal photo is, that the long days of tropical heat often create clouds all across the Caribbean in the late afternoon, and more often than not these clouds block the sun just when its orange light begins to bathe our hillside scene, or worse yet, just when the train comes around our Grand Curve. Imagine the frustration!

So here we were back again, climbing steeply through that dry thorn brush, looking down from the hillside at the lush green valley below, savoring the fresh air and natural scents in the shimmering heat.

Then someone from the farms below called out to us, so right away I answered back, thinking perhaps it was our friend Rafael, whom I photographed last year with his oxen. It felt good to approach the little clearing where we usually set up our cameras, and we were eager to recline and enjoy that favorite scene in meditation and silence.

Then I noticed three individuals slowly making their way uphill from where we'd heard the shouting, probably figuring we were friends. "When they get here, I'll pretend I can't understand a word of Spanish and maybe they'll leave us alone," I told Okan. It was a selfish response, but this particular hilltop was the only outdoor place we've found in all of Cuba where we can sit for more than a few minutes without being disturbed.

"Don't forget that these are people from the land, like us," Okan reprimanded me, "so at least try to be a *little* friendly." I swallowed hard and agreed, knowing he was right, but still not fully prepared to give up my quiet retreat.

The first one to reach us was a muscular fellow with black hair and mustache, fancy trousers, good running shoes on his feet, his chest bare, and a typical friendly Cuban smile on his face. He shook hands and asked our country, along with some other questions. He had my attention so fully that I barely noticed the other two fellows quietly smiling in the background. He looked and talked like one of those suave hustlers around tourist areas, so I asked him where he was from.

"Havana," he said, to which I burst out laughing. It seemed ridiculous to be way out here in such a beautiful, remote part of Cuba, where everyone seems so personable, only to encounter a city-dweller from such a huge place. Somewhat disappointedly I said, "So you are not a campesino?" He shook his head, then pointed at the other two and said, "*They* are campesinos."

It was then that we met Emilio and Enrique, first cousins, poor dirt farmers, neighbours on adjoining bits of land, users of a common ox for plowing and hauling. They had been coming up here to our favorite hillside since childhood and enjoying the same beautiful view. When I told them how much we liked it there and showed them pictures of a somewhat similar scene from our own homeland, we suddenly discovered a very strong mutual bond. For the next while we smiled, talked and even hugged, forgetting all about the Havana dude, who turned out to be a visiting in-law. Not only did these two guys grow up and live in our fa'orite spot, but Emilio's father, with the same name, just retired after a lifetime career running engines on the favorite narrow gauge railroad. Cousin Enrique, who was older, ironically *lost* his dad on the railroad, on that very same curve, when he drank too much homebrew one night and didn't get off the tracks in time. "No bitterness," said Enrique. "It was sad, but we knew that it was his own fault."

The four of us visited as though we were long-lost friends, with hardly a thought to the fact that they spoke not a word of

English and between Okan and I there wasn't a kindergartener's worth of Spanish. Yet with many hand signs and lots of enthusiasm the stories and ideas just flowed, as we learned about each other and explored some pretty deep topics. I was amazed at how

Three Amigos. During one of our pleasant hillside visits looking down at the farming community of La Caridad de Bariay, in northeastern Cuba. In the straw hat is Enrique Santiesteban Fernandez, a poor but happy farmer who lives with his wife and two children in the little cluster of buildings just beyond his left shoulder. In the distance between Enrique and I is the home of his younger cousin Emilio Ramos Santiesteban, better known as Pancho, who farms with his dad. Their plots of vegetables and bananas are down at the bottom of this hill. Okan and I like to come here with our cameras, often just to sit quietly and enjoy the fantastic view, a highlight being the passing of an occasional steam-powered sugarcane train on the narrow gauge line curving through the midst of it all. The distant pointed peak between Enrique's head and mine is appropriately named "La Tetta."

smart and wise these two dirt farmers were. It helped that I had
our family album in the camera bag, with their version already
spread out for real all around us. The two trains came and went
during our long conversations, everyone pausing and watching
quietly during the brief time of their passing while we picked up
our cameras and went to work.

As we got ready to pack up and leave, Enrique asked how
many more days we'd be in the area. When I told him, he invited
us back for our final evening and said his family would serve us
a meal. We agreed, and I mentioned that we might still be trying
for that "perfect photo." The clouds had shaded the scene both
times that afternoon when the trains arrived, but our visit made
everything otherwise seem exceptionally bright.

Thus, our last day in the countryside of Cuba turned out to be
our very best. Up on the quiet hillside of La Caridad de Bariay it
was easy to get lost in good thoughts, forgetting the world beyond, contemplating the beautiful scene before us, as splendid as
any artist could possibly put on canvas. A green carpet rolled out
from beneath our feet, dappled light and dark by the various
stands of brush and palm, here and there accented by the huts of
campesinos and their nearby fields. A few kilometers away stood
the Serros, three rocky outcrops directing one's view up into the
vast blue sky. La Teta is the most conspicuous of them, rising up
into a wooded mound, a knob of rock at its top, as if it were the
beautiful breast of a reclining woman.

A spiral of smoke rising from behind one of the secluded
farmhouses down below indicated where our new friends and
their family were roasting a pig in our honor. They said they'd
expect us after the second afternoon train passed through the
Grand Curve with its load of sugar. That's why we were back up
on that hillside, tripods set up and cameras mounted for the
fourth time this week. I thought last year's four day effort to
capture that "perfect picture" was stretching things, but the appeal of it is much stronger than my sense of reason, so every
possible afternoon this year we've pulled off the road nearby,
taken a few last swallows of bottled water (hot by that time of
day), then headed up through thorn bushes and other plants in

order to see the two trains go by, usually an hour or two later, around four or five.

Enrique and Emilio had joined us each afternoon up on the hill, but for this final occasion they stayed down below and worked their fields instead. They understood our attachment to the place - their place - and they knew from experience that the hillside is best enjoyed alone, without talking. Even on days when they did come up to sit and visit with us, there were quiet times when we all just studied the scene. Besides that, they also had the rare but much appreciated consideration to keep quiet whenever it was time for us to concentrate on our photo work. Other people at such times are quite distracting.

The two cousins headed up as soon as the second train passed

Emilio Ramos - campesino, father, grandfather, and retired engineer of Rafael Freyre's famous "Little Horse" narrow gauge locomotive - coming home from another day of working his fields with the prized family oxen, Barandero and Cassadorre. All day long the surrounding community could hear him calling out directions to his two strong workers and pals. Now and then his voice would be drowned out by the huffing, puffing, and rumbling of a steam powered sugarcane train, whistling for the crossing down in the dip behind them.

and they saw us folding up our equipment, which they wanted to carry. They seemed to rejoice with us that we'd finally had sunlight on a late afternoon train, a fitting end to our fourth and final attempt this second year. It made the upcoming meal and visit all the more poignant and unforgettable.

The older Emilio greeted us with an eager wave as we reached the tracks on the far side of the curve. Shirtless, brown and muscular, he didn't look like a retired steam engineer, especially with his slim figure and boyish grin. Adding to his macho image was the pair of husky, grey bullocks that he was leading with ropes tied to steel rings in their noses. They were the family's tractors and servants combined, clean and lean, looking healthy and

Homegrown Cuban Meal. It's been a long hot day of photo work for Okan and I, so this fresh meal brought big smiles. We had to work hard at enjoying it fully because only we were served while the rest of our extended family stood and watched - and cheered our eating! In addition to the pig, the farm food includes lettuce, yucca (somewhat like potato), tomato, cucumber and of course, a big plate of rice and beans, without which no Cuban meal is complete. Cool water was from a nearby well.

strong. It was obvious that they were a most valuable asset, helping the family to maintain their basically self-sufficient lifestyle, testimonials to their success in difficult times and challenging situations. A Kansas farmer with a new John Deere tractor couldn't be any more proud than Emilio was of them.

The family compound consists of several wooden cabins with palm thatched roofs and various little sheds. Everywhere is neat and tidy, with stone arrangements and multitudes of plants carefully tended. We were brought to the central patio and shown to a picnic table with only two chairs. On top of a pink and white flowered tablecloth were two plates with utensils, two glasses, and a pitcher of cold water. Upon our arrival, they brought out bowls of sliced tomatoes, cucumbers and lettuce, along with fried red beans, plus a plate of sliced bread. Then Enrique and young Emilio proudly brought the pig, a juicy brown suckling on a long pole and dripping from an afternoon of roasting over the open fire. Everyone made sounds and motions of delight.

We had thought this was to be a big family dinner to which we'd been invited, but it turned out instead to be a big family watching a dinner, *our* dinner, with all the eating being done just by the two of us! We said nothing, simply following their instructions, which were given frequently and with much gusto, telling us to fill up our plates, to eat as much as we could, and preferably to eat much more. They cheered and whooped whenever one of us asked for a refill - or agreed to take it as they offered it, which was constantly the case. They jeered and looked dismayed whenever I said, "Enough, I'm too full." Back home in native society there are places that have customs like this, left over I suppose from more primitive times when eating was often a case of feast or famine. We ate and ate that evening, having fortunately fasted all day, so the meal found room within both of us. The family of 12 or 14 obviously took great delight in being able to host such a couple of interesting new friends - seldom seen foreigners, at that - right inside their own home. There was not a hint of wanting to gain anything by it other than friendship. In fact, through the whole week neither Emilio nor Enrique in any way suggested that they were poor or that, to them, we were rich.

The food was finally cleared away, after we convinced them that there was absolutely no space left in our stomachs for more. Then we all sat in the fading light and exchanged pleasantries for a while through various levels of Spanish, aided by the usual hand signs, along with one brother-in-law's hotel-learned bits of English, which mostly consisted of shouting, "Okay!"

Eventually I sent Okan out to our car and told him to bring in a big blue hockey bag from the trunk. I'd spent the night before going through our remaining luggage to fill up this one with all the stuff we didn't really need back home. This included clothing, medicines, tools, food, even a toy truck for the 10 year old son of Enrique. I first gave Papa Emilio a copy of my coffee table book about Canada's most famous train, "The Canadian," with colour pictures taken by Okan and I on trips made some years ago, when he was much younger. They had apparently never seen such a fancy book before, much less had one in their farm house. The old Papa railroader nearly burst with pride, as everyone tried to look over his shoulders while he kept going back and forth through the pages. It was a great way for us to end another successful visit to the island of Cuba.

Fourth Visit to Cuba

Hotel Plaza - La Habana
March 3, 1996

Hello Okan:

You're the first one I'm going to write to this time, since you were with me on the last two trips and I sure miss your company already. No navigator or photographic assistant, no companion and best friend; I'm both excited and a bit intimidated by the thought of going around in Cuba all by myself. Am dreading the moments of loneliness, yet I know that to balance them there will also be places and people that I can get involved in without wondering if you might be getting bored. Of course, in just ten days another best friend of mine should be showing up at the airport, assuming your mom doesn't chicken out at the last moment for our 25th anniversary "vacation."

The new flight from Vancouver saved me having to go way out east to Toronto, but instead of going directly to Varadero as I'd been led to think, we stopped over for "house cleaning" at Cancun, Mexico, all of us passengers having to get off the plane for an hour - at five in the morning! Needless to say, I got little sleep on the overnight flight, the change from my soft bed in a silent mountain cabin to the barely-reclining seat in a pressurized sky cabin being simply too radical for my system. When we arrived in Varadero I walked out of the plane and into the Caribbean sunshine, not sure if it was real or just another wilderness dream. Even waiting in line for the passport check didn't feel like total reality - much different from my first time through, when I was pretty nervous about the "communist system," your brother Iniskim and I not being sure what sort of reception to expect.

Nearly fell asleep waiting for my baggage to arrive at the carousel; it took over an hour this time, and my two bags just *had* to be the very last. I was the final tourist to check out, with all four uniformed guards waiting to leave and end their shift. I fig-

ured that meant smooth sailing, especially since there were no
chalked X's on either bag, but one guy apparently hadn't
stopped anyone else yet (he was nearest to me, so I'd watched
him during my wait). He must have decided to try looking like
he was doing his job, with results similar to those in past years.
That is, he made me open the baggage, then he dug around a bit,
found one or two things of peculiar interest for which he wanted
explanations, after which he even helped zip the tightly packed
bags up. He was most curious about a plastic bag full of Quaker
Harvest breakfast cereal, which he finally poked open with a finger so that some of it spilled into my folded clothing, from
where he started scooping it up apologetically to put back in. I
got him to stop, preferring the mess in my clothes to having my
future food get sifted by his airport hands. He didn't notice the
huge pile of photo prints, for which I might have been charged a
duty, since I hear that all items to be left in Cuba are now assessed at 100%. It's pretty obvious that I brought these pictures
to leave here (along with several dozen shirts, socks and other
clothing, plus two spinning rods and reels).

Had a good visit on the flight down with a bearded and di-
vorced contractor from northern British Columbia who "accidentally" visited Cuba for a few days last year while taking a side-
tour to his vacation in the Bahamas. He met a Cuban translator
on the tour bus who has since become his lady-friend. He was on
his way for a third visit with her in Havana, telling me he stays in
her apartment and has no problem doing so. When he heard that
I was heading for the big city too, he offered a ride in his taxi,
but I explained that for my work it was necessary to make the
trip on the Hershey electric train. He said to let him know if I
changed my mind.

Well, lo and behold, he and the taxi were still waiting outside
the airport door when I finally got out, while most everyone else
had already left on the various buses. When he called out, "You
sure you don't want a ride," the weariness from our overnight
flight suddenly won out over my determination to work - especially since I wasn't sure how to get to the electric train station
and was dreading the burden of my two heavy bags, along with

an overloaded camera case (two 35's and the Hi-8 video, plus film and accessories) along with a small backpack holding immediate toiletries, grub and clothing. An awesome load for a crowded Cuban transportation system, so you won't be surprised to hear that my dazed head was soon being pummelled by strong ocean breezes rushing in through both wide-open front windows while I sat in the back seat of a new Nissan taxi. It was too hot to ask for a change in the windows, so I just pulled on my cap and hunkered down. Couldn't sleep because the driver was trying to set a new speed record on the lightly-travelled highway. My mind kept seeing that crushed car we looked at a couple of years ago, in which two Russian tourists died after hitting a cow on this same road, also at high speed. Suffice it to say the guy was a good driver and got me here in seemingly no time without making us into hamburgers. By ten in the morning he had me and my bags at the front desk of the Hotel Plaza. Coming direct from the airport to the hotel lobby was like stepping back into the 1920's, when this place was built. It doesn't seem to have changed a lot since then.

The driver listened to news on the radio all the way up, switching back and forth between Radio Marti, beamed over from Miami, and Cuba's own Radio Rebelde. Both were in Spanish so I had some difficulty following along, but the driver repeated the main things in simpler Spanish, plus a touch of English. No doubt at home you're following the news as well, to see what will be the outcome of Cuba's shooting down those two small planes. The driver feels sure the whole situation will blow over soon, and says it's of no great concern to the average Cuban like himself; that it will cause no long term harm. He feels certain that Cuba did the right thing by shooting the planes down, even if they were unarmed. He said no other country would allow repeated violations of its airspace like they had made, especially since everyone seems to know they've also been showering propaganda leaflets on Havana. It was strange for us to be travelling along the coast on this particular day, since the friends and relatives of the lost pilots had threatened to arrive in Cuban waters nearby with a big anti-Castro flotilla that had the potential to further inflame

A typical street in Old Havana, with many buildings going back to the 1700's, making this '47 Chevy seem comparatively new.

present tensions between Fidel and the U.S. I heard later on CNN news (beamed to my hotel room by satellite) that stormy weather forced the boaters to postpone their plans, which makes me guess (and hope) no one will care anymore by whatever time they re-schedule it. Still, while riding in the taxi I kept half a lookout for fireworks and aerial forces, though all I saw was the stormy sea crashing against a rocky and deserted coast.

My plans to get a hotel room immediately upon arriving in Havana for a badly needed nap were spoiled by an unsympathetic old desk clerk, who insisted that check-in time was not until 4:00 p.m. and that he wouldn't be sure if there were rooms available before then. This place intrigued me enough that I really wanted to stay, and I didn't relish the thought of moving all my baggage, though our old Hotel Inglaterra is within sight, just across the park from here. They're both important buildings in Havana's history, the Inglaterra being the country's oldest active hotel, while the Plaza maintains its Roaring Twenties flavour. Both of them were closed down and completely overhauled in recent years, so they're nice to sleep in too, besides having great character.

With almost six hours to wait for a room (the somber clerk finally let slip the encouragement that there would "probably" be one available). I checked my bags into the hotel's luggage room and set out for a walk. Those of you who have travelled long distances and lost a night of sleep, then emerged on foot in some totally foreign city, will have some idea of how the next couple hours in downtown Havana went. It was a busy Saturday, midday, and of course the hotel is right in the heart of Old Havana, the Unesco declared heritage site, whose narrow streets and fascinating assortments of old and older buildings date back to the 1600's, like an architectural bridge between Old Europe and New America.

The moment I stepped out through the huge round-topped doors onto the crowded sidewalk a pleasant middle aged fellow asked if I was American or German. When I said Canadian, he right away asked if I'd like some information about the city, telling me proudly, "I am a historian!" I wasn't sure if he was legit or just trying some con angle, so I asked his occupation, to which he again insisted, "I am a historian." This time I said to him: "I am also a historian," then we shook hands and became friends.

He works at a nearby cultural institution, dealing with old and new art, loves his city, and studies its history as much as he can. For the next couple of hours we walked up and down the old streets together, talking, stopping now and then for photographs.

At one point I said to him, "Well friend, how is it with you in life" He laughed and replied, "Terrible!" I laughed with him, then we walked a while in silence. We tried to stay on the sidewalks, but these are only wide enough for one person so we were constantly stepping down to make room for girls and ladies. Among his interesting tales was one of the more unusual explanations I've heard for the fact that he can speak fairly good English. "My grandfather came to Cuba from Germany," he said, "and my grandmother came from Italy, so they couldn't understand each other, nor could they speak Spanish; instead, they both learned English and that's how they talked to each other all the time. Back then many people in Cuba knew how to speak English, before we joined with Russia."

He was carrying a bag of cloth that he had just brought to a tailor for the making of a pair of pants. But the tailor said he had no material with which to make pockets, so my friend was taking the stuff back home until he can find pocket material. Or, as he later admitted under my insistent questioning, until he can find a few American dollars to help the tailor find what was needed. I said a personal guided tour of Old Havana was worth to me about the same as what would cover this extra cost, so there was my first chance at playing Santa Claus again.

At one point we were coming up to a busy intersection while discussing some serious political topic. In order to make his point more clearly, my friend stopped in the middle of the sidewalk and looked earnestly in my eyes, waving his hands and arms while he talked. Suddenly I noticed behind him a pair of uniformed cops heading our way through the crowd, so I said loudly, "Yes, that is indeed very interesting history, so let us see some more of Old Havana," then we moved on, while the cops stayed behind. He brought me to street markets, where people were selling food, and many more were selling artwork, along with leather things, clothing and souvenirs for tourists. Foreigners made up a small but noticeable contingent of the overall traffic. Lots of sellers, lots of items and lots of lookers, but very few buyers. I felt sorry for those people, many of whom were looking longingly at me, no doubt wishing I'd turn the tide for their day's business and shell out some cash.

A strange custom was that many of the vendors joined together in making rhythmic noises with little wooden sticks like the ones used in Latin bands, which make clacking sounds that travel up and down the crowded streets, joined in by one or two conga drums. Of the craftwork being sold some was of pretty good quality, including inlaid wooden boxes and fine carvings of wood or stone, beautiful knitted dresses, even saddles and spurs, but also a lot of shmuckey "junk" that I can't imagine anyone wanting to haul back home. In one 17th century churchyard and plaza there was music and dance being performed by a skillful troupe, some of them on stilts towering way above the thickly massed crowd. There was sort of a party atmosphere, and I'm not talking about Fidel's party, at least not his official one. On the other hand, as the leader of a nation where people are allowed to gather happily in this way, he can take some credit for this party as well. U.S. Senator Helms might consider spending a little time among those people of Cuba that he seems so determined to punish.

On one side street we saw a 1938 Bondomobile, a red monster of a car with bulbous headlights and a fairly new roof of ordinary tin, whose lumpy body appeared to have bondo filling up its dents from one end to the other, none sanded very thoroughly, though the overall car still managed to possess a certain charm. It looked like the limo of a gangster; over the doorway behind it was a sign announcing the neighborhood watch committee, the government's eyes and ears. Apparently a member of this group goes around in this outrageous machine. A neighbor said he thought the car was basically a Mercury, while his son volunteered that it was built in 1938. They said it runs okay, but sucks gas like crazy.

At two o'clock I went back to the hotel, feeling pretty tired and even more spaced out than before, marvelling at how I hadn't slept since my family brought me to the airport, far away from the streets of Old Havana. On the street outside I met an elderly gent with a 1933 Model A who said it was for hire, so I told him I'd be back when I wasn't so sleepy. Think I'll have him drive me to the railroad station.....

The grumpy guy at the desk was real busy this time, so I went to a young fellow who was just finishing with a guest and asked him about a room. He started checking the files so I quickly added my story about flying down all night from Canada and desperately needing some rest, at which point he cheerfully said, "Sure, no problem," and pulled a card from the file. In Spanish he said to grumpus, "Here's an empty room, can I let this guy have it?" Grumpus looked annoyed, studied the card, apparently knew he was beat and said to go ahead. Nice room, facing an inside courtyard - and thus very peaceful for downtown Havana - though for me a bit costly at $68 a night. Then again, worth the extra bucks for its cleanliness; if not for the new TV with CNN, a movie channel and Muchmusic thrown in. Even a room phone, which for the first time in Cuba I'll be using, though it should be fun with my rough Spanish. I guess at worst somebody will hang up on me.

After a short, sound sleep I showered, re-dressed and got ready "to go out." My first real solo venture in Cuba, having always had either you or your brother with me before. Actually, my main goal for this first day was to meet the photographer "Wildy," whose letter I picked up on the way to the airport, just in time to get his address and a neighbor's phone number - plus the information that he'd be leaving tommorow morning for a week of photographing out in the countryside. He said I'd have to meet him on the day of my arrival or not at all. Left a message for him with his neighbour (and I cheated by asking the hotel operator to do the talking).

Wildy is a friend of a friend, and he's the first known Cuban train enthusiast, a photo journalist by trade, who is working on a

The Malecon, Havana's Sunset Strip, a wide curving boulevard famous for its spectacular waterfront views, dramatic sunsets, and colourful crowds. This old building's facade is getting a much needed facelift - slowly and mostly by handwork. Stormy seas send waves that force closure of the road and send saltwater spray against these buildings.

photo book of trains that he'd like to have us publish. Sounds like an interesting fellow and a worthwhile project, so I really wanted to connect.

Hearing nothing back to my message, I figured it best to head for his place and at least leave him a written reply to his letter. The young desk clerk said it was a *long* walk, partly along the waterfront Malecon, which he said can be dangerous for tourists at night. So I decided to go out on the street near the hotel and look for a private car, an old "Americano." I had gone about a block without seeing the right kind (an especially old or classy rig is what I wanted), when I realized that all I had with me was a roll of twenties. The kind of car I was looking for probably wouldn't have that much American money on board, so I headed back to the hotel to get change.

When I asked grumpus if he could change a twenty he shook his head and said, "We've already totalled the day's take, so you have to wait for the next shift." After thinking this over for a bit, I decided not to wait and started heading for the front door when I noticed a young, black-bearded fellow sitting quietly on the lobby bench. On a hunch I walked up in front of him and asked, "Are you Wildy?" He was indeed! I said, "Boy, I'm just trying to get to your apartment, in fact I should already be on my way there. I was just going to leave you a letter and then go out for the night! What a lucky coincidence that we've now met!" He let me look through a small portfolio of photos that he's taken along some of the sugar railroads, telling me that his best photo work is right now at an exhibition in Holguin. He's made himself into sort of a one-man Cuban steam support effort, trying to raise awareness in his country about the historic treasures still working in their land. His photos emphasize the exciting and unique shots of smokey engines at sunset interspersed by close ups of driving wheels, spokes, and throttle levers, along with portraits of the workers. He was with a friendly Swiss chap named Andreas, a fellow photographer, enthusiast, and traveller, whose Cuban girlfriend was anxious to get going. Wildy looked mighty pleased when I gave him a stack of my train books for a parting present. He hasn't seen books like that except advertised in the train magazines that friends sometimes bring him. Foreign tour groups occasionally take him along to interpret, which really helps his work since he doesn't have a car to get around, and you and I know what that would be like when trying to reach isolated sugar mills.

After Wildy and his friend left I walked through Old Havana looking for a place to eat and darned if the first spot to catch my eye didn't turn out to be El Bodeguita del Medio, hangout of the famous writer Ernest Hemingway, literary hero of Cuba. A narrow, crowded, two-story place that's also famous for having signatures and graffiti from seemingly every customer who's ever eaten there - including mine now, neatly embossed with dozens of others on the round wooden table where I was served. The meal was typical for Cuba and not very expensive. A trio with guitars came along and added just the right seasoning...

In the heart of Old Havana at twilight. On the left is Cuba's Capitolio, faced by offices and apartments, with towers of the National Theatre in the distance. Parked between opposing lanes of the wide main street are a varied collection of old American cars waiting to be hired.

March 6, '96

....Well Okan, a couple days in downtown Havana have passed so fast that there wasn't even time to sit and write. Although I dislike big cities and would rather not be stuck here just now, I'm always amazed at the pull they have on my senses, at how I can think I'm just going out for a short walk only to find myself heading up one block and down another, seeing new things at each turn and meeting lots of interesting people.

Right now I'm riding inside a green '52 Dodge whose bad shocks and worse alignment makes us bounce so much that my penmanship is barely readable. This might as well be a convertible, since only the windshield has glass left in it and the tropical winds are blowing through here in gale force. I have great misgivings about my planned adventures for today, since we're not even out of the city yet and the driver has already complained about several problems. My goal is to reach two sugar mills located way out in the country west of Havana, then to follow a couple of their trains over heavens-knows-what kind of roads.

I took your advice to rent a private car with driver for one day of photographing, though I didn't exactly get the pick of the lot. I actually had a beautiful dark blue 1948 Cadillac lined up for this trip, with original chrome and upholstery, but its well dressed young black owner never showed up like he promised me last night, when I talked to him on the street. I waited this morning for over an hour, while a cool dude named Miguel, with baseball cap on backwards and a thin gold necklace, kept bugging me about finding another car and driver so that I could get going. "You're friend is not going to show up," he kept saying in smooth and fairly convincing English, "let me find you a good car close by." He's a high school history teacher who has given up regular work in order to earn U.S. cash as sort of a downtown agent-hustler for tourists. When I made a joking comment about chicas he looked at me earnestly and said, "My mother is a woman and my daughter is a woman, so that's where I draw the line. No women! But everything else I can get for you."

At the moment, "everything else" includes having him sit up

in the front seat by the driver, even though I told him that I have no money to pay him as an interpreter. "That's alright, " he assured me, "I like you and want to come along for the experience. I can practice my English and get out of this city for a while." He said he was born in the country near where I want to go, and that he worked for some years at a sugar mill, though when he told me, "I was a maquinista on a steam locomotive," I think he was pushing the truth.

What you probably had in mind was that I should rent that baby blue Caddy limo you and I rode in last year, but one of the other old car drivers told me it's getting motor repairs, which is why I haven't seen it around. There were other choice rigs cruising past the hotel last night, including that green '33 Ford Model A, but its elderly driver said he wouldn't dare go so far out of town with it. This morning at nine there wasn't much selection on the street, so Miguel persuaded me to accept this old homely Dodge.

Actually, he first had to persuade the driver, a slim fellow who said he doesn't know where the two sugar mills are. Miguel assured him that *he* did, and that they weren't very far.

There is one consolation to the drafty interior - it provides fresh air to offset the poisoning I'm slowly getting from this car's loud and leaking exhaust system. But the wind also pummels me with dust and grit, so that I'm already feeling as grubby as I normally would at the end of a train-chasing day, though we're still in the first hour. Just now, when I again questioned the car's ability to make the torturous miles ahead, Miguel tried to reassure me by bragging up the driver, patting his shoulder and saying, "He's been a car mechanic for 33 years, since the time he was a boy, so don't worry, no problems."

A short while later, and we're just pulling away from the first sugar mill - the wrong one, adding to my hunch that Miguel doesn't really know much more about our trip than the driver, whose sudden silence makes me think he has just figured out the same thing, and is probably wondering what he got himself into. All the more so since his motor has now died twice, very suddenly, though he got it started again each time. Anyway, the mill

High noon in downtown Havana, as an old Model A Ford taxi waits outside the front doors of Estacion Central, the capitol city's main train station. Adventurous travellers can join the throngs of Cubans who leave from here daily aboard a variety of passenger trains heading for all parts of the island.

where we stopped had only a short little narrow gauge railroad with a couple of ugly orange and black diesels.

......More time has passed and I'm now basking in the air conditioned comfort of a luxury tourist bus! My hunch came true, as Miguel turned out to be way off in his guess as to how far it is to the two mills I want to visit. With each kilometer the driver had more complaints, while the motor continued to die until finally it just wouldn't start anymore. Thank heavens we had just reached the first of my two mills - barely - making a photo finish by drifting to a halt on the dirt road outside the mill's locomotive shop, where to my surprise not one, but two little narrow gauge locomotives sat steaming. Work comes first, so I ignored the broken car and rushed about getting vintage portraits in the nice light, discovering in the process that the two engines were fired up mainly because of an arranged visit by a German tour group, whose camera-toting members were already lined up - and surprised to see me - along a stretch of double track on the far side of the shop. The two engines - one smaller (and more rare) than the other - were then run down those tracks in unison to provide an interesting picture for the visitors, which to my delight, suddenly included me.

Back at the car, our driver had the hood up and was perspiring while taking a forlorn look inside. Whatever was wrong apparently couldn't be remedied by his 33 years of experience. Through Miguel he asked for the $40 we'd agreed on in Havana, but I had to point out that we were only halfway through the trip, and hadn't even reached the second mill, which to me was quite important. I didn't bother to bring up the train chasing we were supposed to do so I could get my photos; he was having enough problems and probably would have considered it an outrageous request. So I offered half payment for half a trip, which set up a quiet storm of protest. He'd paid $25 in cash for gasoline alone, a purchase I had witnessed on our way out of the city, so that my $20 offer would leave him worse than broke. That I wasn't at my requested destination didn't seem to matter, all he could think about was being broke down way out in the country, which for him was surely a problem.

Meanwhile, I had a quick talk with the German tour group's leader, explaining my transportation predicament, so he offered a seat on the half empty bus, which would not only bring me back to my hotel later on, but was on its way next to the same mill I wanted to visit, where they'd already made advance arrangements. I went back to the driver for one last offer of twenty dollars, but upon seeing his dejected look I felt guilty, so I compromised at thirty, which he accepted.

Although hesitant to bite the hand that fed me (or in this case, that gave me a ride), I would be remiss not to mention what a sterile method this tour bus seemed to offer for travelling through the Cuban countryside, totally isolated from the people and their reality, with not even a window to roll down. The 15 or so passengers just arrived from Germany last night, intent on seeing as many steam engines as possible over the next ten days, showing no care or understanding for Cuba and its society. Mill visits had been arranged and paid for in advance, so they just needed to hop out of the bus for a few minutes of sweating and picture taking, without needing to meet the local folks in order to make friends or obtain permissions, like us. The small engine at the first mill would not have been running without their request, so group visits are a good way to document these old machines, but they keep participants completely isolated from the human angle that makes Cuban railroading especially unique and memorable. Here's hoping my three hours as a German rail-fan tourist will be the extent of that experience for my whole life!

There was a Cuban government representative aboard to make sure the mill visits went smoothly, getting off the bus before the rest of us to check with the mill boss as to the special requests. She was an elderly black lady who seemed highly educated and spoke fluent high German. The job is obviously a perk in government circles, as she received tips in American cash from the group and will no doubt get more in the next ten days. Her staunch support of the system was obvious from the way she used the p.a. system to give us a running commentary on places that we passed, all of it having to do with the history and success of the revolution, with most passengers ignoring her and talking to each other, having no doubt noted the blatant tones of East Bloc style propaganda.

It was just after noon when we got to the second mill and there was not a train due to steam out until the crew had eaten their lunch, so the tour leader asked what the group wanted to do. "Find something to drink," cried out several voices, no doubt picturing a little latin beer garden hidden in the nearby palms. The government lady was consulted, so she stepped out for directions, coming back minutes later with a mill worker who said he'd guide us to a "snack bar." It was in the palms alright, about half a kilometer from the mill, a thatched hut serving - you might have guessed it - guarapo, or genuine sugarcane water! Warm, and in one of four glasses they had on hand.

A throng of Cubans had been busy drinking from those glasses when we drove up, all of them eyeing our tour bus suspiciously, wondering what the tourists could want, since apparently none had ever stopped there before. Groans were heard throughout the bus when the menu was announced, after which the tour leader said that those who wished to avail themselves of this respite should go and line up right away. Not a soul moved, so the leader said, "Alright, then I shall tell them we have changed our minds." I felt embarrassment for the sake of the Cubans, though I knew they couldn't see us behind our tinted windows. Someone in the group felt the same, as he got up and followed the leader outside, shrugging his shoulders and muttering, "Why not?"

The Cubans parted for our leader and the one who was coming behind. A single glass was seen being wiped, filled with a milky looking substance, then drained by our fellow traveller, who smiled and failed to keel over dead as was perhaps expected. At that, another fellow in the bus rose and said loudly, "That looked delicious," whereupon most of the crowd suddenly got to their feet and filed out, the Cubans perhaps regretting that they'd given up their place in line so willingly, as we now spent 20 minutes draining their supply of cane water. I didn't join the parade, having learned the hard way more than 30 years ago in Guatemala to keep unfamiliar country liquids out of my system while travelling. Not to worry, the fancy bus had a spiffy toilet.

We spent the next couple of hours standing around in the wind and sunshine waiting for the sugar train that was "due any minute," after our bus had brought us back to trackside. We eventually got hauled some distance out into the country by a very beat-up homemade rail-bus normally used to transport track workers. It left us at the top of a long grade, a tight scenic spot that might have allowed two or three people to stand tightly side by side for one of those stereotypical three-quarter views of the approaching train, but not this whole crowd. Somehow most did manage to jam into that space together, elbow to jowl, while I went down a steep embankment and across a bean field for a broadside view. Not only did those guys manage to hold their camera positions during the long wait that followed, but they also didn't notice what effect the tropical sun was having on their peachy pale skins, most of them wearing short sleeves, short pants, with hardly anyone's head covered by a hat. You can imagine what kind of hot flashes they had in bed that night!

For the past couple of days I've been phoning around to find a rental car, but so far without luck (unless I want a Mercedes, at oil baron prices). I could rent from one of the newer car outfits that don't have many agencies around the island yet, but that would be a problem in case of breakdown. Finally I went to the nearest office myself and told the young manager - to whom I'd already spoken by phone - that I was getting desperate for a vehicle with which to get out of town. He smiled, then said, "I *could* phone around for you to see if anyone has a car, but in that case, would you be willing to pay a small commission?" I nodded my head, not worrying about a few extra bucks, but disappointed that even government agents in Cuba will now emulate Latin countries with the ever-present 'mordida," or bite.

A bigger boss walked in before the phone calls got started, smiling when he heard the situation, then asking me bluntly, "How much commission will you pay?" My ten dollar offer was found acceptable and it conveniently turned out that he'd been driving around town in a dark blue Nissan that he said I could rent on the spot.

With my new mobility I headed right for the sugar ministry offices across town, another place where phone calls had gotten me nowhere. At a crowded downstairs desk one of three secretaries called the only official whose name I knew, then handed me the phone. With a bad line and a noisy environment I was suddenly forced to try using my rough Spanish to convince this big shot that he should let me up to his office so that I could plead for authorization to take a couple of special sugar train pictures.

To my surprise, it worked! Within a few minutes the official whom I'd called was there, along with a second man, both leading me away from a crowded room filled with many Cubans who were also hoping to be heard.

Upstairs it quickly turned out that my contact was not official enough to give the required authority, therefore he called anotheer boss who was higher up yet. Unfortunately, this elderly man had a rather grim look on his face as he listened to my story, caused partly, I later learned, from his years as an officer in the Cuban military. His first response was negative, but after an hour of stonewalling he finally looked at our family photo album (and a few of my railroad photo books). There was a pause, then suddenly he came up with ideas and questions of his own as to how I might help his work with tourism, ending the meeting by offering far more help than I'd expected. We'll see how this turns out when I get to the designated mills.

"Always, always, the Motherland"

March 14, 1996
Rancho Luna Hotel, Cienfuegos

Well, your mom finally arrived, so you'll no doubt be interested to hear how she's responding to our tropical adventureland. Twenty-five years ago, when she and I got together, it never occurred to me that we could be celebrating our anniversary in Cuba, especially not aboard a smoke-belching, hard working, narrow gauge steam locomotive. For an introduction I brought her on a round trip from Mal Tiempo to Potrelillo. Coming back with a heavy train load, the locomotive's drivers spun out of control frequently, while I stood right behind the engineer and your mom hung on for dear life up on the tender. Two brakemen kept her company, exchanging loud shouts, keeping their eyes on the newcomer, just in case she needed help.

We had driven through the small town of Guarerras on the first morning after she arrived. There was a photo scene I wanted to check out at a major intersection on the way, where our highway crossed several railroad tracks. It was guarded by a fellow up in an old time wooden elevated tower, who operates an array of levers for the track switches and signals. I stopped on the shoulder of the road in front of a small house and told your mom I'd be back in five minutes, wanting an inside picture of the tower. I was startled on return to find our car sitting empty. Then I heard her call my name from that small house, where she had gone and knocked, then gotten a family of five enraptured by family photos that she brought, even though no one there could speak English and her Spanish is still pretty much limited to 'buenos dias' and 'si!' The lady of the house told me right away, "Your wife is the first Indian woman we have ever seen - we want her to stay longer and tell us about her people. We want to cook a meal for her and introduce her to more of our family." It was hard for me to tell them that we had to leave at once, as we still had a long drive ahead.

Your mom did get to see her husband as steam engineer for a while, on the way down to Potrelillo with the empties. It was an easy run, though Raul insisted on standing behind me the whole way, he being among the most careful of Mal Tiempo's engineers. His father was locomotive shop foreman in the years before our old friend Pepe, so he was raised to respect those old machines. Do you remember meeting his dad last year, the old man who talked about the days when he and other Mal Tiempo workers used to gather food and clothing for the revolutionaries up in the mountains?

This was a late afternoon run, which I thought your mom would enjoy as it heads towards the mill into the orange sunset. But our overloaded train did so much stalling that we ran out of daylight only halfway home. This, of course, made the ride all the more exciting, but also more dangerous. In addition, the air turned quite cool right after the sun dropped behind the distant horizon, with Mama dressed only in short sleeves, sitting unprotected up on the wide-open tender. I called her down from there and had her stand behind the fireman, whose spare shirt I then borrowed for her to wear, though it was of a small size. The windowless cab was still pretty drafty, but its walls at least provided her some protection from the wind and there was the glowing warmth from the firebox. She was awed by the flames reflecting off everything, throwing her silhouette against the blackened trees and bushes that we passed in the outside night.

The climax of our run was that final big curve and steep grade just a couple kilometers below the mill, where Raul opened the throttle wide, causing sparks to shoot from the chimney, while the firebox boomed and pulsated like thunder, from the combustion of fuel, causing our ears to plug and throwing wild locomotive shadows against the adjacent tall stands of sugar cane. It was pretty scary to hit that big curve, with the locomotive swaying and bucking wildly from side to side. Together we placed ourselves at high risk, having more faith in the old machine and its rickety tracks than common logic would dictate, but it ended well and your mom says she'll never forget the experience.

This morning started out a bit rough for us, after hanging around the beach here longer than we should have. We then ran late for two promised visits with friends. The first was to woodcarver Edel, in downtown Cruces, who'd sent word through our mutual friend Maykel this past winter that he was carving something special for us. I had forgotten how many other homes looked similar to his, so we ended up cruising several blocks before I finally gave up and asked somebody. The name Edel got no response from the two teenaged girls I stopped, nor did the information that he was a wood carver, but when I said he was a *big* handsome, black Cubano who works out with weights, (which I mimicked to their delight), they immediately pointed to his place, a block further down. Sure enough, we found him working out in his funky backyard gym of welded junkyard parts. He asked for you right away, says he sends greetings, and was enthused to meet your mom. He gave her the carved mask of an Indian chief, while for me he had a beautiful stick of red Cuban mahogany, with the head of a chief carved at the top - his thick long hair forming the curved handle - then a snake winding its way down to a very delicate and pointed foot - a *black* foot, he said proudly, in honor of our family's tribe, and "as a symbol of friendship between Canadian people and Cubans."

We left there and went next to Efren's for lunch, but got held up in downtown mid-day traffic: pedestrians, bicycles, horse-drawn carriages, and finally a black Lada hearse that was stopped and blocking most of the narrow street. Half a block beyond there we got flagged down by our little friend Daisby, looking even more frail than usual, crowding into our Nissan's small back seat with three others, including one of his sisters. The other day I gave him some money to help with urgent family trips they've been making back and forth to Havana, where his other sister has been in critical condition at a hospital. The moment he got settled in the car he said, "Adolfo, my sister is right there behind us. She has died." And with that, both he and the remaining sister began to wail and sob pitifully, while I tried to steer my way through the traffic with very watery eyes, haunted by the sight in my rear view mirror of that black hearse right behind us. Daisby rolled down his window and waved for it to follow, the driver being from Havana and unfamiliar with the small town and its back country roads.

We ended up at the Mal Tiempo community hall, where the

late sister was taken inside with her simple coffin, so that friends and relatives could bid her farewell before the next day's funeral. It goes pretty quick in Cuba, usually without much of any religious service. She had died that previous night. One of our other railroad friends came over to talk, while we waited for Daisby to finish inside (he'd asked me to wait so he could pick up a picture of the same sister that I happened to have brought with me from last year). The friend said that the poor sister had committed suicide by drinking battery acid, because of her husband's infidelities. Everyone in the small community was upset by this, especially since she left behind two little kids.

After our meal with Efren I was to have taken my special photo of two engines facing each other at the crossing, complete with buggies, cowboys and an old car in the road. But the yard was very silent during the time we ate, then we learned that this was caused by the derailment of the yard engine, sitting quiet and somewhat sideways across a switch, with nearly two dozen track workers and others gathered around to assess the situation. Shop foreman Fabio was among them, and since he was needed to arrange the road crossing photo, I knew the derailment had cancelled it. Not only that, he said in disgust, but in addition the day's other locomotive - due back at this time with a load of cane - was actually broke down at a reload halfway along the mainline. Two reloads were already in need of more empty cars, so the crew would have to rush back, with no time to stop for photos. Oh well, you know how those kinds of frustrations keep coming up.

Hotel Casa Grande
Santiago de Cuba
March 27, 1996

What a relief it is to be here, resting on the third floor of this classic old downtown hotel, after one crazy long day of travelling. You'd think my energy would be about drained, but I'm eager to go on with the next stage, which will be the long postponed cross-country train trip from here to Havana. By now your mom should be in Varadero on her way back home. I think she had a great time here. She promised to write a letter about it, but you'll probably hear all the details first-hand long before that.

My day began at about four this morning, when the whining diesel motor on Rafael Freyre's blue rail-bus No. 50 slowly invaded the otherwise quiet air of La Caridad the Bariay, the sound growing louder as the bus reached the tracks on this side of the hill and began to work its way around our "Grand Curve", moments later rumbling over the road crossing down-hill from the family farm house, where I've been staying this week. I knew No. 50 would take slightly over an hour to continue up the mainline to Altuna, from there down the winding branch-line to Jobal, then back to our farm crossing. It would stop to pick up workers along the way, sometimes also their families, bringing them back to the mill and town. I tossed and turned a while longer in bed, a mosquito net protecting me from bugs but doing nothing for the excitement of upcoming train travel that filled my head, keeping at bay whatever sleep my exhausted body still yearned for.

When I finally got up and dressed in the dark, then headed down to the crossing. My dozing senses got startled wide awake by a voice calling my name from the darkness when I got to the tracks. It was Enrique, who had beat me there from his own house up on the other hillside. Roosters were beginning to crow from various farms, while from across the distant range of mountains came the first vague hint of daylight, like a faint line painted by a grand master of the dark skies.

Enrique was congratulating himself for persuading his cane

cuttting boss that one more day off work was a worthy contribu-
tion to international relations, and that he as a poor farmer
should be allowed to enjoy this short time with his dear Canadian
friend. I know we feel the same about each other, as though we'd
been together all our lives, a rare thing to encounter in these
modern times, satisfying to know that in a supposedly totalitarian
country it was no big deal for him to miss one more day of work
to experience our friendship.

Then slowly the soft sound of crickets and other insects got
drowned out by a distant drone that turned louder as the rail bus
came closer, while at the same time we could hear the crunching
of quick footsteps coming down the road. It was the ever-
punctual Hector, oldest son of Emilio Sr., heading for work as
conductor on the train I'd be riding for much of the day. He
called out a pleasant greeting just as the headlight from No. 50
caught both Enrique and I momentarily in the face as it rounded
a final curve and began to slow down for us. Hector climbed up
the steps first, carrying a little backpack for his papers and other
things needed at work. Enrique and I followed him with my
camera bags, the driver barely coming to a stop before accelerating again for the "Grand Curve" and steep grade ahead.

The bone-jarring sensation of riding this 1940's bus was
greatly enhanced by the fact that its steel wheels found no soft
spots in their constant rolling over the iron rails. Inside, some 40
passengers held tight to their stiff plastic seats as a dim light bulb
bathed the scene from overhead in a deep orange glow, at least
during the times when its faulty wiring allowed it to stay lit for
more than a few seconds.

Ahead of the passengers, in a small, glassed-in compartment
of his own, sat the tousle haired driver, concentrating his eyes on
the tracks in order to get us over the mainline safely, holding
tightly to the steering wheel even though the bus was guided
along its path by the winding rails. When he turned the wheel to
the right it applied the brakes, to the left released them. Gas and
clutch pedals were on the floor, along with a gangly gearshift
lever that caused a lot of grinding during its frequent moves.
Conversation among the crowd was necessarily limited due to the

loud racket and the constant jolting, with many of the people seeming to be still somewhat asleep. Cuban life is full of late nights, and this was awfully early in the morning. The windows were all open and some of the riders leaned out regularly, either for better viewing or to get blown more wide awake. Enrique and I were certainly no longer sleepy, out on the cool back porch, where drafts came up the stairwells and then rushed passed us to go out the back window, whose wooden frames lacked glass. This was experiencing passenger train travel at its grittiest, with both of us grinning from ear to ear, unable to talk above the noise, mesmerized as the scenery and farms flashed by.

The mill yard was a dimly lit, blue-cast dawn scene of much activity, with constant streams of workers crossing the tracks on their way from town to the big sugar mill, from which hissed the

Back in the 1920's and 30's many North American shortlines were saved from bankruptcy by replacing steam-hauled passenger trains (requiring full crews and equipment) with simple railbuses operated by a single driver. At Rafael Freyre such service still exists - more due to local need than because of any bankruptcy threat to the state owned rail line. We've just made a round trip on a branchline to the village of Jobal. The driver is standing with a friend while waiting by the phone for the dispatcher's clearance to proceed.

sounds of hard working steam machinery. Mechanics were already busy in the locomotive shop, repairing two steam engines and one of the two 1939 General Electric diesels, while on a nearby track three other steam engines were slowly coming to life, their crews working hard to grease and fire them up for the day's work. Boilers rumbled, tall stacks belched smoke, as steam pressure went up slowly inside the boilers and caused white clouds of steamy mist to fly about. Some of the men oiled and tightened the moving parts, while others used brooms to sweep off dirt and soot, or handfuls of rags to wipe everything down. Such respectful treatment of locomotives was standard on many railroads in years gone by, but is a rare thing in this day and age, even in labour-intensive Cuba. A direct result of Rafael Freyre's continuing custom of assigning locomotives to particular engineers for the long term, thus building up pride in each crew to keep its machine looking good.

After about an hour of these "warm-ups," the three crews got ready to head out on the line, first off the mark being the train I'd gotten authority to ride. Our engineer was a friendly fellow named Yoel Peres, with Armando as fireman, Hector as conductor, and the brakemen Rafael and Alexander, all of them working pleasantly and efficiently together. For the next few hours we travelled towards the little sugar reload village of Uvila, at the end of the "mountain line," stopping at several other reloads, two of them at the end of picturesque branch-lines. As you can well imagine, my hand was on the throttle much of the time, thus fulfilling some of my longest-held railroading fantasies. This alone made those extra days of waiting for Ministry authorization in Havana well worth the effort.

The plan was for our train to be back at the mill by noon, but that didn't take into account a rebellious cane car that decided to derail more than halfways out, then refused to get back on the tracks, though we spent a couple of hours trying. Not only did this throw off my day's busy schedule, but it also fouled up a very special picture I had arranged with all three trains combined upon their midday arrival at the mill, thus making a unique "triple-header." In the lead was to have been old Emilio's pride

Snapshot of Hector, Yoel and the crew at a Chucho. For many decades fresh sugarcane was loaded aboard railroad cars through a simple chain and pulley system based on angular overhead frames like the one seen at the right of this picture. This is a slow, labor intensive system that nearly caused a country-wide change from train to truck hauling of the cane. But then some engineers designed the acopio, a more complicated and mechanized setup wherein the fresh cane is first chopped, then loaded aboard cars with a conveyor belt, while big fans blow off the leaves and chaff, thus creating a much cleaner and more compact load for delivery to the mills. The fabulous narrow gauge line of Central Rafael Freyre has among the last old time chuchos still in operation, all the more noteworthy because a lack of repair parts for their diesel motors has forced crews to bring back even more primitive ways, as several of these motorless chuchos are again powered by teams of oxen.

and joy, engine 1388, but its crew had already finished lunch by the time we arrived and they were overdue at the reloads with empty cars, waiting only for us to clear the mainline before blasting out of town. Seeing the look of disappointment on my face, Rodolfo got a couple of fellows to fire up one of the reserve engines, so that I still got shots of a triple-header, as I had been arranged in Havana, but the session was more rushed and less dramatic than planned.

On our way back from that long morning trip, way overdue because of the load and our derailment, I whistled proudly as we approached the crossing downhill from the family farm at La caridad de Bariay, with a bunch out on the road to wave at our passing. I was let down to see young Emilio - all fancy-dressed for town - telling me in signs that it was getting too late and he'd have to leave. Our plan had been that he would ride with me as far as Holguin, and I'd really been looking forward to this final chance for a visit. Enrique and I eventually caught a ride back out to the farm with the second afternoon train, where I was pleased to find that Emilio had changed his mind and was still waiting for me.

I hurried up to the house, where my bags were fortunately packed, and peeled my clothes off on the way into the corner bath stall, where Emilio's hard-working sister Eulalia already had a bucket of warm water waiting for me. In less than five minutes I felt fresh and clean, taking two more minutes to get dressed and three more to run down to the tracks and back uphill on the far side in order to have a short lunch with Enrique, who had told me with a sad look the day before, "Can you come and have at least one meal at *my* house?" So, even with the long drive to Santiago still ahead and my schedule really late, the request of friendship had to come first. Both Emilios walked with me, father and son, but everyone's concern was that I should "eat lots!" As soon as I felt full, I simply smiled at their protestations, and shook my head when they insisted I have more. I knew that a full stomach would not make the upcoming drive any easier!

For the first stage of my trip to Holguin, things went smoothly on the wide open road. Time passed fast with Emilio and I talking continually, knowing how hard it will be to communicate by mail. He directed me to his army barracks, and darn if I didn't get a flat tire just as we got there, which we quickly changed. Unfortunately, when I rented the car I didn't look closely at the spare; someone had obviously hit a big rock or sharp object with it, denting the inside edge of the rim and gouging a marble-sized hole from the tire side. Just what I needed - a bad tire and no spare, with sunset approaching and many miles of rough roads ahead. On hindsight, I was crazy to continue, but the alternative would have been to seek out the Havanautos agent in Holguin. It was suppertime and he would have been gone to eat. No one else usually has the equipment to repair the tubeless tires used only on rental cars.

The numerous potholes, rocks and unexpected breaks in the road that I encountered after dark kept me constantly on edge, especially since the headlights were both weak and crooked. More than a few times the tires squealed as I stood on the brakes when one or another obstacle suddenly came into view. In addition, two times the highway made a major change, with no warning or signs of further direction. On one I guessed right; the other had a guardian angel in the form of a bicyclist, who shouted as I passed in the dark. I stopped and backed up, whereupon he said that if I wanted Santiago (he guessed by seeing a rental car way out in the dark) I'd have to go back three kms to where the highway was all torn up from construction. I would then follow a dirt road for a ways, not the nicely paved stretch that I had picked. You can imagine my sigh of relief when I finally entered the city itself, all four wheels and my nerves still fairly intact.

There are very few places left in the world where you can still see American-style narrow gauge railroading from the turn of the century, with Cuba being the best and closest. Here's old Santa Lucia No. 6, working hard uphill on the 30-inch gauge Rafael Freyre line with a swaying train of fresh sugar cane.

Letters from Cuba

Hotel Palma de Sol
Varadero
March 28, 1996

Dear Husband,
  You asked me to write down my thoughts about Cuba, so I'll do it here on the beach before I go home tomorrow. It feels strange to travel in Cuba alone, especially knowing you're somewhere else on this interesting island; where, and doing what?
  As an aboriginal person of North America I came to Cuba wondering how the people would treat me and what they would think of my kind. It turns out many of them are pretty curious, and usually puzzled by my origins. So much racial mixing in their own society has made them aware that there are many blendings, but they can't decide what mine is. They seem to know at once that I'm not Cuban, and that I'm neither white nor African, the two races they know best. Their lack of contact with Native Americans sometimes causes them to ask if I'm Chinese or some other Asian.
  Luckily, the whole issue has been kind of interesting rather than bothersome to me. There wasn't the kind of racial superiority that I still sometimes feel from narrow minded white folks closer to home, both in the U.S. and in Canada.
  Actually, what Cubans often noticed about me more than any racial differences is that my height and weight stand out. Cuban men are often shorter than me, while men and women both are usually smaller. Since my whole family consists of large people, I can just imagine the looks we'd get if we all came here together, though Cubans like rodeos so they'd be interested to meet my brothers, and with their love of sports they'd also want to hear about my dad's wrestling days. Most of all, it seems every Cuban I've met has wanted to know more about native people, and how they are doing these days in North America. They're always surprised when I tell them that compared to Cuba, the native tribes are actually quite well off.
  The social life of Cuba reminds me a lot of my young days on the Blood Reserve in Southern Alberta during the 1950's. They

really help each other, and there's a lot more interaction between people than what I see back home nowadays. When modern conveniences like televisions and automobiles became available to us, we began yearning for them and this broke up our interactive tribal life, whereas Cubans that I saw live with few modern luxuries and have little chance to get any, so their focus is more on social life, which they still seem to value highly.

One of the best visits I had in Cuba was with Yolanda and her family in the little town of Palmira, that day you left me and went riding with your railroad friends at Mal Tiempo. There were people coming and going in her life all day.

It was nice for me to experience this kind of social life again, while at the same time it made me see Fidel's whole system in a new light. Until now I thought his people were really oppressed, suffering badly; that they could barely take their eyes off the ground; that they could never enjoy a beautiful day. What I saw

A sunny morning on the plaza at Palmira, with Beverly saying farewell to her friend Yolanda (at left) and neighbor Milagra (on the right), who is an English teacher. Yolanda's little grandson is in the foreground.

instead was a very friendly and strong people enjoying for the maximum what little in the way of material things they have and accepting their lack of any more by considering it in part a sacrifice to make for their beloved country. A strong love of country was noticeable everywhere, especially out *in* the country, where most Cubans still live.

Great lessons could be learned by those of us in more modernized places from the way Cubans get maximum use out of old things that we would have thrown away long ago. Most obvious are the many vintage American cars, which are kept running with few funds or parts because they are needed, not as a weekend hobby. Some of those cars brought back childhood memories of my brothers and events in my life; I got a rush seeing an old '49 Ford with its hood up beside the highway, as I recalled my dad in that same predicament with the same kind of car, long ago.

Machismo is one major part of the Cuban personality that I wasn't looking forward to. I found it everywhere, just like I'd imagined, but to my surprise, I never really felt myself threatened by it. It seemed much safer being among the obviously macho Cuban men than it sometimes feels among the more uncertain characters of North America.

Having to show your passport everywhere you go must annoy a lot of tourists, who probably consider this a typical hassle of communism. But for Indians of my age and older, it brings back memories of carrying an Indian I.D. card and having to get the agent's written permission to travel away from our reserve, or to get a job, go to school, sell a horse, and so forth. No communism in rural Alberta, just bureaucracy working to control a people. Same old story, in a different setting.

The worst thing I experienced in Cuba was that night drive to Holguin and Rafael Freyre. I was amazed at the risks people were taking on the highway in all kinds of vehicles. Riding bikes without lights right in our path seemed to be the ultimate in lunacy. Seems like all these bike riders carry bags besides, to make their riding even more awkward. Or they have passengers with them, often a husband pedalling while his wife rides behind with a baby in one arm and a bag hanging from the other. I had to laugh at one bike rider who was barely visible under his cargo - a baby mattress. On a motor bike there was a person apparently moving to a new household, with all sorts of things tied on, including, literally, a kitchen sink.

In the small town of Cruces, near Cienfuegos, lives our friend Edel, one of many practicing artists in Cuba. We are looking in at his backyard workshop, which has painstakingly equipped with many homemade tools. In his hand is the carving of an "Indian chief" that he has just finished as a gift for Beverly. Nearby is his backyard gymnasium, with a variety of weight-lifting and exercise equipment built mostly from scrap car parts.

Aboard Train No. 2
March 28, 1996

This will be my last letter from Cuba, as I'm now on my way
home, rolling along at a good 65 or 70 kms an hour, about 100
miles out of Santiago and with over 400 yet to go.

I'm on the overnight express to Havana, the only tourist
among some seven or eight hundred Cubans riding this fairly
long train. All the cars are coaches, not a sleeper, lounge or dining car in the consist, though fortunately the seats are fairly spacious and there's lots of leg room. *Real* fortunately, since the
overhead rack is too small and crowded for my duffel bag, which
is down here with me. My neighbor Carlos has his guitar beside
him in the same way, and neither of us are uncomfortable. He's
a quiet musician and an interesting talker. I'm lucky to have him
rather than the lady just ahead whose little kid keeps screaming
and climbing all over their neighbour - who doesn't like it.

Back in Santiago de Cuba I got chauffeured to the train station from the Hotel Casa Grande by - get this - a 1935 Graham-
Paige convertible, a classic with the top down, that could have
been driven by the likes of Clark Gable when it was new. The
driver said it is one of only two in Cuba, and that it's not easy to
get parts for it. He had it parked in the downtown plaza and for
five dollars gladly took me for a tour that included the infamous
Moncada barracks and ended at the railroad station. Rough riding old beast, everybody staring at it in passing, just as they
would have done if I'd walked by without it. Several people
shouted their black market offers to me, like money exchange
and cigars, while the driver just smiled and kept driving. But he
acknowledged all the good looking women who tried to flag us
down, waving to some and honking at others.

My neighbour Carlos plays folk music with a trio down in
Santiago and is on his way to Havana for a test that may move
him up to a higher pay scale, although he says it's the dollar tips
from tourists that really count. The raise is mainly for status and
some special privileges, including the possibility for travel and
recording. "I would love to come up and sing in Canada some-

We're approaching the Moncada barracks, where Fidel Castro began his revolution with an attack by student friends and followers in 1954. A national landmark, the place is today also an elementary school. Photo was taken from the back seat of my taxi, a 1935 Graham-Paige convertible.

time," he said real sincerely, speaking good English and seeming to understand the world at large way more than Cuba's critics would have us think Fidel allows.

"Now that the big cold war has ended, the Americans want to keep going with their little cold war in the Caribbean," Carlos said sadly. "I have relatives in the U.S. and they agree with this policy, can you imagine? Something so hurtful and oppressive to their relatives, their own people." He said he writes poems about things like this, but so far hasn't sang any of them in public with music. Bob Dylan and Leonard Cohen are two of his heroes. He said there are already some singers willing to speak out through their songs, including one with the same first name as his, whose song about Wilhelm Tell I mentioned earlier.

"The United States treats Cuba as if this was still 1960, when they were able to dictate to a lot of countries how they should govern themselves. That's changed, so now Cuba is almost alone in this, being kept in America's shadow. If you want to have light in a house, you don't close up the doors and windows." He said the young have a great yearning to know America better and it frustrates them that both sides won't allow this. "I think the Americans would see Cuba changing much more to their liking if they would try to improve relations with us, instead of passing more restrictions." Since I haven't heard any news lately, he surprised me by saying President Clinton has announced that he will tighten the old embargo against Cuba because of the two planes that were recently shot down.

Back in 1992 New Jersey Representative Tortecilli bragged when his anti-Cuba bill was passed that it would bring Fidel down in weeks. Four years later Fidel's still there, and this plan to further tighten the embargo will keep him there even longer. The embargo is America's obsolete and crazy obsession with one man, a man who is showing the whole world that even with such a mighty power trying to destroy him he is still the country's leader after 35 years.

That Fidel has survived all these years right next door to the U.S. is something close to a miracle, even if you just count his survival of CIA assassination attempts. Perhaps that survival was already foretold at the time when he gave the revolution's first victory speech, as a white dove inexplicably landed on his shoulder in front of a huge crowd. One may disagree with many parts of his politics, but Fidel Castro is definitely not just some tinpot dictator that America can dethrone.

Over the years Fidel has often been accused of leading Cuba "by trial and error," but how else can a nation of people learn a new way of life after being subjugated for so many generations by an endless line of tyrants? Even in its recent attempts to allow some forms of capitalism, Cuba has no real precedents. The problems experienced by Russia have convinced Cubans that this is no model to copy. Iron Curtain countries like Hungary and Poland look more promising, but they both have a democratic past to help guide their way while Cuba has no such experience. For this they need good examples and encouragement from their nearest neighbors, not more threats and bullying.

In the face of constant immense challenges, Cuba stands alone in this western hemisphere as a country where the people live with less and less in order to maintain their national pride and principles. If they stay at it long enough, the day is liable to come when economic and environmental causes force the rest of the world to live much more simply than we do now, at which point it might just be that Cuba will be the nation setting the precedents.

For now it's getting too dark on this train to write, so I'll close my eyes and try to sleep a bit. When the night is through I will get off in Havana with the rest of this crowd. But only *I* will be allowed to keep going to the airport, from where a plane will whisk me away, once again, from the struggling reality of daily life in Cuba, and from all the warm friendships that nonetheless continue to be offered so freely everywhere I've gone.

A.H.W.

Here's the Graham-Paige taxi parked on the cobblestone street outside the blue and white train station of Santiago de Cuba. Trains pull in on the other side of this building, while beyond the tracks there are warehouses and wharves for international ships.